FROM POST-MAOISM

T & F /ROUTLEDGE
DISTRIBUTION CENTER
2360 PROGRESS DRIVE
HEBRON, KY 41048

3 LBS   1 OF 1

SHIP TO: WEDEMAN, ANDREW
UNIV OF NEBRASKA-LINCOLN
POIS
513 OLDH
LINCOLN NE 68588

UPS GROUND

TRACKING #: 1Z X45 099 03 1158 6545

BILLING: PREPAID

INV# 15246531
PO# 42401
DATE: 04/25/01

CTN: 1 of 1   WGT: 2.1
ID# 1158654   DOC: RO

022/042

%
04/25 N #005070

11158654

WEDEMAN, ANDREW
0700 - 15246531 - 04/25/01
2.1 - UPS

FROM POST-MAOISM
TO POST-MARXISM

The Erosion of Official Ideology
in Deng's China

KALPANA MISRA

Routledge
New York and London

Published in 1998 by

Routledge
29 West 35th Street
New York, NY 10001

Published in Great Britain by

Routledge
11 New Fetter Lane
London EC4P 4EE

Library of Congress Cataloging-in-Publication Data

Misra, Kalpana.
    From Post-Maoism to Post-Marxism: the erosion of official
ideology in Deng's China / Kalpana Misra.
        p.   cm.
    Includes bibliographical references.
    ISBN 0-415-92032-9 (cloth). — ISBN 0-415-92033-7 (pbk.)
    1. Communism—China.   2. Socialism—China.
    3. Ideology—China.   4. China—Politics and government—1976–.
    5. Teng, Hsiao-p'ing, 1904–.   I. Title.
    HX418.5.M57   1998
    320.951—dc21   97-45758
                                                              CIP

Contents

1976	September	Mao Zedong, chairman of the Communist Party of China (CCP) dies.
	October	Broad-based coalition within the successor leadership carries out a coup against the Gang of Four (Jiang Qing, Yao Wenyuan, Chang Chunqiao, and Wang Hongwen). With the purge of the most radical-leftist group in Chinese politics Hua Guofeng succeeds to the two highest offices in the Communist hierarchy: the chairmanship of the CCP and premiership of the State Council.
1977	February	*Renmin ribao (People's Daily), Hongqi (Red Flag), Jiefang ribao (Liberation Army Daily),* joint editorial emphasizing the need to "adhere to whatever policies were set by Chairman Mao and implement whatever instructions were given by him." The editorial that earned the name Whatever Faction for its proponents was aimed at resisting Deng Xiaoping's rehabilitation and any reassessment of past events or policies that could extend to a criticism of Mao himself.
	July–August	Deng Xiaoping reappears in public and assumes his old positions as vice-chairman, CCP Central Committee, vice-premier, State Coucil; chief-

of-staff, PLA; and vice-chairman, Military Commission.

September

Media campaign to revile the Gang of Four broadens its target to the "pernicious" influence of radical leftism in general. Chen Yun's speech commemorating the first anniversary of Mao's death extols the principle of "seeking truth from facts" and openly criticizes dogmatism.

1978 May

The ideological reorientation movement led by Hu Yaobang begins to gather momentum. *Guangming ribao* publishes its Special Commentator article, "Practice Is the Sole Criterion for Testing Truth," which begins a nationwide media campaign to undermine Hua Guofeng's position and the blind obedience and submission to Mao's directives advocated by the "whateverists." The reformist-led media also begins to publish articles castigating the Maoist view of "bourgeois right," while promoting the principle of "distribution according to work."

November–December

A Central Work Conference and the meeting of the CCP Central Committee Third Plenum following in its wake authorize reversal of verdict on the 1976 Tiananmen incident, rehabilitate Peng Dehuai, and open the door to reassessment of the hitherto unassailable persona of Mao himself. The formal rejection of the Dazhai agricultural model in favor of decollectivization, sideline occupations, and rural-trade markets is underscored by the proposal to terminate disruptive political campaigns and shift the emphasis to economic modernization.

1979   January–April   Hu Yaobang, promoted to secretary-general of CCP Central Committee and director of the Propaganda Department, convenes a Theory Conference to continue the task of ideological readjustment and facilitate the draft of a comprehensive appraisal of the CCP record in power and the role of Mao. In the first half of the Conference dominated by radical reformers, Wang Ruoshui's speech assails the Cultural Revolution as a "great catastrophe" and assigns the main responsibility for it to Mao. Other delegates make devastating critiques of China's feudal autocracy and stress the need for institutional and legal checks on abuse of power. Su Shaozhi and Feng Lanrui publish their article on "undeveloped socialism." The latter half of the conference is marked by rallying of the moderate leadership, crackdown on the Democracy Wall movement, and Deng Xiaoping's speech on the Four Cardinal Principles, which lays down the parameters of debate on political issues.

1980   November   Hua Guofeng is replaced as premier of the State Council by Deng Xiaoping's protégé Zhao Ziyang at an enlarged meeting of the Politburo. Deng assumes chairmanship of CCP Military Commission. Rift widening between radical reformers seeking a thorough repudiation of past errors, and moderates like Chen Yun, Hu Qiaomu, Ye Jianying, and others wary of too negative an evaluation of previous policies and Mao's leadership.

1981   April   Short-lived campaign against "bourgeois liberalization." Criticism of Bai Hua's *Unrequited Love* meets resistance by radical-reformist media.

	June	"Resolution on Certain Questions in the History of Our Party Since the Establishment of PRC," adopted by the Sixth Plenum of the 11th Central Committee. The final form of the Resolution marks a tactical retreat on the part of Deng and his followers with a much watered-down critique of Mao and the Communist Party's failings.
1982	September	Twelfth CCP Congress endorses Chen Yun's emphasis on readjustment and the elimination of sectoral imbalances by more efficient and rational macro-control mechanisms. In the aftermath of the Congress, Hu Yaobang and Zhao Ziyang step up their urging of radical-reform oriented intellectuals to provide a "theoretical basis" for the expansion of reform into the urban-industrial economy.
1983	March	Follwing the lead of Wang Ruoshui and Ru Xin, Zhou Yang's speech commemorating Marx's death centennial addresses the problems of bureaucratism, authoritarianism, and political corruption in terms of alienation. Wang Ruoshui's decision to publish Zhou's speech in RMRB in defiance of Hu Qiaomu and Deng Liqun results in the former's dismissal as deputy editor.
	June–October	Moderate offensive against ideological revision. At the Second Plenum of the Twelfth Central Committee Deng Xiaoping criticizes theorists spreading "spiritual pollution" by their attacks on the Party's leadership and the socialist system.
	November	Campaign against "spiritual pollution" reined in and restricted to the sphere of ideology.

1984 **January–August** Hu Qiaomu's speech at the Central Party School brings the campaign to a formal close for the time being. CASS economists begin to distinguish between a "fixed" Soviet-socialist economic model and the Yugoslav and Chinese systems. Their purpose is to invalidate the identification of the Soviet centrally planned command economy with a classical socialist model, and to legitimize the departure of the Chinese variant from the "borrowed" or "dated" Soviet one.

October The Resolution on Economic Structural Reform incorporates the principles of a "planned commodity economy" and "separation between state ownership and management." These pave the way for the contract responsibility and lease systems in industry and the implementation of managerial control over production decisions, above-quota goods, and profits.

1985 **September** The effects of urban-industrial reform and rising sectoral, regional, and individual disparities heighten moderate apprehensions regarding "peaceful evolution to capitalism." Chen Yun's speech at the National Conference deplores the substitution of socialist ethics by the values of market-based distribution. Radical reformers attempt to alleviate concerns about reemerging socioeconomic polarization by arguing that antagonistic contradictions have been overcome in Chinese society and "social struggle" has replaced class struggle as a motivating force. "Culture Fever" erupts as a host of younger writers and artists trace the sources of current shortcomings and failings in the socioeconomic order to Chinese tradition and culture.

1986   April–   Articles and speeches commemorating the Thir-
       September   tieth Anniversary of the Hundred Flowers
                         demand political structural reform along with
                         economic change. Yan Jiaqi, Yu Haocheng, and
                         others press for freedom of expression, checks
                         and balances, and rule of law. Su Shaozhi and
                         Wang Yizhou point to the similarity between
                         the bureaucratic structure of the proletarian dic-
                         tatorship and feudal despotism.

       October   Fang Lizhi steps up attacks on Marxist ideology
                         and the Chinese leadership in speeches across
                         university campuses.

       November–   Student demonstrations begin at Keda in Anhui
       December   Province and spread to Xian, Tianjin, Nanjing,
                         Shanghai, and finally Beijing in December.
                         Demands of the students include freedom of the
                         press, independent student unions, and human
                         rights in general.

1987   January   Hu Yaobang is assailed for toleration of intellectual
                         dissent and failure to restrain student demonstra-
                         tors, and dismissed from his post as general-
                         secretary at an enlarge meeting of the Politburo.
                         Demands for institutional change are rejected by
                         Deng Xiaoping as "bourgeois liberalization." Fang
                         Lizhi, Liu Binyan, Wang Ruowang, Su Shaozhi, Li
                         Honglin, et al., are criticized for advocating West-
                         ern political values and institutions.

       October   Zhao Ziyang's speech at the Thirteenth Party
                         Congress unveils the third phase of reform and
                         employs the term, "primary stage of socialism" as
                         a theoretical justification for bold and unortho-
                         dox economic policies.

1988

Widespread public discontent at rising levels of material differentiation and cadre corruption revive discussion on social equity and fairness. Radical-reformist intellectuals and members of Zhao Ziyang's think tanks identify the monopoly of state ownership and bureaucratic manipulation of the partially privatized economy as the root of all problems. Zhao's advisors propose a "new enlightened despotism" for guiding the country's transition to a full-fledged market economy. Their theory of "Neo-authoritarianism" is opposed by Hu Jiwei, Su Shaozhi, Yan Jiaqi, and others who advocate immediate democratization as a way out of the reform/crisis/reform cycle.

1989   **April**

The death of Hu Yaobang sparks off a wave of student demonstrations in favor of freedom, democracy, and human rights.

June

Military crackdown on the Tiananmen movement. Jiang Zemin replaces Zhao Ziyang as general-secretary.

**September–
October**

Deng steps down as chairman, Military Commission in favor of Jiang Zemin. Deng Liqun and his associates take over major newspapers and the propaganda apparatuses to direct an ideological offensive to repudiate both liberal-democratic intellectuals and proponents of new-authoritarianism (many of whom are either in exile or under arrest).

1990

Neoconservatives like Xiao Gongqin and Wang Huning criticize the naive romanticism of the liberal democrats and revive the notion of a "visible hand" and an elite-guided process of modernization. Although the Seventh Plenary Session of the Thirteenth CCP Central Committee marks a reassertion of Deng's economic program neoconservatives continue to emphasize the need for gradualism.

1991		Leaders like Chen Yuan point out the dangers of weakening central authority and the destabilizing consequences of devolution of authority. *Zhongguo qingnian bao* (*China Youth Daily*) prints "Realistic Responses and Strategic Choices for China After the Soviet Upheaval." The document, ostensibly meant for internal circulation, recommends appeals to nationalism (rather than Marxism-Leninism) as a rallying force within an ideological framework combining Western rationalism and traditional Chinese culture.
1992	**January**	Deng Xiaoping travels south to tour Guangzhou and Shenzhen and shore up support for reformist policies.
	October	Fourteenth Party Congress demonstrates a victory for Deng and his policy preferences. The principle of a market economy is incorporated into the Party Constitution and Jiang Zemin stresses the need for continued "deepening of reform."
1993	**October– December**	The publication of volume III of the *Selected Works of Deng Xiaoping* is described as a major political event by Xinhua. Jiang Zemin is quoted as praising Deng's seeking truth from facts and eschewing a "dogmatic bookish understanding of certain Marxist principles, the unscientific or

even distorted understanding of socialism and the incorrect ideology that skips the first stage of socialism." The Third Plenum of the Fourteenth CCP Central Committee asserts that China's reform has entered new stage and points outs that "to establish a socialist market-economy system is to let the market play a fundamental role in allocating resources under the state's macro-economic regulation and control."

1994   March–June

Jiang Zemin's speech at a national party school work conference recalls Deng's injunction, "don't think that Marxism-Leninism–Mao Zedong Thought will disappear, become useless, and fail...there will be no such thing." Media articles discuss the importance of theoretical study and correct handling of contradictions that have emerged among the people as a consequence of reform. "Reconciliation, coordination, and mediation" are recommended as the means for resolving new contradictions. The book *Looking at China Through a Third Eye* focuses attention on the adverse destabilizing consequences of reform, the alarming decline of public morality and the reemergence of class conflict and polarization in Chinese society.

1995   January–March

Corruption and lax discipline in Party ranks becomes a source of renewed concern. Jiang Zemin voices the need to maintain the Communist Party's "progressiveness and purity," against the influences of decadent ideology and culture.

October

Deng Xiaoping's theory of building "socialism with Chinese characteristics" is touted as a second historical leap (after Mao) in combining the fundamental tenets of Marxism-Leninism with Chinese reality.

1996   July–September   *Renmin ribao* (*People's Daily*) article cautions against "Confucian craze" but urges the integration of Confucian ethics with Marxism. The notion of "self-cultivation" and the Confucian "humanistic ideology of upholding virtue and stressing education" are suggested as the keys to higher ethical standards. Other media articles deplore the lack of understanding of the theory of building "socialism with Chinese characteristics" and draw attention to the corrosive effect of "Western bourgeois ideology" in fomenting skepticism toward Marxism and the socialist system. A "10,000-character statement" attributed to Deng Liqun by the Hong Kong Press addresses the implications of the shrinking public sector for China's socialist economic foundation and points to the emergence of a "nongovernmental bourgeois class and a petty bourgeoisie."

1997   February   Deng Xiaoping dies at age 92.

Acknowledgments

I began writing this book at a time when ideology in China was not a particularly fashionable topic. For first teaching me to take the role of ideas seriously and fostering my interest in Chinese Marxism during my years at Delhi University I wish to thank Professors Tan Chung, V.P. Dutt, the late O.P. Kaushik, K.K. Misra, M. Mohanty, K.R. Sharma, Mira Sinha, and Huang I-shu.

The greatest credit for encouraging me to begin and continue work on this project at the University of Michigan goes to Michel Oksenberg, Alfred Meyer, and Donald Munro. For their intellectual guidance, rigorous standards, and challenging but supportive criticism through the successive stages of writing, I am profoundly grateful. Tu Wei-ming, who graciously gave of his time to read and reread the different drafts has also been a special source of inspiration and encouragement.

My analysis and writing have been immeasurably improved and enriched by the advice and assistance of several professional colleagues, friends, and anonymous reviewers. I deeply appreciate Su Shaozhi's time and help in clarifying certain theoretical issues. To David Kelly and Melanie Manion I owe a special debt of gratitude for their insightful suggestions and exceptional generosity in sharing sources with me. Sophia Lee has gone beyond the call of duty as friend and colleague to help me locate rare resources and contacts.

Special acknowledgement is due to Michael Mosher and Paul Thomas for their enthusiastic support and timely assistance. For their helpful suggestions, I also wish to thank P.J. Ivanhoe, James Tong, Richard Matthews, David Shambaugh, and Ray Wylie. The extraordinary efficiency of Melissa Rosati, Eric Nelson, and Lai Moy at Routledge is greatly appreciated, and I consider myself extremely fortunate to have worked with such a superb editorial team. The timely completion of this book was facilitated by the generous financial support provided by University of Tulsa research and travel grants, and the expert secretarial assistance of Toy Kelley.

Finally, I am most grateful for the patience, forbearance, and unqualified support of my family and friends that has nurtured and sustained me through every stage of this project. Whatever refinements of analysis and lucidity the book contains owes much to the insights and advice of my father, K.K. Misra, a favorite mentor and perennial source of inspiration, and my husband Murali Iyengar whose intellectual companionship has been indispensable to the evolution of my ideas and scholarship. My mother Kamal, my sisters Kamana and Kajal, my brother Kovid, and my children Kabir and Karnika have been dazzling critics and the most exuberant supporters—but for their impatience, I would still be writing this book! Narayani Ganesh, Melanie Rich, Perry Simons, and Lois Bartlett have also been invaluable allies in sustaining my enthusiastic commitment to my endeavours and relieving the tedium of work. This expression of gratitude for an exceptional circle of family and friends is a meagre return for all that they have given me.

Introduction

Mao's passing and the subsequent return of Deng Xiaoping to the forefront of Chinese politics marked the beginning of sweeping changes within the Chinese system. The shift away from the ideological preferences of the late Chairman was evident in the practical thrust of policies introduced by the immediate post-Mao regime although the successor leadership of Hua Guofeng went to great lengths to affirm the Maoist legacy and resist any criticism of radical leftism at the theoretical level.[1] The ascendancy of Deng Xiaoping and the political decline of Hua and his cohort brought a much sharper break with the past for Deng's agenda included far-reaching economic, political and cultural change. The hallmark of the new approach was its focus on economic development accompanied by a recognition of limits to state control, which translated into an extensive depoliticization of social life and the cultural and literary spheres.

Within a decade China's economic landscape had been transformed by the emergence of special economic zones, rural markets, private enterprises, stock exchanges, and Sino-foreign joint ventures. Legitimization of consumerism and profit making accompanied the implementation of the contract responsibility system in agriculture and industry, while internationally the reformist leadership vigorously promoted extensive linkages for the purpose of attracting foreign technology, trade, and investment.

Although the reforms in the economic realm were more spectacular, changes that marked the social, political, and cultural arenas were by no

---

1. William Joseph, *The Critique of Ultraleftism in China, 1958–1981,* Stanford: Stanford University Press, 1984; Brantly Womack, "Politics and Epistemology in China Since Mao," *The China Quarterly,* no. 80 (1979), pp. 768–792.

means insubstantial. By the early 1980s, the political system had experienced some liberalization in an attempt to institutionalize policy making and procedures and prevent future crystallizations of "cults of personality." The partial retreat of the state acknowledged a measure of distinction between the public and the private and facilitated what many observers term the tentative emergence of a civil society, characterized by a loosening of the constraints of the *danwei* (work unit) system and a rapid expansion of new voluntary associations, formal and informal intellectual networks, unofficial journals, salons, study groups, and think tanks. Relaxation of state controls brought forth an infusion of popular culture from Hong Kong and Taiwan and a tremendous flowering of indigenous artistic and literary creativity exemplified in the works of the Star artists, Menglong poetry, new novels, short stories, and the productions of filmmakers like Chen Kaige and Zhang Yimou.

The crackdown on the student demonstrations and the events of 4 June 1989, raised doubts about the continuation of liberal policies associated with leaders like Hu Yaobang and Zhao Ziyang. However, the leftist ascendancy in the initial post-Tiananmen period was countered by the reiteration of continued "deepening of reform" following Deng's celebrated southern tour in early 1992. With the 14th Party Congress convened later that year the principle of a market economy was incorporated into the Party Constitution illustrating that a drastic reversal of reform was no longer considered a desirable or feasible option even among so-called hard-liners within the leadership. Cultural and intellectual pluralism which avoided the "forbidden zones" and occupied the spaces defined by Tang Tsou as "zones of indifference" continued to thrive.[2]

Ideology and Legitimacy

In the initial years of the post-Mao era, interpretations of the change of course favored by the successor leadership centered on the question of whether China was going revisionist. As the magnitude of the transfor-

---

2. Tang Tsou, "Introduction," in *The Cultural Revolution and Post-Mao Reforms: A Historical Perspective*, Chicago: University of Chicago Press, 1986, p. XXIV.

mation became more apparent, the focus shifted to the People's Republic's abandonment of Marxism.

Given the crucial defining role of ideology in Chinese society the need for a theoretical explanation of dramatic policy changes would seem to be self-evident. And, indeed, the reformist leadership headed by Deng Xiaoping perceived from the outset the significance of fashioning a doctrine or refurbishing the existing one to rationalize its critique of the past and establish its own legitimacy and the unfettered pursuit of modernization.

By late 1978, the disjunction between affirmation of Mao's intellectual legacy and the reversal of his policy preferences was being addressed by a cautious toleration of muted criticism of the late Chairman and the adoption of the position that his radical innovations of the Cultural Revolutionary period were the misguided wanderings of a senile mind. The debate on epistemology launched in 1978 epitomized Deng Xiaoping's strategy of "discrediting the tendency to seek legitimacy primarily from the classics" (the quote is Brantly Womack's) in order to direct the Party toward a "more flexible and utilitarian standard" to assess new policies. The move was regarded by observers as nothing short of brilliant. By stressing practice as the criterion of truth, Deng adroitly manipulated a key tenet of the early Mao to discredit his later ones and neatly undercut the position of residual Maoists, Hua Guofeng, and the "whatever" faction (Wang Dongxing, Wu De, Ji Dengkui, and Chen Yonggui).[3] This heady start notwithstanding, the limitations of Deng's ideological victory were exposed within a decade, as the Chinese Communist Party failed not only to renew its legitimacy, but also to arrest the cynicism and "crisis of faith" that had pervaded the population since the closing of the Maoist era.

The focus of this study is the ideological reorientation and intellectual evolution that began in the late 1970s and spanned the entire Deng era, and that marked the transformation of the regime's theorists from supporters and legitimizers of "existing socialism" to advocates of a new post-Maoist and post-Marxist intellectual discourse. The book addresses one of the most significant and paradoxical political developments of the Deng

3. Brantly Womack, "Politics and Epistemology in China Since Mao," in *The China Quarterly*, no. 80 (1979), pp. 768–792.

Xiaoping era in China, viz., the decline of regime legitimacy during a period in which its performance had, in fact, exceeded expectations and achieved astonishing levels of economic growth, and enhanced living standards in both material and cultural terms.

The central thesis of the book is that the attempt to find an ideological basis to justify the dramatic change of course was ultimately unsuccessful, and it was this failure that explains the leadership's inability to consolidate its legitimacy in a way that could garner support among its most crucial constituency—the elite intelligentsia.[4] A symptom of this failure was the standoff between the more moderate/"conservative"[5] and radical factions within the leadership each of whom checkmated the ability of the other to develop a theoretically consistent framework to support its policy positions. A detailed analysis of key ideological debates illustrates that the root of the problem lay in that there is no long-term sustainable middle ground between socialism and capitalism (so ardently sought by Chinese reformers and their counterparts in Eastern Europe and the former Soviet Union), and thus no way to express it in ideology either. China's intellectual establishment could not articulate a coherent, persuasive set of beliefs

---

4.   The focus on ideological debate is crucial to understand the paradox referred to above. Studies of regime legitimacy in authoritarian systems have focused on mass legitimacy or a broad-based acceptance of the regime and its goals by the "population as a whole." Legitimacy in the eyes of the general populace is closely linked to performance and in that area the Deng Xiaoping leadership clearly scored high. It is also true, however, as Ding Xueliang has noted astutely, that even more crucial than the perception of the masses in general may be the allegiance of the intellectual elite and its support for officially sanctioned doctrinal norms. In the post-Mao period the failure to accomplish the ideological revitalization necessary to supplement performance-based legitimacy was linked directly to the disaffection of the intelligentsia, its decreasing dependence on the political leadership, and its growing awareness of its own specific interests as a group.

5.   This study employs the term "moderate" to refer to individuals such as Chen Yun, Peng Zhen, and Hu Qiaomu because the use of terms such as "conservative" and "reformist" in the context of change in the Communist Party-led countries in recent years is a problematic one. Arif Dirlik points out how such usage fails to distinguish between reforms that are informed by socialist norms and those that simply aim to bring about change. "Anyone who is serious about socialism, or is hesitant to abandon the legacy of the revolution is immediately dubbed a conservative." See Arif Dirlik and Maurice Meisner ed. *Marxism and the Chinese Experience*, Armonk: M.E. Sharpe, 1989, p. 22.

to support a set of policies that lacked internal consistency and coherence. The oscillation of policy and theory was thus inevitable and legitimacy essentially impossible to achieve because of the inherent contradiction of the mix.

The major consequence of China being left in a situation of undergoing massive transformation without a sufficient theoretical basis or guideline was the pervasive cynicism and apathy that has been widely noted. My study, however, draws one other significant conclusion that has been generally overlooked. The fundamental weakness of the ideological reorientation lay in its inability to satisfactorily and conclusively set aside the Maoist legacy. Privatization of the economy, deepening socioeconomic polarization, and particularly the emergence of the cadre capitalist all confirmed Mao's fears of capitalist restoration and vindicated his preoccupation with the phenomenon of the Communist Party itself becoming the major obstacle to progress and socialism (which led among other things to his decision to launch the Cultural Revolution). The consequences of the socioeconomic policies so enthusiastically embarked upon by the Deng Xiaoping leadership had, in fact, been predicted with extraordinary foresight by the Maoists in 1975 when Yao Wenyuan argued that consolidation of "bourgeois right" and expansion of material incentives would lead to a situation where

a small number of people will in the course of distribution acquire increasing amounts of commodities and money through certain legal channels and numerous illegal ones; capitalist ideas of amassing fortunes and craving for personal fame and gain, stimulated by such "material incentives" will spread unchecked; phenomena such as the turning of public property into private property, speculation, graft and corruption, theft and bribery will increase; the capitalist principle of the exchange of commodities will make its way into political and even party life, undermining the socialist planned economy; acts of capitalist exploitation such as the conversion of commodities and money into capital, and labor power will occur....As a result, a small number of new bourgeois elements and upstarts...will emerge from among Party members, workers, well-to-do peasants, and personnel in state organs. When the economic strength of the bourgeoisie has grown to a certain extent, its agents will demand political rule, demand the overthrow of the dictatorship of the proletariat and the socialist system, demand a complete changeover from socialist ownership, and openly restore and develop the capitalist system.[6]

Throughout the 1980s and 1990s the Maoist prognosis returned to haunt both the moderate leadership that agonized over China's "peaceful evolution to capitalism," as well as the radical reformers and liberal intellectuals who echoed Maoist and ultraleftist denunciations of a new exploitative class of Communist Party bureaucrats in socialist systems. Mao's critique of Soviet-type societies (and his assertion that nonantagonistic contradictions among social groups and leaders and masses could turn antagonistic in post-revolutionary society) ultimately was affirmed directly or indirectly by both moderate and radical reformers. Thus, even after his death, Mao's shadow loomed large as the chief critic of his successors and of Chinese socialism. In light of this conclusion, I argue that the Mao fever of the 1990s, aside from its eccentric and commercial manifestations, underscores and reflects at a deeper and more serious level the shortcomings of the ideological reorientation attempted in the Deng Xiaoping era.

Thus, the central assumption of this study is that issues of ideology and intellectual debates over policy are extremely significant. There is a fairly well established tradition in some fields of academic inquiry of discounting the role of ideas, values, and beliefs. This is either because of the problematic nature of the relationship between behavior and consciously expressed verbal assertions of belief and intentions or because of the "power-interest" perspective.[7] The latter employs a cynical approach to ideological assertions as a cloak for power struggles or as ex facto rationalizations of practical measures to advance personal, group, or national interests.

Studies of China during the Maoist era recognized that Mao's predominance within the system stemmed from the authority of ideology more so than from specific power centers within party, state, or military bureaucracies. Since the ascendancy of Deng Xiaoping in Chinese politics, it has been more fashionable to argue that practical flexibility rather than ideological

6.   Yao Wenyuan, "On the Social Basis of the Lin Biao Clique," in *Hongqi*, no. 4 (1975), pp. 20–29.

7.   Benjamin Schwartz, *Communism and China: Ideology in Flux*, Cambridge: Harvard University Press, 1968, pp. 7–10.

considerations has driven the reform program, and interest in ideological developments has waned considerably. However, there are significant exceptions. Arif Dirlik, Maurice Meisner, Mark Selden, and Joseph Fewsmith, among others, have continued to provide some of the most insightful reflections on the deradicalization of Chinese politics and its implications for socialist theory and practice.[8] In their incisive and definitive study of *Chinese Marxism in the Post-Mao Era, 1978–1984*, Bill Brugger and David Kelly underscore the continuing importance of ideological discourse and illustrate how "abstruse philosophical argumentation has great political relevance."[9] Commenting on the reason why ideology is still vitally important in China, Tu Wei-ming points out that "even if we choose to believe that the power struggle in China is more a political game than an ideological debate it is worth noting that the widely accepted way to exercise power in this political game is through ideological debate."[10] The "art of persuasion" through intellectual discourse, he goes on to say, "is not so much moralizing propaganda as an essential ingredient that defines Chinese society."[11]

These views are strongly supported in the recent scholarship of individuals from the mainland like Ding Xueliang, Gu Xin, He Baogang, Yan Sun, and others. In particular, Ding Xueliang's *The Decline of Communism in China* confirms the importance of ideology by reiterating that the legitimacy of a regime depends less on popular perceptions and more on the acceptance of doctrines of legitimacy and the norms derived from them by the intellectual elite.[12]

My own study demonstrates that in postrevolutionary societies such as China the interaction between ideas, ideology, power conflicts, and policy

8.   Arif Dirlik and Maurice Meisner, ed. *Marxism and the Chinese Experience*, Armonk, N.Y.: M.E. Sharpe, 1989; Mark Selden, *The Political Economy of Chinese Development*, Armonk, N.Y.: M.E. Sharpe, 1993; Joseph Fewsmith, *Dilemmas of Reform in China*, Armonk, N.Y.: M.E. Sharpe, 1994.

9.   Bill Brugger and David Kelly, *Chinese Marxism in the Post-Mao Era, 1978–1984*, Stanford: Stanford University Press, 1990, p. 93.

10.   Tu Wei-ming, "The Modern Chinese Intellectual Quest," in *Way, Learning and Politics: Essays on the Confucian Intellectual*, Albany: State University of New York Press, 1993, p. 175.

11.   Ibid., p. 173.

12.   Ding Xueliang, *The Decline of Communism in China: Legitimacy Crisis, 1978–1989*, Cambridge: Cambridge University Press, 1994, p. 16.

formation is much more complex than is conceded by the power-interest and bureaucratic politics approaches. At the mass level, it may be true that in the immediate post-Mao period cynicism and apathy rendered most discussions of official doctrine more or less irrelevant, and prompted the leadership—both moderate and radical reformist—to stress a greater measure of performance-based legitimacy. But within the elite (political leaders as well as the intelligentsia) and its rank-and-file constituency, ideological considerations played a significant role in determining the acceptability of certain policies over others. Moreover, the intellectual dynamism and vitality that accompanied the ideological reorientation effort belies the claim that the regime's theorists were merely articulating and legitimating the existing socioeconomic order. Since the late 1970s the new intellectual discourse that has emerged in China has not only questioned and challenged but also attempted to transcend the ideological framework within which it is expected to operate. The rise of a "communal critical self-consciousness," to use Tu Weiming's eloquent phrase, led to tensions between the intelligentsia as a group and the political leadership, and eventually a modification of the relationship between intellectuals and the state.[13] Yet, in the midst of rapid socioeconomic transformation, declining social mores, public order, and popular confidence in the authority structure, both political leaders as well as a major section of the intelligentsia have reiterated the need for a theoretical consensus that can provide an overarching value orientation, set goals, determine means, and provide an overall direction to China's quest for modernity.

Moderates Versus Radicals: The Clash Over Ideology

Intellectual debate in the post-Mao period has both shaped and been influenced by the intense competition between contending sets of elites over

13.   Tu Wei-ming, "Intellectual Effervescence in China," in *Exit From Communism, Daedalus*, Spring 1992, pp. 251–292; Marle Goldman, *Sowing the Seeds of Democracy in China: Political Reform in the Deng Xiaoping Era*, Cambridge: Harvard University Press, 1994; Ding Xueliang, *Decline of Communism*. Lin Tongqi, Henry Rosemont, Jr., and Roger T. Ames, "Chinese Philosophy: A Philosophical Essay on the 'State-of-the-Art,'" in *The Journal of Asian Studies*, vol. 54, no. 3 (August 1995) pp. 727–758.

the issues of political, economic, and cultural change. The theoretical controversies that began in the late 1970s and continued through the 1980s focused on epistemology, historical stages, and feudal culture in an attempt to trace the philosophical premises and the social structural origins of ultraleftism and distortions in Chinese socialism. The aim of the discussions on class and class struggle, which took place simultaneously, was to deny the validity of the Maoist radical intellectual discourse altogether as a deviant phenomena.

Rival groups in the leading coalition agreed upon the disruptive consequences and, therefore, the undesirability of the Maoist stress on continuous revolution and unceasing class struggle. Similarly perceived was the need for a public admission of errors in policy and ideological orientation in the past few years, both on the part of the Party collectively and Mao individually as its dominant leader.[14] Emphasis on "seeking truth from facts" was, in the early post-Mao period, as much a preference of Chen Yun as it was of Deng Xiaoping.[15] The Practice Criterion discussions of 1978, directed against absolutization of ideological authority and in favor of a more flexible orientation in policy making, therefore, had the full support of both radical and moderate reformers. Differences between the two groups centered on the extent of deMaoification and implications of specific policies for stability, elite legitimacy, and compatibility with the prevailing doctrine.

The moderate agenda that came to be identified with Chen Yun, Bo Yibo, Peng Zhen, Deng Liqun, and Hu Qiaomu included measures to vitalize the stagnant Chinese economy and allow a greater role for the pro-

---

14. A Central Work Conference held in Beijing from 10 November to 13 December and the Central Committee Third Plenum following in its wake were landmark events. They authorized reversal of verdict on the 1976 Tiananmen Incident, rehabilitated Peng Dehuai, and opened the door to reassessment of the Cultural Revolution and criticism of the hitherto unassailable persona of Mao himself. The formal rejection of the Dazhai agricultural model in favor of decollectivization, sideline occupations, and rural trade markets was underscored by the proposal to terminate disruptive political campaigns and shift the emphasis to economic modernization.

15. Chen Yun, "Uphold Seeking Truth from Facts—Commemorating the First Anniversary of the Death of the Great Leader and Teacher Chairman Mao," in *RMRB*, (28 September 1977).

fessional intelligentsia in the policy-making process without conceding any real political authority and without major departures from the tenets of the official Marxist-Leninist and modified Stalinist tradition. Discussions on epistemology, class, and class struggle were favored by moderate leaders and ideologists for the purpose of demonstrating their own doctrinal correctness as opposed to the distortions allegedly introduced by ultra-leftists. The slogan "practice is the sole criterion of truth" established a theoretical justification for modifying Maoist economic policies, while the revised assessment of classes and class struggle in socialist society legitimized the elite agents of change as well as permitting the rehabilitation of millions of others who had been persecuted during the Anti-Rightist Movement and the Cultural Revolution. These practical measures and the ideological offensive launched against ultraleftist radicalism gained a wide measure of popular support for the new leadership.

Members of the radical reform group also rejected Mao's extreme politicization of Chinese society, his confrontational leadership style, and his preoccupation with cleavages and antagonisms in favor of stability, unity, and law and order. However, Zhao Ziyang's advocacy of an increasingly market-oriented economy and Hu Yaobang's commitment to preventing future political catastrophes disposed both leaders to emphasize more fundamental institutional change as well as ideological and political pluralism. Critiques of the political hegemony of the Party were in accordance with reformist policies and served the interests of patrons like Hu and Zhao and their intellectual followers. Attacks on bureaucratism not only addressed the problems of arbitrary leadership, corruption, and nepotism (seen increasingly as brakes on reform and a major cause of popular disenchantment), they also facilitated rectification drives to replace Cultural Revolution recruits of the Communist Party with supporters of Hu and Zhao.[16] Calls for democratization and legal and institutional constraints (rather than ideological or normative ones) on the use of power expressed the intelligentsia's need for guarantees against violations of personal and professional autonomy.[17]

16. Ibid.

17. A Theory Conference convened in early 1979 under the aegis of Hu Yaobang highlighted the divisions between the radical reformers and the moderates by raising a number of serious questions concerning not merely the origins of erroneous policies such as the

Unlike the moderates, radical reformers did see themselves as revisionists (and this is why they sought to remove the stigma from revisionism in the Practice Campaign) who borrowed from diverse strands within the Marxist tradition and other non-Marxist writings to remove discrepancies between theory and practice, and redress the deficiencies that they perceived in the official ideology. Radical-reformist critiques of Maoist policies and the Soviet-Stalinist political and economic structure ranged from denunciations in the orthodox tradition of Karl Kautsky, Georgy Plekhanov, Rosa Luxemburg and, more recently, Pavel Campeanu to the humanist revisionists who found inspiration in the early Marx. Thus, while Hu Qiaomu and Deng Liqun tried to defend and perfect the 1950s model of central planning and administrative control and minimize deviation from the official Marxist doctrine, their rivals Su Shaozhi, Hu Qili, Du Runsheng, Yu Guangyuan, and others looked to the writings of Nikolai Bukharin and Janos Kornai and the more heterodox examples of Yugoslavia and Hungary.[18] For the latter, the Soviet experience offered

Great Leap Forward and the Cultural Revolution, but more fundamental ones regarding historical development and the nature of the Chinese Revolution as well. Conversation with Su Shaozhi, 25 April 1990. For detailed accounts of this Conference see Merle Goldman, pp. 47–61 and Ding Xueliang, pp. 91–99. During the Conference and in the period following it Hu's supporters (theorists in the Theory Research Office of the Central Party School, editors of *Renmin ribao*, *Guangming ribao*, and some members of CASS, notably, Su Shaozhi, Liao Gailong, Li Honglin, Yan Jiaqi, Sun Changjiang, Ruan Ming, Yu Guangyuan, Wang Ruoshui, Guo Luoji, Hu Jiwei, and Yang Xiguang) called for sweeping evaluations of the experience of the entire Communist movement beginning with the Bolshevik Revolution, and reassessment of its leaders including the most sacrosanct, Lenin in the USSR and Mao in China. Taking at face value Deng Xiaoping's call for "emancipation of minds" these theorists advocated developing research on Marxism, abandoning Soviet perspectives on imperialism, capitalism, socialist construction, the role of the vanguard party, etc., and absorbing other influences from the works of Milovan Djilas, Rudolph Bahro, Althusser, and the Frankfurt School. See for example Yu Guangyuan, "Develop One Step Further the Study of Marxism," in *Makesizhuyi yanjiu*, no. 1 (1983), pp. 1–6; Su Shaozhi, "Earnestly Study the New Situation in the New Period and Advance Marxism," in *Xuexi yu tansuo*, no. 1 (1983), pp. 17–22; "Marxism Must Study the New Situation in the Contemporary World," in *Xinhua Wenzhai*, no. 3 (1983), pp. 11–12.

18. Yu Guangyuan, "Develop Economics for Even Better Construction of Socialist Modernization," in *Jingji yanjiu*, no. 10 (1981), p. 8; "Perceive the Reform of the Period of Socialist Construction From the Point of View of World and Chinese History," in

very little of relevance to China.[19] Yu Guangyuan denied even that the
early economic successes of the 1950s were due to the "correct" policy of
the First Five Year Plan, but gave the credit to the enthusiasm of the people and the cadres in the euphoric first years after the CCP came to
power.[20] Policy makers in socialist countries, it was argued, needed to recognize that "as far as the building of socialism by different countries is
concerned, there should be no 'standardized' model; as far as the building
of socialism in one individual country is concerned, there should be no
'immutable' model."[21]

Deng Xiaoping's determination to mediate a series of compromises
between the moderate and radical reformers produced an eclectic official
doctrine incorporating traditional and innovative tenets and reflecting the

Zhongguo shehui kexue, no. 1 (1985), pp. 53–68; Su Shaozhi, "Tentative Views on the Reform
of the Economic Mechanism in Hungary," in *Selected Studies on Marxism*, ed. Institute of
Marxism-Leninism, Mao Zedong Thought, CASS, 1988; Su Shaozhi and Guo Shuqing,
"The Relationship Between Marxist Theory and the Yugoslav Self-Management System,"
in *Dangdai quowai shehui zhuyi*, no. 2 (1984), pp. 9–16.

19.   These analysts argued that the absolutization of the Soviet model and the intolerance
of the international communist movement for diverse paths to socialism stemmed from
Stalin's failure to recognize the specificity of the Russian situation and his canonization of
the Soviet social economic structure (*tizhi*) as the basic socialist economic system (*zhidu*).
According to Su Shaozhi, the petrification of the post-NEP Soviet strategy emerged after
Stalin's victory over fascism "ostensibly" demonstrated the validity of centralization, rapid
industrialization, and agricultural collectivization. Henceforth, it became virtually impossible to critically examine the Soviet developmental strategy, and its "blind implementation" in other socialist countries inevitably brought problems and imbalances. See "The
Resolution Is a Guiding Document of Marxism," in Renda *Fuyin*, no. 3 (1985) pp. 5–11.

20.   Yu Guangyuan, "Perceive the Reform of the Period of Socialist Construction From
the Viewpoint of World and Chinese History."

21.   Su Shaozhi, "Develop Marxism Under Contemporary Conditions—In Commemo-
ration of the Centenary of the Death of Karl Marx," in *Selected Studies on Marxism*, Beijing: Institute of Marxism-Leninism-Mao Zedong Thought (CASS), 1988, p. 23. See also
Chen Daisun, "Study Modern Economies of the West and Socialist Economic Modernization of Our Country," in *RMRB*, 16 November 1983; Huang Fanzhang, "Take a Correct
Approach Towards the Contemporary Bourgeois Economic Theories," in *GMRB*, 20
November 1983; Ma Hong, "Marxism and China's Socialist Economic Construction—
Written to Commemorate the Centenary of Marx's Death," in *Social Sciences in China*,
no. 3 (1983).

inconsistencies and tensions of the contradictory half-way policies of reform that it was meant to explain. The validity of the moderate position was undermined simultaneously by concrete departures from the Soviet model in practice and the radical reformist, persistent efforts to raise questions that had long troubled the international Communist movement: Why had the socialist system been unable to resolve satisfactorily the question of the relationship between ruler and ruled? Why had not the superiority of socialism manifested itself in the economic system, or how were Marxists to explain the backwardness of socialist economies and the staying power and flourishing of capitalism?

The discussions on practice, stages of socialism, classes, and class struggle (which were summed up in programmatic documents like the 1981 Resolution and Zhao Ziyang's Speech to the Thirteenth Party Congress) revealed that neither group was able to sustain its critique of Maoist deviations with any consistency without in the process undermining its own position as well. The extolling of scientific methods and practical verification provided critics like Fang Lizhi an avenue to press for complete intellectual autonomy and to refute the "guiding role" of any "supreme principles," including those of Marxist philosophy. Moderate reformers themselves realized early on that critiques of ultraleft dogmatism, skipping of stages, and voluntarism could just as easily and logically be extended to the pre-Liberation period and, thereby, undermine the legitimacy of the Chinese Communist revolution itself. Radical reformist policies proved vulnerable when emphasis on the economic determinants of class pointed to the reemergence of private property and new classes as a consequence of economic liberalization and decollectivization. The shift in focus from class to individual subject in the emerging discourse on alienation, subjectivity, and practical philosophy was understandable from the perspective of those who sought to move China in the direction of a market economy and a pluralist democratic system. However, the replacement of class as a social category eliminated the raison d'être of the CCP's leading role and function in Chinese society and quite effectively undercut the validity of the Four Cardinal Principles.[22]

22. These were: Uphold the socialist road, the dictatorship of the proletariat, the leadership of the Communist Party, and Marxism-Leninism and Mao Zedong Thought.

In general, the radical reformers proved more able at undermining prevailing dogma than at furnishing a new theoretically consistent and persuasive ideological framework. The need to package recommendations so that they would be ideologically acceptable to rivals led establishment intellectuals like Liao Gailong and Yu Guangyuan to frequently employ tautological arguments to promote policies. For instance, having driven the point home that socialism, public ownership, and "laborers being masters" are terms that have been little understood by official Communists themselves, Yu Guangyuan's claim that Lenin's definition of socialism needed to be revised to include commodity production offered no better reason for us to prefer this new definition over Lenin's, other than the fact that a commodity economy existed in Eastern Europe and in China—in countries that had been declared socialist by their leadership.

The dismantling of the Maoist legacy was at best partially accomplished. The problem was not only moderate opposition, but also the structural flaws that the radical reformers identified in the Stalinist system struck chords with the Maoist critiques of bureaucratic socialism. Like Mao and his followers, the radical reformers also attacked privilege seeking and the monopoly over power by a new bureaucrat class. The crucial difference, of course, was that while the Maoist panacea was heightened social mobilization and a strengthened dictatorship of the proletariat, the reformist intellectuals pressed for limits to state power, firm demarcation of public and private spheres, and eventually restitution of private property to undercut the power of the bureaucracy and its control over resources.

The failure of the intellectual establishments of both groups to enunciate an ideological or intellectual rationale for either radical or moderate reform contributed to the vacillating policies of the post-Mao era. The intellectual contingents of neither set of the contending political elites could fashion a coherent, compelling, and ideologically acceptable framework to serve the interests and policy preferences of their patrons and, at the same time, satisfactorily put the Maoist era behind them. Ultimately it was this shortcoming along with a persuasively articulated appeal for pluralism and democracy (ideologically justifiable but politically unacceptable) that denied Mao's successors the renewal of legitimacy sought by them, and enhanced the attraction of non-Marxist and post-Marxist alternatives.

The significance of the discussions on epistemology and social structure lay in their exposure of the inconsistencies and contradictions inherent in the reform process. Moreover, it was the inability to find satisfactory answers to the dilemmas highlighted by the reforms—individual versus collective, equity versus development, growth versus stability, economic decentralization versus political and economic monopoly—within the limits proscribed by the leadership which led to a search for alternative paradigms and the emergence of the intellectual currents of neo-authoritarianism, democratic liberalism, and Confucian humanism.

The critical reappraisal of China's experience with Marxism and the renewed interaction with the West made it possible, perhaps even necessary, to address once again issues that had been raised decades earlier during the May Fourth Movement—tradition and modernity, indigenous values and Western culture (symbolized by science and democracy), a national search for identity, and the full emancipation of the individual. The iconoclastic anti-tradition spirit of May Fourth has found adherents in Liu Xiaobo, Bao Zunxin, and Gan Yang, and in art, literature, and film. However, the intellectual mainstream represented by Su Shaozhi, Wang Ruoshui, Hu Jiwei, Li Honglin, Li Zehou, and others retains its commitment to Marxist ideals and goals at varying levels, and even the most vociferous critics of the regime like Fang Lizhi profess their approval of the fundamental goals of democratic socialism.[23] Those who have more self-consciously denounced the erstwhile dominant intellectual framework, on the other hand, are not as distant from the "Marxian dogmatists" that are the object of their criticism. For these new converts the model of modernity offered by the West is in the words of Tu Wei-ming "deceptively simple."[24] The pluralist capitalist telos has been substituted for the socialist one and their faith in the inevitable march towards that ideal future is predicated on an identical historical determinism. In this way, the intellectual discourse that has emerged in the Deng era is not

23.   James Williams, "Fang Lizhi's Expanding Universe," in *China Quarterly*, no. 123, (September 1990), pp. 459–484

24.   Tu Wei-ming, "Intellectual Efferevescence," p. 258.

simply post-Mao, neo-Marxist, or non-Marxist, but quite distinctively post-"Maoist" and post-"Marxist."[25]

The broad conclusion that can be drawn from these developments is that as early as the mid-1980s ideological reorientation had clearly proved unpersuasive or unacceptable. The attempt to base legitimacy solely on performance also ran into trouble by the late 1980s as the adverse socioeconomic consequences of reform gained visibility and the Party resorted to increasing repression to silence its critics and opponents.

The ability of dissidents, within and outside the Party, to point to discrepancies in the official ideology, between theory and reality and between the words and actions of the Party elite, have seriously undermined its credibility and claims to leadership. The abandonment of socialist goals (at least in the short and medium term) in favor of unrestricted economic growth removes the raison d'être of the CCP's existence even as it validates the claims of other individuals, groups, and political organizations to lead the country towards the same goals of modernization, wealth, and prosperity. Paradoxically, the ritualistic "upholding" of socialist ideals make the CCP a legitimate target of criticism for pursuing policies and lifestyles inimical to those ideals.

The steadily narrowing social base of the CCP—the new bureaucratic capitalists comprised of cadres, and their friends and relatives—makes it vulnerable to attacks from both the left and the right for deviating from socialism and for a less than thorough accommodation of capitalism. So far, the major challenge to its authority has come from proponents of liberal democracy. However, in the light of increasing disparities in wealth and opportunities, one cannot rule out a more broad-based opposition of workers and peasants who may prove less willing than their leaders to give up the values of equity and social justice. It is not clear how successfully the army can be called upon repeatedly to quell domestic disturbances that may arise, and the Party's survival may require more than the flow of

25. I am using the term in the way in which Ernesto Laclau and Chantal Mouffe describe themselves. "If our intellectual position is 'post'-Marxist, it is also post-'Marxist.' It has been through the development of certain intuitions and discursive forms constituted within Marxism, and the inhibition and elimination of certain others, that we have constructed a concept of hegemony...a useful instrument in the struggle for a radical, libertarian, and pluralist democracy." See *Hegemony and Socialist Strategy*, London, 1985, p. 4.

political power through the "barrel of a gun." No longer armed with revolutionary theory, the next casualty of the Chinese revolution may be the vanguard itself.

Outline

Chapter One analyses the discussions which began in mid-1978 on "practice as the sole criterion of truth." Focusing on the timing of the discussions, their political significance, and philosophical essence, this chapter points out the limitations of the new leadership's emphasis on practice as a reaffirmation of a basic tenet of Maoist thought. It concludes that the discussions, in fact, prepared the ground for proceeding in an entirely different direction.

Chapters Two and Three deal with the discussions on feudalism, debates on the "source of knowledge" and the "primacy of matter," and the controversy over stages of socialism. Focus on these issues was prompted by the reinterpretation of the nature and requirements of the new period by the Third Plenum of 1978, and, through these debates, radical reformers attempted to rationalize policies of economic liberalization on the one hand and provide an explanation of past errors like the Great Leap Forward (GLF) and the Cultural Revolution on the other. The attempts to provide a reassessment of Chinese society from the viewpoint of sociological determinism or an epistemological critique of ultraleft voluntarism failed as a consequence of the interplay of ideology and politics.

Chapter Four begins with an overview of the evolution of Mao's ideas on class and class struggle in socialist society and goes on to analyze the post-Mao perspectives for understanding class and social contradictions. It argues that the thesis on the disappearance of exploiting and exploited groups in socialist society put forward by advocates of moderate and radical reform served to legitimize the elite agents of change and new economic policies and to justify the replacement of the nomenclature of Dictatorship of the Proletariat with a mellower-sounding People's Democratic Dictatorship. However, the attempt to define class primarily in economic terms was short-lived. The Maoist ideological and political definition of class was ultimately retained by radical-reform theorists for the contrary purpose of denying the sociological implications of a privileged intelligentsia and a newly emerging group of wealthy proprietors.

Chapter Five focuses on the ideological and political significance of the modifications introduced by the post-Mao leadership on issues such as a new bourgeoisie or bureaucrat class, the emergence of an intellectual counter-elite, and the respective appeals of socialist democracy and neo-authoritarianism.

Chapter Six concludes with an elaboration of the major thesis supported by this study. The attempt to outline a new coherent, internally consistent and persuasive ideological perspective to support post-Mao policies was ultimately unsuccessful. In putting forward an appeal for democratization, advocates of reform offered the political leadership a solution which would obviate the need for an officially sanctioned and rigidly enforced doctrine, permit a degree of ideological pluralism within specified limits, and allow the leaders to draw their support from the improvements and changes that they had initiated. It was, however, a recourse that the politically conservative chose not to take. They opted instead for the ambivalence of retaining an ideology that could neither logically sustain the policies that they had espoused nor provide them with the legitimacy they sought.

ONE

The Criterion of Truth

The death of Mao and the purge of the Gang of Four removed the most strident voices of Chinese radicalism. Hua Guofeng's political decline, along with that of other beneficiaries of the Cultural Revolution, further undercut the predominance of ideological rhetoric in Chinese politics. Deng Xiaoping's return to politics in 1977 marked a new stage in intra-elite conflict and policy debate. Back in Beijing, Deng lost little time in launching an offensive to (a) assure a dominant place for himself in the policy-making process, (b) eliminate any residual opposition to the single-minded pursuit of the "four modernizations," and (c) thoroughly and systematically repudiate the ultraleft radicalism that constituted the Maoist legacy to Chinese politics.

The campaign on "practice is the sole criterion of truth" played a crucial role in legitimizing flexibility and the reorientation of ideology to the demands of economic construction.[1] However, the scope of the discussions also revealed that neutralization of Maoist and neo-Maoist forces did not usher in a unanimous consensus on theoretical issues. On the question of dealing with the Marxist-Leninist-Maoist legacy, in particular, significant divergence continued to exist within the bureaucratic and intellectual elite.

The Political Background

The debate on epistemology that unfolded in the spring of 1978 was no mere exercise in esoterics. In July–August, while the Chinese Academy of

---

1. I would like to thank Melanie Manion for the generous use of her bibliography and resources on the post-Mao epistemology debates.

Sciences held discussions on the criterion of truth, Zhou Yang underlined the importance of the debate as one that "affects our party's and our country's future.[2] In his speech at the closing session of the Central Work Conference of November, Deng Xiaoping reiterated

> . . . the current debate about whether practice is the sole criterion for testing truth is . . . highly important and necessary. When everything has to be done by the book, when thinking turns rigid and blind faith is the fashion, it is impossible for a party or a nation to make progress. Its life will cease and that party or nation will perish. . . . Only if we emancipate our minds, seek truth from facts, proceed from reality in everything and integrate theory with practice, can we carry out our socialist modernization programs smoothly, and only then can our Party further develop Marxism-Leninism and Mao Zedong Thought. In this sense the debate about the criterion for testing truth is really a debate about ideological line, about politics, about the future and the destiny of our Party and nation.[3]

In broad terms, the object of the campaign on seeking truth from facts and stressing practice as the sole criterion for testing truth, was to provide a theoretical basis for the change in course which was being maneuvered by the new rehabilitees, Chen Yun and Deng Xiaoping. Specifically, it was directed against the attitude reflected in a joint Renmin ribao *RMRB*, (HQ) *Hongqi*, and *Jiefang ribao JFRB* editorial published on 7 February 1977, which stressed: "We must adhere to whatever policies were set by Chairman Mao and implement whatever instructions were given by him."[4]

The proponents of this "whateverist" approach at the higher levels[5] opposed the rehabilitation of Deng Xiaoping, the reversal of verdict on the 1976 Tiananmen Incident, and criticism of the radical leftist position

2. Hu Jiwei, "Report on a Series of Struggles in the Top Echelons of the CCP," in *Zhengming* no. 34, (1980), pp. 55–63.

3. Deng Xiaoping, "Emancipate the Mind, Seek Truth From Facts and Unite as One in Looking to the Future," 13 December 1978, *Deng Xiaoping, Speeches and Writings*, Pergamon Books 1987.

4. "Study Documents Well, Grasp the Key Link," Joint Editorial *RMRB*, (also *JFJB*, *HQ*), 7 February 1977, p. 1.

5. In addition to Hua Guofeng the group included Wang Dongxing, Ji Dengkui, Chen Yonggui, Chen Xilian, Zhang Pinghua, and Li Xing.

on bourgeois right, proletarian dictatorship, continuous revolution, and the theory of productive forces, on the grounds that such initiatives violated Mao's words and actions. Although these individuals had disassociated themselves from the extreme left group around Jiang Qing and participated actively in the persecution of the so-called Gang of Four, they refrained from criticism of leftism as a deviant phenomenon.[6] They understood full well that a direct attack on the real ideological orientation of Jiang and her cohorts, and any reassessment of past events or policies would logically extend to a criticism of Mao himself. Such a development would be catastrophic for a leadership group that owed its political advance to the Cultural Revolution and based its legitimacy on being Mao's chosen successors.

Thus, advocates of reform realized quickly enough that even though, as demonstrated by Tiananmen, the masses may not be averse to debunking "whatever" the Chairman had said and done for the last decade or so, entrenched vested interests, especially in the bureaucracy, would not countenance too rapid and/or drastic a move away from Maoist orthodoxy. Such change needed to be justifiable within that tradition. By reminding their audience that seeking truth from facts and stressing practice as the sole criterion of truth were key Maoist slogans Deng Xiaoping and Chen Yun displayed their political acumen by skillfully employing selective Maoist tenets to discredit other ones. According to the *RMRB* editor, Hu Jiwei, the principle of taking "practice as the sole criterion for testing truth" was first singled out by the Central Party School in the winter of 1976, when it began to "expose and criticize Lin Biao and the Gang of Four.[7] By September 1977, Chen Yun and Nie Rongzhen began openly criticizing dogmatism and extolling the party style of seeking truth from facts, just as the ideological reorientation movement led by Hu Yaobang started to gather momentum.[8] Termed the "third campaign to criticize the Gang of Four" this reorientation attempted to broaden the focus of

6. William Joseph, *The Critique of Ultraleftism in China 1958–81,* Stanford: Stanford University Press, 1984, p. 160.
7. Hu Jiwei, "Report on a Series of Struggles."
8. Chen Yun, "Uphold Seeking Truth From Facts," *RMRB*, September 28, 1977, pp. 1–2. Nie Rongzhen, "Restore and Develop the Party's Excellent Style," *RMRB*, 5 September 1977.

earlier attacks on what Hu and his followers considered the "erroneous and pernicious" theoretical influences of radical leftism.[9] The spearhead of attack was the journal *Lilun dongtai*, edited by Ruan Ming and and published by the Central Party School, which carried a series of articles aimed at refuting the "two whatevers." Having circumvented the censorship of Wang Dongxing and the Propaganda Department by this device, these were subsequently reprinted in *GMRB*, *RMRB*, and *JFRB*, as Special Commentator contributions indicating a considerable measure of support within high-level journalistic and theoretical circles.[10]

In March, *RMRB* published an article entitled "There Is Only One Criterion for Testing Truth."[11] On 11 May *GMRB* published "Practice Is the Sole Criterion for Testing Truth" under the title of Special Commentator.[12] This article, which was to spark off the nationwide campaign on "practice," was privately submitted to the paper by Hu Fuming, a philosophy professor at Nanjing University, and passed on by Editor in chief Yang Xiguang to Sun Changjiang and Wu Jiang in the Theory Research Office who modified it and arranged for its publication in *Lilun dongtai* on 10 May.[13] The reprinting of the article in *GMRB* on the following day (and in *RMRB*, *JFRB*, and through the New China News Analysis (NCNA) on 12 May) was authorized by Hu Yaobang himself.

The publication of the practice-criterion article caused a stir even among some of Deng's reform-minded colleagues. Hu Qiaomu tried to persuade Hu Yaobang to suspend the debate and discontinue the publication of controversial articles in *Lilun dongtai*.[14] However, the "antidogmatism" message of the article was reiterated on 2 June by Deng Xiaoping in his speech at the All-Army Political Work Conference, thus sanctioning

9. New Year's Day Editorial, *Peking Review*, no. 1 (1978), p. 10.

10. Goldman, *Sowing the Seeds of Democracy in China*, Cambridge: Harvard University Press, 1994, p. 36.

11. "There Is Only One Criterion for Testing Truth," *RMRB*, March 1978.

12. Special Commentator, "Practice Is the Sole Criterion for Testing Truth," *GMRB*, 11 May 1978.

13. Michael Schoenhal's article, "The 1978 Truth Controversy" gives a detailed account of the politics behind the publication of this article. *The China Quarterly*, no. 126 (1991), pp. 243–269. See also Merle Goldman, *Sowing the Seed*, p. 36–39.

14. Goldman, *Sowing the Seeds* p. 39.

his support of the movement to combat ideological rigidity.[15] Deng exhorted his audience to "restore and unfold the good tradition of seeking truth from facts," and his call was soon picked up by the media sources supportive of his political position. On 24 June *JFRB* and *RMRB* carried a Special Commentator article entitled "One of the Fundamental Principles of Marxism."[16] With this article (written by Wu Jiang, then section head at the Central Party School, and endorsed after modifications by Luo Ruiqing, secretary-general of the Military Commission) the dictum that " 'practice is the sole criterion of truth' is the quintessence of Mao Zedong Thought" became a constant theme of these two newspapers and scholarly journals under the influence of Hu Yaobang and his associates. By August–September, the propaganda barrage against what was now coming to be recognized as the "whatever faction" had intensified. At this time, the practice campaign reached national proportions as, one by one, the provincial leaderships began to endorse Deng's line and convene conferences to publicize it.

Meanwhile, Wang Dongxing, Zhang Pinghua (the Central Propaganda Bureau Chief), Wu Lengxi (the former editor of *RMRB*), Xiong Fu (the general editor of *Hongqi*), and Hu Sheng (the assistant general editor of *Hongqi*) maneuvered behind scenes to resist what they perceived as a concealed revisionist onslaught against Mao's radical theoretical innovations.[17] Their opposition to the reformist campaign underway[18] and the factional conflict brewing within leadership circles was illustrated by *Hongqi's* refusal to publish articles on the practice criterion and by the *Zhongguo qingnian* episode. On 6 September, *RMRB* had carried a report about the announcement of the publication of *Zhongguo qingnian* after a gap of 12 years. The first issue scheduled for distribution in mid-September was, however, abruptly confiscated ostensibly on the orders of Wang

15.   Deng Xiaoping, "Speech at the All-Army Political Work Conference," *RMRB*, 6 June 1978, pp. 1–2.

16.   Special Commentator, "One of the Fundamental Principles of Marxism," *JFRB*, *RMRB*, 24 June 1978.

17.   Hu Jiwei, "Report on a Series of Struggles." Qi Xin, "The New Power Struggle of the Chinese Communists," *Qishi niandai*, no. 106 (1978), p. 6.

18.   In private speeches and communications, the group criticized the theoretical campaign as an attempt at de-Maoification and a "cutting down of the banner."

Dongxing. The reason for confiscation, although not stated publicly, was its positive portrayal of the Tiananmen incident. The journal also carried an important article entitled "Smash Superstition, Master Science" signed by a staff Special Commentator, and written by Hu Yaobang himself.[19] The article accused Lin Biao and the Gang for creating a decade of "modern superstition," i.e., the cult of Mao, and could therefore be interpreted as one of the first indirect attacks on the Cultural Revolution in an official publication. The confiscated issue was ultimately released a few weeks later indicating that the "whateverists" had lost another round.[20]

The support rendered to Deng by military commanders and most provincial party secretaries and the gradually improving position of what the Hong Kong press referred to as the "practice faction" was demonstrated around the same time by the replacement of Beijing party chief Wu De with Lin Hujia. Wu De's dismissal was directly linked to the Tiananmen issue. Since the first anniversary of Zhou Enlai's death in January 1977, wall posters in Beijing had incessantly called for criticism and dismissal of Wu De for his involvement in the quelling of the 1976 riots and his earlier long-standing identification with the Cultural Revolutionary group.[21] The demands at this time of the Democracy Wall activists coincided with Deng's own political needs: the dismissal of Wu De and the "reversal of the verdict" on the Tiananmen incident, which not only eliminated one more leftist, but also represented another instance of an erroneous decision of Mao that needed to be rectified. Such developments could not fail to throw doubt on Mao's capacity for sound judgment and thus undermined Hua Guofeng's legitimacy which was based on the Maoist injunction, "with you in charge I am at ease."

Furthermore, the wide publicity given by the Democracy movement to the problems of the Maoist period—arbitrary rule, social and political repression, and economic stagnation —strengthened Deng's case for a sharp breach with the past and demonstrated widespread popular support for his policies of political reform and economic liberalization.

---

19. Qi Xin, "The New Power Struggle of the Chinese Communists," *Qishi niandai,* no. 106 (1978), pp. 6–13.

20. Ibid.

21. SWB/FE/5980/BII, 28 November 1978, pp. 5–7.

The cumulative effect of the developments in the summer and autumn of 1978 was a great surge in the political fortunes of the Dengist camp. A Central Work Conference that convened in Beijing from 10 November to 13 December prepared the groundwork for the more famous Central Committee Third Plenum by frank discussion of hitherto politically sensitive questions (the 1976 Tiananmen Incident, the role of Mao, and the Cultural Revolution), and by tabling important policy changes related to agriculture and industry. The reversal of verdict on the Tiananmen incident, decided by the Work Conference was officially announced by the newly constituted Beijing Party Committee on 15 November.[22] The Conference also proclaimed the end of "the era of turbulent mass struggles" (thus reversing Hua's emphasis on "taking class struggle as the key link") and proposed the termination of disruptive political campaigns and a shift in emphasis to economic modernization.

At a more concrete level, the delegates rejected the Dazhai agricultural model in favor of a policy stressing the production team as the basic unit and private plots, sideline occupations, and rural trade markets as necessary supplements of the socialist economy.[23] Hua Guofeng's industrial targets and plans for ambitious construction projects were dismissed as unrealistic and the conference proposed an addressing of the more urgent problem of imbalanced development. This agenda of economic reform had already been hinted at in the preceding months in the speeches and writings of Deng Xiaoping, and supportive intellectuals and military leaders. One of the most significant of these policy statements had been put forward by Hu Qiaomu at a meeting of the State Council in July 1978—but not published until October—where Hu urged paying attention to objective laws and letting economic mechanisms replace administrative ones for state regulation of the economy.[24]

The Third Plenum of the Eleventh Central Committee, which met from December 18–22, thus marked a triumph for Deng Xiaoping's camp. It formalized the changes recommended by the Work Conference. A draft

22. *Zhongguo geming shi*, "The Truth About the Tiananmen Events—History Turned Upside Down Through the *People's Daily* by the Gang of Four Is Turned Right Side Up," *RMRB*, 21 and 22 November 1978 pp. 140–143.

23. *Zhongguo geming shi*, pp. 140–151.

24. Hu Qiaomu, "Act According to Economic Laws," *RMRB*, 6 October 1978.

of New Working Regulations for Rural People's Communes paved the way for far-reaching changes in rural policies and the responsibility system in agriculture. Politically, it seriously undermined the position of Hua Guofeng and the "whatever faction" by a very positive evaluation of the practice debate and by intimating that Mao, too, was capable of committing mistakes.[25] Consequently, the Plenum reversed the 1959 verdict on Peng Dehuai and rehabilitated Tao Zhu, Bo Yibo and Yang Shangkun. The Communique admitted that mistakes had also occurred during the Cultural Revolution but a reassessment of the event itself was shelved for the time being.

Despite the reversals of the Third Plenum Wang Dongxing and his associates continued to attempt to broaden the inner-party struggle and focus criticism on "empiricism" rather than dogmatism. The move by the Philosophical Study Institute to extend the discussions on practice to the grassroots also met with some resistance. The need for a renewed campaign to "make up the missed lessons in the criterion of truth" later in the summer indicated the foot-dragging that had characterized important areas and organizations in the first round.[26] On 20 February 1979 a big character poster on Democracy Wall, signed by Gong Xiangdong, attacked the Third Plenum for "trampling on Chairman Mao's line and reversing the verdict on the right deviation in 1957 and on Peng Dehuai." A few days later another poster by a Marxism-Leninism–Mao Zedong Study Society criticized Hu Yaobang and Hu Qiaomu's revisionism.[27]

25. "Communique of the Third Plenum of the Eleventh Central Committee of the CPC, *Peking Review*, no. 52 (1978), pp. 6–16.

26. Staff Commentator, "Deepen and Expand the Scientific Study of Marxism-Leninism–Mao Zedong Thought," *Zhexue yanjiu*, no. 11 (1978), p. 207. Special Commentator, "Win Complete Victory in the Struggle to Expose and Criticize the Gang of Four, *RMRB* 4 October 1978, pp. 1–2; Contributing Commentator, "Talk on the Question of Abstract Affirmation and Specific Negation," *RMRB*, 22 September 1978; Zhang Chunhan "Overcome Narrow Thinking, Deepen the Discussions on the Criterion of Truth," *HQ*, no. 11 (1979), pp. 11– 14; Zhang Lizhou, "Deepen the Discussion on the Criterion of Truth," *Sixiang zhanxiano* no. 4 (1979), pp. 1–5; "Making up the Lesson Must be Applied to Reality," *RMRB*, 13 September 1979, p. 1.

27. Qi Xin, "The New Power Struggle of the Chinese Communists."

However, the momentum lost by Hua and the "whateverists" in early 1978 was never regained. Despite a temporary setback to the reformers in the first few months of 1979, the leftists were already on the retreat. The meeting of the Fifth National People's Congress (NPC) which took place from 18 June to 1 July 1979, reaffirmed the need to speed up agricultural reform, revise the overly ambitious target set for the Four Modernizations, and enact a legal system for the promotion and protection of socialist democracy.[28]

By year's end, the "whatever faction" was decidedly in troubled waters as the reformers and the practice theorists successfully challenged the stigma attached to criticizing leftism and extended the responsibility for catastrophic errors such as the Great Leap Forward (GLF) and the Cultural Revolution directly to Mao himself.[29] By February 1980 the "whateverists," now also known as the Little Gang of Four, had all been ousted from their political offices.

Even in retrospect, the relative ease with which Deng and other reform-minded associates disposed of the radical leftists and embarked on a course which the CCP under Mao Zedong had denounced as revisionist for over a decade is quite remarkable. Apart from attempts at political intimidation, remnant Mao loyalists offered practically no theoretical resistance to the discussions on practice. The question then arises: Was the lack of a systematic and coherent response to the theoretical challenge posed by the practice theorists reflective merely of the ineptitude of the "whatever faction"? Or, was it indicative of the validity of the claims to doctrinal fidelity by the practice theorists and their assertion that the stress on practice was indeed a reaffirmation of a basic tenet of Mao Zedong Thought? Secondly, and more importantly, did the campaign accomplish the reformist leadership's goal of establishing a new ideological consensus and addressing the crisis of legitimacy looming before the Party as a whole? To answer these questions, it is necessary to understand the philosophic essence of the campaign on "Practice Is the Only Criterion for Testing Truth" and it is to this that we turn next.

28. Hua Guofeng, "Report on the Work of the Government," *Beijing Review*, 6 July 1979.

29. Ye Jianying, "Comrade Ye Jianying's Speech at the Meeting in Celebration of the 30th Anniversary of the Founding of the PRC," *Beijing Review*, no. 22 (1979), pp. 7–32.

Practice Is the Sole Criterion for Testing Truth

In the international Communist movement, debates on Marxist philosophy were, more or less, an established tradition at crucial historical junctures. The first serious challenge to what had yet to be termed Marxist orthodoxy arose with the attempt by a few leaders of the German Social Democratic Party to channelize the working-class movement into a legalistic and constitutional direction, and to provide a philosophic dimension to the new policies by positing new discoveries in the natural and social sciences and in philosophy against the ideas of materialism and dialectics. Bernstein's attraction to Kantian dualism and his advocacy of gradual reform within the existing system was interpreted by Lenin and others as an opportunist attempt to revise the theories and views associated with Marx and Engels. Consequently, there arose, as the latter perceived it, the need to canonize, i.e., outline authoritative tenets of Marxist philosophy, which alone could serve as the theoretical basis for genuine revolutionary activity. Any attempt at modification or reformulation of the elements of this "orthodox" system could henceforth be labeled "revisionism."

The "humanist" and "historicist" Marxism which sprouted in the wake of de-Stalinization in Europe once again directed attention to questions of epistemology and philosophy, as men like Louis Althusser attempted to reassert the scientific character of Marxism and refute the validity of "socialist humanism" as an adequate response to the challenge of Stalinism.

In China, the success of the Maoist strategy of peasant bases and guerrilla warfare was celebrated in the philosophical writings of Ai Siqi and Mao Zedong as a vindication of dialectical materialism. "On Practice" and "On Contradiction" summarized the worldview of the Chinese Communists and legitimized their strategy of revolution. In the late 1950s, the failure of the GLF and the rumination that followed brought epistemology back into ideological discourse. "Where Do Correct Ideas Come From?" restated Mao's ideas on the nature of truth and the process for discovering it and marked the philosophical evolution that had taken place since 1937.

The 1978 discussions on practice shared a similar concern for validating a given set of policy preferences by a restructuring of the established tradition. The task before theoreticians was the retention of certain concepts and the discarding of others, and the problem they faced was that of establishing the credentials of their criteria of selection. Recourse to epistemology was needed to authenticate their restructuring of the Marxist-Maoist legacy and counter orthodox criticism of such "revision." The *GMRB* article of 11 May 1978 argued:

> Undoubtedly we must adhere to the most basic principles of Marxism, the Marxist standpoint, viewpoint, and method. But the Marxist theoretical treasure-house is not a petrified, unchanging dogma, it must in practice, continuously add new viewpoints, new conclusions and discard those specific old viewpoints and old conclusions which are not suited to the new conditions.[30]

The identification of social practice as the criterion of "scientificity" by this article set the tone for a media barrage reiterating and elaborating the main themes set out in the original: Dogmatism is the main obstacle to progress and policy making geared to the development and modernization of China. Ideological fetishism or an overly theoretical approach should be replaced by the spirit of "seeking truth from facts" and recognizing "practice as the sole criterion for testing truth."

The process of verifying truth outlined during the campaign was based on Mao's exposition in "On Practice." According to this text, the process of acquiring knowledge begins with the perceptions received from the objective world by human sense organs.[31] After a sufficient amount of perceptual information has been accumulated, a leap occurs in consciousness from perceptual knowledge to the formation of ideas, i.e., conceptual knowledge. This marks the first step in the whole process of cognition—the movement from objective matter to subjective consciousness. Whether or not such conceptual knowledge is a correct reflection of reality is not ascertainable at this point. Verification takes place in the second stage of the cognitive process when ideas, plans, measures are translated into practice. If preconceived aims (predictions of objective results) are realized in that course of practice, one's ideas are an accurate representa-

---

30. Special Commentator, "Practice Is the Sole Criterion for Testing Truth."
31. Mao Zedong, "On Practice," *Selected Works of Mao Tse-tung*, Peking: Foreign Languages Press, 1967. (*SW*), vol. 1, pp. 68–69.

tion of reality. If not, then consciousness lacks correspondence with the external world.[32] However, Mao went on to add:

> Generally speaking, whether in the practice of changing nature or of changing society, men's original ideas, theories, plans, or programs are seldom realized without any alteration . . . ideas, theories plans, or programs are usually altered partially and sometimes even wholly, because of the discovery of unforeseen circumstances in the course of practice. That is to say it does happen that the original ideas, theories, plans, or programs fail to correspond with reality either in whole or in part and are wholly or partially incorrect. In many instances, failures have to be repeated many times before errors in knowledge can be corrected and correspondence with the laws of the objective process achieved and consequently before the subjective can be transformed into the objective, or, in other words, before the anticipated result can be achieved in practice. Nevertheless, when that point is reached, the movement of human knowledge regarding a certain objective process at a certain stage of its development may be considered completed.[33]

Needless to say, Mao in this exposition left unaddressed the crux of the issue, that is, on a practical level, of the many different or even totally contradictory viewpoints that emerge from theories summed up on the basis of practice, which interpretation is to be regarded as the authoritative one? Does the choice depend on who or how many are advocating what? The fact that verification requires time, and a proposition may need to go through repeated testing in practice before it is proved true further compounds the problem. The next question that arises is, how many times would the practice have to be repeated before a particular choice could be eliminated and another accepted in its place? Lastly, one can argue, in Mao's conception of the knowledge process there is *never* any definitive knowledge of truth. In the "endless cycles" of practice, knowledge, again practice, and again knowledge, the "results" of practice at any given stage are simply perceptions that need to go through the rational stage and then applied for verification, over and over again.[34]

32.   Ibid, p. 67.
33.   Ibid, pp. 78–79.
34.   In their article "Marxist Theory and Socialist Transition: The Construction of an Epistemological Relation," Michael Dutton and Paul Healy criticize the post-Mao theorists for this but the problem exists in Mao's presentation itself. See *Chinese Marxism in Flux*, 1984, ed. Bill Brugger, New York, M.E. Sharpe, 1985, p. 27.

The problem of conflicting assessments of practical results and the consequent need for a second criterion was raised by practice theorists in the 1978 discussions. The notions of "benefit," "majority interests," and "people's welfare" were put forward by Wang Ruoshui and other writers as criteria for evaluating the results of practice.[35] Theorists like Ma Ming, however, distinguished between practice as an epistemological category and "welfare" or "benefit" as political criteria, and resisted a conflation of the two, pointing out that this would lead to the confusion of Marxism with pragmatism or utilitarianism.[36] Although left unresolved at the time the point raised by Wang et al., was related to the crucial "facts cannot interpret themselves" argument which relates revolutionary goals to practical results.[37] The differences between the two groups would be manifested more clearly in the following decade between humanist Marxists who would go on to refute the Leninist theory of reflection and others who would equate the criterion of practice with that of productive forces.

For the most part, the late-1970s discussions on practice followed the positivist-Marxist tradition begun with Engels and Kautsky which treated Marxism as a theory whose truth could be established by universally recognized criteria of scientific validity and involved neither social, i.e., class commitment nor value judgment. Knowledge was regarded as a product

35. Wang Ruoshui, "The Aim of Practice Is the Criterion to Evaluate the Success or Failure of Practice," *GMRB*, 12 May 1980, p. 3. Contributing Commentator, "All Things in the Subjective World Must Be Verified by Practice," *RMRB*, 25 September 1978. Contributing Commentator, "Open Up the Broad Prospect of Theoretical Work," *RMRB*, 22 December 1978. Lei Zhenwu, "Uphold Materialism, Thoroughly Implement Practice as the Criterion of Truth," *Zhexue yanjiu*, no. 9 (1979), pp. 3–9. Meng Xianzhong, Wang Yanbing, Liu Renke, Wang Youdang and Hu Hao, "It is Necessary to Reflect Correctly the Results of Practice," *Zhexue yanjiu*, no. 6 (1980), pp. 54–56.

36. Ma Ming, "Neither Purpose nor Interest Is the Criterion to Test the Truth," *Zhexue yanjiu*, no. 8 (1980), pp. 13–16, 12. Articles denying the charge of pragmatism included, Wang Ruoshui, "The Theory of Knowledge Must Not Forget People," *GMRB*, 12 February 1981, p. 4, also in David Kelly ed. "Wang Ruoshui," pp. 101–12; Chen Xiuzhai, "Clearly Demarcate Between the Marxist Criterion of Practice and that of Pragmatism," *Zhexue yanjiu*, no. 3 (1979), pp. 210–24, Wang Jianwei, "The Principled Difference Between the Marxist Criterion of Practice and that of Pragmatism," *Zhexue yanjiu*, no. 6 (1980), pp. 56–58, 51.

37. For a more detailed exposition see Brugger and Kelly, *Chinese Marxism*, and my unpublished doctoral dissertation, *Rethinking Marxism in Post-Mao China: The Erosion of Official Ideology, 1978–84*, Ann Arbor Michigan: University of Michigan, 1992.

of scientific experiments so designed that the result would be causally dependent on the nature of the real object and assertainable by an "a-theoretical mode of observation governed by a preestablished harmony between language and the real."[38]

However, in Mao's thought, by the early 1960s, the whole notion of objective criteria for establishing the "scientificity" of revolutionary Marxist theory had been superceded in favor of deciding on political grounds. At this time Mao, following Ai Siqi, (and unlike Yang Xianzhen) explicitly rejected the simple theory of reflection outlined in Lenin's *Materialism and Empirio-Criticism* in favor of the more sophisticated *Philosophical Notebooks'* view of the mediating role of consciousness.[39] In "Where Do Correct Ideas Come From?" he wrote:

> (In the process of verifying ideas in practice) generally speaking, those that succeed are correct and those that fail are incorrect, and this is especially true of man's struggle with nature. In social struggle, the forces representing the advanced class sometimes suffer defeat not because their ideas are incorrect but because, in the balance of forces engaged in struggle, they are not as powerful for the time being as the forces of reaction; they are therefore temporarily defeated, but they are bound to triumph sooner or later.[40]

38. Collier, "In Defence of Epistemology." In *Issues in Marxist Philosophy,* edited by John Mephan and David-Hillel Ruben, Brighton, England: Harvester Press, 1979, pp. 65–6. Barry Hindess, *Philosophy and Methodology in the Social Sciences*, Hassocks, 1977, p. 186. Such an assumption has been challenged quite successfully by the conventionalist approach in the philosophy of science, which argues that the body of established scientific theory at a particular moment is "underdetermined" by empirical evidence and formal reasoning. See Benton, *The Rise and Fall of Structural Marxism*, p. 23. Thus, it is always possible in full logical consistency to account for available empirical evidence in terms of more than one set of theoretical assumptions. Theories of perception, too, may be employed to establish the incoherence of the idea of "theory neutral" observation, which would be required if empirical evidence were to play the kind of role of final arbiter between competing theories to which empiricism generally assigns it. Thomas Kuhn has argued that "in answering any scientific question, the particular conclusions that the researcher arrives at are probably determined by his prior experience in other fields, by the accident of his investigation and by his own individual makeup." See *The Structure of Scientific Revolutions*, 2d edition, Chicago: University of Chicago Press, 1970, p. 4.

39. Joshua Fogel, *Ai Ssu-ch'i's Contribution to the Development of Chinese Marxism*, Harvard Contemporary China Series, no. 4. Cambridge: Harvard University Press, 1987, p. 25.

40. Mao Zedong, "Where Do Correct Ideas Come From?" *SW*, pp. 502–504.

In the wake of the criticism that he had undergone for the failure of the GLF, this essay was an obvious attempt to reconcile Mao's belief in his own correctness with the "reality" of his defeat. Truth for Mao now became not simply a correspondence of ideas to fact, attainable by any practitioner of scientific experimentation. Like Georg Lukacs and Karl Korsch before him, Mao in 1963 was reasserting the epistemologically privileged position of the proletariat to argue that true knowledge of the social process and historical development could be attained only by that class.[41] The validity or truth of Marxism as a scientific theory of reality was not comprehensible to just anyone since it was essentially the self-awareness of a revolutionary class changing reality in the process of knowing it, and not a passive assimilation of a ready-made external world. From this Mao and the radicals went on to argue that knowledge could serve specific class interests and therefore truth was class truth.

The question that arises at this point is whether truth which is attainable only from the vantage point of a certain class is also inherently true. The Maoist insistence in the late fifties and sixties that truth can emerge only through struggle, and the tendency to define the proletariat increasingly in political terms lead me to argue that Mao's use of terms such as class knowledge or class truth was misleading. During this time his concern was not with truth or falsehood in the ordinary sense, i.e., as errors of cognition, but rather, true or false consciousness, where the latter confirms the state of human servitude to impersonal objective-historical processes and the former leads to an awareness of the possibility of emancipation, de-alienation, recovery of species essence, and so forth. The issue was not one of evaluation by any universal criteria of scientific accuracy since such scientific criteria are scarcely value free with their emphasis on efficiency, technological rationality, etc. One either sided with the bourgeoisie or with the proletariat. Truths revealed by the failure of the GLF according to the radicals were "bourgeois truths" because they demoralized the proletariat and hence served the interests of the bourgeoisie. Since the proletariat rids itself of "delusion" and "mystification" and acquires "true consciousness" during the struggle for emancipation, the

41. Lukacs, *History and Class Consciousness*, London: Merlin Press, 1971, pp. 224–225; Kolakowski, *Main Currents of Marxism*, vol. 3, p. 320.

emphasis on revolutionary change, class struggle, and cultural revolution was seen by Mao as the means by which his own view would be vindicated over that of his rivals.

The post-Mao theorists made an important departure from Mao by negating the idea of class truth:

> Truth refers to a correct understanding of objective things and of the laws governing them, "correct" here meaning conforming to reality and tested by practice. Whether or not knowledge conforms to reality is a matter quite apart from an individual's class standpoint or a class's attitude towards that knowledge or towards the reality it reflects.[42]

These discussions followed the Kautskyte and Stalinist tradition, which conceived of truth as emerging through participation in the production process or scientific experimentation and becoming ever more refined with the advance of technology. Given the new leadership's emphasis on undermining the salience of class struggle, the epistemology discussions chose to disregard Mao's view that truth could develop only from struggle with falsehood, and opposition was necessary for the discovery of truth since a correct line could only be formulated in a struggle with an incorrect line, the two constituting a unity of opposites.[43]

The lack of emphasis on the dialectics of the struggle between truth and error (the emergence of truth through class struggle) fitted in with Deng Xiaoping and Chen Yun's preference for stressing harmony and unity and downplaying the role of conflict. Furthermore, the intent of the epistemology debate was to legitimize the "rational" and "correct" policies of the leading coalition. Any acceptance of the idea of temporary defeats due to an adverse balance of forces may have been construed as a potential weapon in the hands of the opposition.

Mao's notion, that "in social struggle, the forces representing the advanced class sometimes suffer defeat not because their ideas are incorrect but because in the balance of forces engaged in struggle, they are not

---

42. Jia Wei, "Is Class Nature an Attribute of Truth?" in *Zhexue zhenglun, 1977–1980 nianchu,* pp. 55–71; *RMRB* 28 November 1978.

43. Mao Zedong, "Speech at CPC National Conference on Propaganda Work," 12 March, 1957, *SW,* p. 292.

as powerful . . . as the forces of reaction,"[44] was not referred to directly but it was quite explicitly rejected at this time. A 1979 *Hongqi* article (i.e., after the journal had begun making up "missed lessons" on the criterion of practice), entitled "Power and Truth," addressed itself exclusively to this issue. Referring to the widespread cynicism that "whoever possesses power will possess truth; whoever has more power will hold more truth"; the author Li Yanshi claimed somewhat unrealistically, "whoever possesses truth will be obeyed; whether he is a worker, toiler of the land, night-soil carrier, or street cleaner, as long as truth lies in his hand he will be obeyed."[45]

Overall, the broader and largely unintended consequence of the stance adopted by the practice discussions was that in underplaying the salience of class and denying the epistemologically privileged position of the proletariat, the party elite, as its vanguard, simultaneously undermined its own hitherto unassailable monopoly over truth. The door was now open for intellectual critics within the elite as well as ordinary citizens to draw lessons from practice and contest the leadership's claims to being the sole arbiters of truth. As Hu Jiwei admitted a decade later:

> As one who had been used to listening to the words of the Party leadership, I began to awaken gradually after experiencing a decade's painful internal strife (during the Cultural Revolution). But it was not until the discussions on the criterion of truth that I was really awakened and began to question the truth of this principle.[46]

Relative Truth, Absolute Truth, and the Problem of Revisionism

The central concern of the epistemology discussion was the legitimization of a set of policies, which the CCP under Mao had denounced as revisionist for over a decade, without compromising totally the prestige of the

---

44. Mao Zedong, "Where Do Correct Ideas Come From?" *SW,* p. 503.

45. Li Yanshi, "Power and Truth," *Hongqi,* no. 11 (1979), pp. 15–17.

46. Hu Jiwei, "Should One Listen to the Party's Words or Not?" in Yu Guangyuan and Hu Jiwei, eds., *The Moment of Sudden Awakening,* Beijing: Zhongwai chuban gongsi, 1989.

leading core and the authority of the ideological tradition. Consequently, definition of revisionism was the focal issue, i.e., what constitutes the essence of Marxism-Leninism–Mao Zedong Thought, which theses is it permissible to criticize and even reject without giving up the right to be the legitimate heirs of the tradition. Orthodoxy, it was argued, did not imply the uncritical acceptance of the works of Marx, Engels, Lenin, and Mao, and revisionism could not be confused with creativity and innovation.[47]

Beginning with the notion that in an infinitely developing universe, man's knowledge of objective reality must always be incomplete; all participants in the discussion agreed, in principle, that even if a scientific theory has been tested in practice and found to be correct it is necessary to revise it again.[48] Since practice at any given stage has a limited sphere of activity the knowledge verified by it in that stage is a relative truth. This relative truth corresponds with the objects reflected by itself, however, this is an approximate correspondence not an absolute one. With the development of science, theoretical explanations of observed facts will be replaced by others more precise and correct, hence, all "proven" hypotheses must be continually tested in practice and revised, if necessary. Such a position, it was argued, was the reaffirmation of a central feature of the Maoist theory of knowledge.[49]

47. Wang Renzhong, "Typical Example of Seeking Truth From Facts," *Zhangguo qingnian,* no. 4, 1978, and *GMRB,* 9 December 1978; Li Honglin, "Science and Blind Faith," *RMRB,* 2 October 1978; "Mao Zedong Thought Is Science" in *Science and Blind Faith,* Tianjin: People's Publishing House (PPH), 1980, pp. 48–56 (the article was written in 1977); Staff Commentator, "Rectify the Attitude Towards Marxism," *RMRB,* 3 October 1979, pp. 1–4; Staff Commentator, "Seek Truth From Facts, Where There Are Errors, They Must Be Corrected," *RMRB,* 15 November 1978, pp. 1, 4; Staff Special Commentator, "Eliminate Superstition, Master Science," *Zhongguo qingnian,* no. 1 (1978), pp. 5–8.

48. However, all participants emphasized a two-tier distinction between general principles and specific principles. The former referred to a category of universal significance, the stand, viewpoint, and method of Marxism otherwise known as the principles of "dialectics" and "materialism." In accordance with such "basic" principles, specific principles of the second category are arrived at to address concrete problems encountered in practice. While "universal principles" were to be considered sacred and inviolable, specific principles could and, indeed, must be revised in response to changing times and circumstances. No writer ever offered any explanation of the epistemological basis of such a distinction. This point will be discussed in more detail later in this chapter.

49. Qi Zhenhai, "The Relativity and Absoluteness of the Criterion of Practice," *Zhexue yanjiu,* no. 7 (1978), pp. 8–14.

The accuracy of this assertion can only be assessed by referring to the Maoist tradition. Since the discussions beginning in 1978 were marked by the "silence" of a Maoist opposition, I have resorted to reconstructing the Maoist argument from Mao's own epistemological essays and from another debate on the theory of knowledge, which had preceded the 1978 discussions by almost a decade and a half.[50] This earlier debate was conducted over a period of two years, 1962–64, primarily in the pages of *Hongqi* magazine. Its focus was precisely the same as that of the 1978 discussion, viz., can a "verified" theory be proven through new practice to be not completely correct and therefore have to be revised?

The controversy was initiated by the natural scientist He Zuoxiu and his main protagonists were Du Lei, Wu Zhunguang, and Tao Delin.[51] The latter group of writers who seem to have been representing the Maoist viewpoint at the time rejected the claim that "proven" hypotheses may be rendered erroneous by subsequent practice on the grounds that this undermined the "dependability" of practice as a criterion for testing truth.[52] The Maoist view was that "a theory is overthrown or revised not because the criterion of practice is relative in character but because the theory has not been really proved or not completely proved by practice." In "On Practice" Mao had argued:

The history of man's knowledge tells us that the truth of many theories is incomplete, and that this incompleteness is remedied through the test of practice. Many theories are erroneous and it is through the test of practice that their errors are corrected. That is why practice is the criterion of truth.

50. I first became aware of this debate through a reference in J.D. Hill, "Epistemology and Politics," University of Michigan Ph.D. Dissertation, 1981. I am grateful to Professor Donald Munro for referring me to Hill's dissertation.

51. He Zuoxiu, "Some Questions of the Criterion of Practice in the Study of Natural Sciences," *HQ*, no. 2 (1962), pp. 13–24. Tu Lei and Wu Chunkuang, "Practice Is the Only Objective Criterion by Which to Verify Truth." Ho Tso-hsiu, "More on the Question of the Criterion of Practice in the Study of Natural Sciences." Chan Ping, "The Situation on the Discussion of the Question of the Criterion of Practice." JPRS 25624, 29 July 1964, *Translation From Hungch'i*, no. 10 (1964). T'ao Telin and Ho Tso-hsiu also took part in the 1978 discussions. Ho's stand seems to have remained the same, while Tao appears to have changed his 1962 position.

52. Tu Lei and Wu Chunkuang, above cited.

If it is thought that a theory which has been proved correct through verification by practice, has to be revised subsequently and that this is a phenomenon in history which conforms to law, then there is no need to show that practice is the criterion of truth.[53]

Unlike theorists during the Practice campaign, Mao did not use the terms truth (knowledge claims verified by practice) and theory interchangeably.[54] Theory in the Maoist usage consisted of conceptual schemes and law-like propositions that can be divided into (1) truths verified by practice, and (2) formulations based on interpolation and extrapolation from other propositions. The latter are as yet unverified by practice and so cannot be regarded as "proven" truth.

The Maoist argument, thus, was a very dogmatic one, maintaining that if a set of propositions are proven empirically to be true at one time (within that sphere of application)[55] they cannot be proven to be false at a later time. Error was restricted to (1) speculative aspects which have not yet been empirically verified (i.e., the summations of results of practice in the rational step of knowledge), and (2) when a theory, which has been confirmed empirically, is applied outside the sphere for which it was tested. It is primarily in this sense that the Maoists discussed the relativity of truth.

Mao's dogmatism can be traced to Lenin's influence. In his philosophically unsophisticated and polemical *Materialism and Empirio-Criticism*, Lenin had observed:

> The criterion of practice can never, in the nature of things, either confirm or refute any human idea completely. This criterion also is sufficiently "indefinite not to allow human knowledge to become 'absolute,' but at the same time it is sufficiently definite to wage a ruthless fight on all varieties of idealism and agnosticism . . . for instance, Bogdanov is prepared to recognize Marx's theory of the circulation of money as an objective truth only

53. Ibid.

54. "On Practice," p. 77.

55. An example of this would be: If surrounding the cities by the countryside was a correct strategy in 1936 then this could be never proved wrong for that situation would never be duplicated. If the strategy failed 10 years later then that failure was in reference to the proposition—"surrounding the cities by the countryside is a correct strategy in 1946."

for 'our time,' and calls it dogmatism to attribute to this theory a 'super-historically objective' truth." This is again a muddle. *The correspondence of this theory to practice cannot be altered by any future circumstances* (my emphasis) for the same reason that makes it an eternal truth that Napoleon died on 5 May 1821.[56]

Lenin's position was in turn derived from Engels who looked at the development of scientific laws as a process in which over a period of time "theoretical explanations of observed facts are replaced by others which do not contradict the former ones but narrow the sphere of their validity"— e.g., Regnaults' discovery defined more precisely the applicability of Boyle's and Marriotte's laws.[57]

The post-Mao practice theorists, on the other hand, adopted a much more flexible position. They accepted the distinction between verified truth and unverified "true" propositions, and significantly, unlike the Maoists, these theorists—or at least some of the more discerning amongst them—did not overlook the perceptual nature of summations of practical results, and categorically denied that "what is summed up from practical experience is, in fact, truth already tested by practice."[58] It was admitted that this was equally applicable to the line laid down by the Eleventh Congress and the goal of the Four Modernizations."[59] The crucial difference between the post-Mao theorists and the Maoists was that, in principle, the former implicitly rejected the finite character of Mao's single process of knowledge.

For the practice theorists the question of revision was also applicable to "verified" true propositions. The truth of a proposition, they maintained, cannot be conclusively proved in a given practice, and "new" practice must not only prove the truth of unverified parts of a theory but must also "retest" proven truths. Thus, through practice one comes to know the

56. Lenin, *Materialism and Empirio-Criticism.*

57. Kolakowski, vol. 1, p. 395.

58. "The source and the testing cannot be separated. . . ." See Liu Ben, "The Origin of Knowledge and the Criterion of Truth," *Zhexue yanjiu*, no. 9 (1980), pp. 12–19. The criticism of Dutton and Healy is, therefore, misinformed, p. 47.

59. Lei Zhenwu, above cited. Xia Guanghua, "The Political Line Must Be Tested Through the Practice of Economic Construction," *Shehui kexue*, no. 3 (1979), pp. 3–4.

truth, but verification as such does not yield definitive truths. Their epistemological position on this issue can be compared to that of the Western philosophy of science tradition associated with Popper and Kuhn that emphasizes that science, far from offering absolute certainty and final answers, is a ceaseless dynamic process. Hence, even hypotheses that have been empirically verified as true possess a relative nature, and scientific data does not prove the "truth" of the hypothesis. It merely suggests that the hypothesis is not false.[60]

The basic divergence within the intellectual elite conducting the discussions and the political leadership initiating and overseeing them became notable at this point. Not only scientists like Fang Lizhi, but other intellectual participants as well, rejected the premise that any scientific approach can and will yield any absolute truths. The 11 May article written by Hu Fuming, and modified by Hu Yaobang, answered the question whether any items of human knowledge can have sovereign validity and an unconditional claim to truth in an unqualified negative. A *RMRB* commentary of 19 September 1978 maintained that "new experiences in practice enrich certain old theories . . . and new theories replace individual theories that through practice have been proved inapplicable."[61] Another article in the November 1979 issue of *Hongqi*[62] claimed:

> Raising questions cannot put an end to the old stage of knowledge. Only the formation of a new theory marks the beginning of a new stage. Raising

60. George Winburg and John A. Shumaker point out, "(o)ne major factor must be discussed at the outset—the fact that evidence that is consistent with a hypothesis can almost never be taken as conclusive grounds for accepting it, whereas evidence that is inconsistent with a hypothesis does provide grounds for rejecting it. . . . The reason for not necessarily accepting consistent evidence is that a finding that is consistent with a hypothesis would be consistent with another hypothesis too, and thus does not necessarily demonstrate the truth of the given hypothesis, as opposed to the other alternatives. . . . Therefore, the finding that is consistent with the hypothesis does not demonstrate its truth. See, *Statistics: An Intuitive Approach*. Monterey, Calif: Brooks and Cole Publishing Co., 1974, p. 156. Originally quoted in Hill.

61. Contributing Commentator, "Uphold the Marxist Scientific Approach," *RMRB* 19 September 1978. Also published in *GMRB* and *JFRB* of the same date.

62. This was the same issue in which the journal apologized for missed lessons in the practice discussion and the change in tenor is remarkable.

questions produces the sparks of new thinking. The seeds of a new concept often fail to peep from under the hardy rocks formed by old concepts. With questions raised, an old theory shows initial signs of collapse. But, unless a new theory takes its place, its defenders will readily repair all the damage done. Therefore questions remain to be developed and must be followed up with the formation of new ideas. Only with the formation of new theories can we ensure the *destruction and elimination of old ones* (my emphasis).[63]

The use of the term (*lilun*) theory instead of (*yuanzi*) proposition, principle, or axiom in some of the articles appearing during this time was neither casual nor an oversight. Clearly, their notion of the development of knowledge went much beyond the "correction, enrichment, and supplementation" that was being advocated by the political leadership (both radical reformers as well as the incrementalists). The intellectual critics of Maoism were not discussing the partial explosion of a theory but the *replacement* of Marxism by other theories more suited to China's modernization. Their explicit purpose appears to have been to present Marxism as a generalization that had served to consolidate a given phase in the development of science but had now assumed the nature of an "epistemological obstacle" to retard further advances.[64] "Marxism has become fossilized," Fang Lizhi opined without mincing words. "It is composed of obsolete conclusions that have led to failure . . . the emancipation of our thought

63. Jiang Niantao, "Questioning and Argument," *Hongqi*, no. 11 (1979), pp. 17–19.
64. The *Hongqi* article cited earlier also hinted at the archaic nature of Marxism by using the following example: "Before the 17C there existed in medical circles the erroneous idea that one kind of blood flowed from the liver to the right ventricle of the heart and then to the lungs and the general system by the veins, and that another flowed from the left ventricle to the general system by the arteries. Such a concept was claimed to have been proven for over a thousand years. Though it was questioned and criticized at various times by Serratus, Vesalius, and other scientists, it remained correct because of the lack of a new theory. Not until Harvey in Britain discovered the circulation of blood was the traditional doctrine of blood flowing from the liver to the general system upset.... Therefore, at a time when a thousand boats are sailing in competition, we should be sufficiently prepared ideologically to get rid of inappropriate arguments and accept new arguments that help Chinese style modernization."

means a search for new theories, not the so-called restoration of Marxism's original face, nor any such thing."[65]

In contrast, others took a more conservative and ambiguous approach. The *Jiefang junbao* (*JFJB*) commentary written by Wu Jiang and endorsed after some modification by Luo Ruiqing maintained:

> Theories are not unchangeable, permanent truths. They must undergo supplementation, revision, enrichment, and development through practice. . . . *The entire theory and fundamental principles of Marxism-Leninism-Mao Zedong Thought are irrefutable. We must adhere to them at all times and never go against them* (my emphasis).[66]

By any definition, to assert that a certain truth or principle is irrefutable is to accord it a permanent status. But such a conception of eternal truth is incompatible with the view that empirical verification cannot prove the truth of a proposition conclusively. To assert simultaneously the "irrefutability" of certain Marxist principles and to acknowledge the possibility of all verified "true" propositions requiring revision and verification is epistemologically inconsistent. In the light of the position staked out by the practice debate as a whole, assertions such as those of the *JFJB* commentary (and the enunciation of the Four Cardinal Principles—to uphold the socialist road, the dictatorship of the proletariat, the leadership of the Communist Party, and Marxism-Leninism–Mao Zedong Thought—by Deng Xiaoping in March 1979) were inherently problematic.

The inability of a section of the leadership and its intellectual establishment to countenance an extension of the concept of revision to Marxism as a whole stemmed from its limited approach to change. In the late 1970s and early 1980s revisionism was still an accepted and pejorative term in the Chinese Communist vocabulary. The Soviet Union continued to be regarded as revisionist[67] and the objective of the discussions on practice

65.   Williams, "The Expanding Universe of Fang Lizhi: Astrophysics and Ideology in People's China," *Chinese Studies in Philosophy*, vol. 19, no. 4 (1988), p. 33.

66.   Contributing Commentator, "One of the Fundamental Principles of Marxism," *JFRB* (also *RMRB*), 24 June 1978.

67.   Gilbert Rozman, *The Chinese Debate About Soviet Socialism 1978–85*, Princeton, N.J.: Princeton University Press, 1987, p. 71; Contributing Commentator, "Talk on the Question of Abstract Affirmation and Specific Negation," in *RMRB*, 22 September 1978.

was, for many in the leadership, more to defend the new policies from the charge of revisionism rather than to deny the validity of the idea of revisionism per se. This would come later not only because it was epistemologically consistent but also because then the political fortunes had changed in favor of the radical reformers.

The definition of revisionism at this time centered on the distinction between the universal/basic principles of Marxism—also referred to as the stand, viewpoint, and method of Marxism—and particular or specific principles which were derived from the experience of applying basic principles to concrete situations. The latter, being specific to time, place and circumstance, could not be applied mechanically, hence, revision of such principles according to need was entirely justified.[68]

Such a distinction was in line with the official Marxist tradition traceable to Lenin and expressed succinctly by Lukacs:

> Orthodox Marxism . . . does not imply the uncritical acceptance of the results of Marx's investigations. It is not the belief in this or that thesis, nor the exegesis of a "sacred" book. On the contrary, orthodoxy refers exclusively to *method* (emphasis in original). It is the scientific conviction that dialectical materialism is the road to truth and that its methods can be developed, expanded, and deepened only along the lines laid down by its founders. It is conviction, moreover, that all attempts to surpass or improve it have led and must lead to oversimplification, triviality, and eclecticism.[69]

Mao's commitment to dialectical materialism had implied the acceptance of the ubiquity and absoluteness of conflict both as phenomenon and as analytical method. According to "On Contradiction," the dialectical materialist-world outlook conceives of a universe in constant flux. However, the universal cause or universal basis for the movement and development of change, i.e., contradiction, remains forever the same. Given the fact that contradiction is unconditional and permanent, man's knowledge of the law of contradiction, i.e., the basic law of materialist dialectic, is permanently valid.[70]

68. Qi Zhenhai and Xu Hongwu, "A Brief Discussion on the Two Forms of Revisionism," in *Shehui kexue zhanxian*, no. 3 (1980), pp. 21–25.
69. Lukacs, "What Is Orthodox Marxism?" in *History and Class Consciousness*, p. 1.
70. "On Contradiction," *SW*, pp. 85–133.

Mao's distinction between basic principles and specific principles was in terms of spheres of application not on the basis of refutability. His epistemological position was that man's consciousness is able to grasp universally applicable absolute truth—the Marxist theory of dialectical and historical materialism being an example of such permanently valid universally applicable knowledge.

In this he was in complete agreement with Soviet thinking on the subject. *A Textbook of Marxist Philosophy* published by the Leningrad Institute of Philosophy held, for instance, that the fundamental distinction between relativism and dialectical materialism is that, for the latter,

> knowledge of the basic law system if it is confirmed by the criterion of historical social practice, enters into the iron inventory of permanent scientific knowledge. . . . The development of practice, the enrichment of factual material, and the development of scientific knowledge, which is connected with these, can make man's knowledge of these basic laws more concrete, or even show that the law system, which was regarded in the past stage as fundamental and universal, is itself rooted in another deeper law system and is its partial form. But all this in no measure destroys the fact that in that law system man had reflected a "little bit" of absolute truth.[71]

In post-Mao discussions, individuals who simultaneously accepted the provisional character of all empirical verification and upheld the "irrefutability" of basic principles were trapped in an ambiguous, dogmatic, and essentially untenable situation. From an epistemological perspective the distinction between universal principles with absolute validity and "relatively true" specific principles, which can be revised according to time and circumstance, implies a hierarchy of practices with different epistemological statuses that yield different kinds of truth. Marxists like Althusser have made distinctions in the epistemological statuses of practice, but inasmuch as the discourse of Chinese theorists did not admit of different practices their position was inherently problematic.

On the other hand, those Chinese leaders or intellectuals who were willing to take Deng's call for "emancipation of minds" to its logical limits

---

71. Leningrad Institute of Philosophy, *A Textbook of Marxist Philosophy*, translated, revised, and edited by John Lewis, London: Camelot Press Ltd., 1937.

did make a radical break with the official Marxist-Maoist tradition. Wang Ruoshui inveighed against "all forms of superstitions, dogmatism, stereo-typed writing, forbidden zones, outdated modes of thought," and pointed out that "according to Marx, all theories must be subjected to the test of practice."[72] A 1980 *Shehui kexue* article claimed:

> The relative and absolute character of truth comes, first of all, from the inherent contradiction in objective things themselves. Everything is in the midst of uninterrupted transformation and development. When the objective object changes, objective truth cannot but change. . . . *One must not conceive of universal truth as eternal truth* (my emphasis).[73]

Hu Yaobang and his intellectual followers accepted the argument that if Marxism is regarded as science and the very criterion of science is revision, then the whole issue of revisionism was of no consequence, whatsoever. Yu Guangyuan argued persausively that one cannot conceive of Marxism as a science and at the same time grant absolute validity to some of its principles, for science ceases to be science once it begins to be worshipped as a set of eternal truths.[74] Guo Luoji deplored the turning of revolutionary leaders into "gods" and the "science of revolutionary theories" into "theology."[75] Such premises formed the rationale for the radical reformers' subsequent efforts to un-dogmatize Chinese Marxism, and their assertion that revisionism was just a historical term for certain phenomena around the turn of the century.[76]

The discussions on epistemology took place in the context of increasing emphasis by the Dengist leadership on scientific and technological modernization. Earnest efforts to revive Chinese Academy of Sciences (CAS) and Chinese Academy of Social Sciences (CASS) research followed

72. Wang Ruoshui, "Marxism and Emancipation of the Mind," *RMRB*, 1 August 1 1980, p. 5.

73. Zhang Shihong, "Eliminate the Metaphysical Poison in the Theory of Truth—Understanding the Relative and Absolute Nature of Truth," *Shehui kexue*, no. 2 (1979), pp. 17–22.

74. Quoted in Williams, "Fang Lizhi's Expanding Universe," p. 468.

75. Guo Luoji, "Commenting on the Crisis of Faith," *Wenhui bao*, 18 January 1980, p. 3. Also in *JPRS*, no. 75320, 17 March 1980, p. 23.

76. Conversation with Su Shaozhi, April 1985.

Deng Xiaoping's keynote speech to the National Science Conference, in March 1978, which included science among the forces of production and praised scientists and other intellectuals as patriotic workers.[77] In this new political climate arguments linking intellectual autonomy to scientific success drew strength from the trend of the practice discussions and incited vigorous debate. Philosophers and historians of science joined their colleagues within CAS and CASS in demanding that scientific arguments be judged by scientific criteria, and to reassess the Marxist philosophy of science in the light of contemporary developments. As the works of Karl Popper, Robert Merton, Thomas Kuhn, Imre Lakatos, Paul Feyerabend, and others became increasingly available, and Chinese scientists explored the implications of the latest discoveries in their respective fields, dialectical materialism, and natural dialectics, in particular, came under special scrutiny.[78]

Within a few years the subject of revisionism had been rendered quite passé by the new controversy over the "guiding role" of Marxism, which erupted in full force in the mid-1980s.[79] At one end in the debate (outnumbered and outmaneuvered) were Hu Qiaomu and the Propaganda Department along with scientists like Zha Ruqiang and He Zuoxiu, who maintained that "no science can ever replace Marxist philosophy," which "remains the ultimate methodology guiding all scientific research."[80] Hu Yaobang and his liberal associates occupied the middle ground by upholding professional autonomy, and asserting that the fundamental principles of Marxism still had real guiding significance but one could not make "absolute concepts" out of them. The radical extreme position was represented once again by Fang Lizhi and others like Xu Liangying, director of the CAS Institute for the History of Natural Science, who resolutely rejected dialectical philosophy as a "museum piece" and pressed for the

77.   Deng Xiaoping, "Speech at the Opening Ceremony of the National Conference on Science," 18 March 1978, *SW*, p. 105.

78.   For an incisive and detailed analysis see Brugger and Kelly, *Chinese Marxism in the Post-Mao Era*.

79.   David Kelly, "Chinese Controversies Over the Guiding Role of Philosophy Over Science," *Australian Journal of Chinese Affairs*, no. 14, 1985, pp. 21–34.

80.   Zha Ruqiang, *Zhongguo Shehui kexue*, no. 4 1982, pp. 9–30; See also Williams, "Fang Lizhi's Expanding Universe," p. 469.

liberation of science from its "guidance."[81] The surging popularity of the iconoclasts illustrated the sea change that had occurred in less than a decade, and could be attributed, in no small measure, to the ground broken by the practice campaign.

The Silence of the Opposition

The unfolding of the Practice Campaign had been a source of great consternation for Mao loyalists. Their retaliation, however, was confined to a few wall posters and some obstructionist and intimidatory tactics all of which proved quite ineffective. The sole exception to the theoretical "silence" of the Maoists was an article entitled "On the Comprehensive and Accurate Understanding and Mastery of the Fundamental Principles of Marxism."[82] Published in *Zhexue yanjiu* in April, i.e., a month after the first article "There Is Only One Criterion" in *RMRB* and a month before the official beginning of the discussion marked by Hu Fuming's piece, the article was, undoubtedly, a response to the discussions that had been initiated in the Central Party School publication *Lilun dongtai* in the preceding year. The thematic content of the article fitted in with the accusations of "abstract affirmation and specific negation" which the "whateverists" were directing against the proponents of practice, and its basic argument was that in the "complete scientific system" of Marxism

> each principle is subordinate to the whole, (and) cannot replace the whole. Therefore, when we study we cannot statically and in isolation look at specific principles without considering the whole. . . . Lenin had pointed out, "when revisionists look at problems, they regard the part as the whole, subordinate the whole to the part, use the part to distort the whole. . . ." From the iron and steel cast of Marxist philosophy we cannot by any means lose any basic premise or any single important part, or else we will deviate from objective truth and fall into the arms of the reactionary bourgeoise.[83]

81. Williams, pp 468–9; also "The Expanding Universe of Fang Lizhi: Astrophysics and Ideology in People's China," *Chinese Studies in Philosophy*, vol. 19, no. 4 1988, p. 61–62.
82. Fan Ruoyu, "On the Comprehensive and Accurate Understanding and Mastery of the Fundamental Principles of Marxism," *Zhexue yanjiu*, no. 4 (1978), pp. 2–8, 22.
83. Ibid.

The author Fan Ruoyu's concern, apparently, seems to have been to emphasize that no revision of even specific principles should be undertaken without taking into account the implications of this on other parts of the doctrine. The point he was making was an important one, present in the writings of Lukacs and Althusser, and in a general sense, in different epistemological traditions. For the French historian and philosopher of science, Gaston Bachelard, scientific transformation is one

> which involves the whole theoretical system of the science—it is not a change which affects concepts one by one, piecemeal. This is because the concepts and problems which make up a theoretical structure are not identifiable independently of their location within the whole.[84]

Fan's espousal of this position is a bit of a mystery. He could have been arguing for the leftists against the entire reformist coalition, whose emphasis on practice rather than theory could be construed to be as one-sided as the leftists they criticized, for the article went on to say

> The whole spirit of Marxist theory also shows that there are close connections between each principle, each principle is not an isolated absolute concept, it must be understood in connection with related principles. . . . But, if we one-sidedly grasp one viewpoint . . . or if in accordance with a deduced momentary need arbitrarily jump from one viewpoint to another, then we will fall into the one-sidedness of metaphysical thought.

What makes this fascinating and plausible is that Fan's emphasis on the integrity of the doctrine is strikingly similar to Lukacs' *totalitat* and his attacks on empiricism—symbolized most eloquently by the Fichtean quote, if "facts" appear to contradict then "so much the worse for the facts."[85] In *Tactics and Ethics*, Lukacs criticized what would be the equivalent of the Chinese slogan "seek truth from facts" by arguing that revisionists and opportunists always appeal to fact *but* facts can be understood only when they are situated in a concrete whole, and the "mediation" between them and the whole is grasped.

84. Benton, *The Rise and Fall of Structural Marxism*, p. 25.
85. Lukacs, *Tactics and Ethics*, p. 30.

However, this stress on the interrelatedness of principles found no echo in articles published on the subject, and Fan himself wrote no more about it. Some months later he appears to have been associated with Yang Xianzhen, but it is unclear whether Fan was further left in early 1978 and subsequently joined forces with the more orthodox elements in the reformist coalition. Or, he may have been allied with Yang from the beginning, in which case also his access to the media might have been restricted by people like Wang Ruoshui who harbored old animosities toward Yang.

In any event, it is hard to understand why Hua Goufeng and his leftist colleagues did not fashion a critique of the practice theorists along the holistic approach suggested by Fan Ruoyu, or by resorting to the theoretical arguments of the Maoists participating in the earlier debate. Their defensiveness, perhaps, can be attributed to the increasing political isolation in which they found themselves and the unpopularity and infeasibility of their policy positions. One might add to this the dilemma posed for them by their espousal of "whateverism," for it ruled out for them the option of joining forces with the incrementalists like Chen Yun and Hu Qiaomu, who were committed to the basic integrity of the received doctrine, but willing to countenance partial modification and adaptation.

Conclusion

The debate on epistemology, which was officially declared to be of far-reaching significance, was in philosophic terms the first major attempt to spell out a new post-Mao stance, which could justify a retreat from leftism and the reorientation of policy toward rapid and sustained economic and technological modernization.

The similarity between the reformer's stress on practice in order to avoid criticism on theoretical grounds and Mao's own position in 1937 was, initially, widely acclaimed. Among others, Brantly Womack argued that "seek truth from facts" (was) a key Maoist slogan and Deng Xiaoping's temerity in departing from received Community Party practice (did) not exceed Mao's own boldness at Chingkangshan, Kiangsi, and Yanan."[86]

86. Brantly Womack, "Politics and Epistemology in China Since Mao," *The China Quarterly*, no. 80 (1979), pp. 768–792.

A corollary to this form of reasoning is the split between a "pre-Liberation" and "post-Liberation" Mao which finds its echo amongst some of Mao's successors also in their attempt to bolster the claim that their line is in conformity with the policy preferences of the "early" Mao.[87]

However, the case for the doctrinal correctness (in terms of Mao Zedong Thought) of the practice discussions as a whole was not as well made as it appeared to be. The "fundamental affirmation" of Mao Zedong Thought (even the version purged of the errors of Mao Zedong) was in essence a highly selective and eclectic one.

Chinese Marxism in the 1930s was close on the heels of Soviet Marxism on the path toward dogmatization. There was no sharp epistemological break between the early Mao and the late Mao. The claim that "dialectical materialism" was a doctrine about the nature of the universe and a "science of the general laws of motion" with all its metaphysical ramifications was never questioned in the epistemological writings of Mao, Ai Siqi, and other philosophers assembled at Yanan at this time. Mao's belief in contradiction as "a universal truth for all times and all countries which admits of no exception" was expressed in "On Contradiction," and the idea of truth emerging out of struggle was reiterated in the fifties as well as the sixties.[88] The basis of Mao's continuing preoccupation with forces of opposition and his belief that forward movement could only be achieved through an intensification of class struggle can really be traced to this early acceptance of the ubiquity of conflict.

The argument that Mao emphasized the role of practice in an effort to legitimize his own position against those of his more doctrinaire rivals with close links to Moscow is also difficult to sustain. If "On Practice" and "On Contradiction" are read in conjunction, as I believe they were meant to be, it is clear that Mao having accepted the genetic priority of practice over theory, affirmed also the very significant theses that the mutual relationship of pairs such as base and superstructure, theory and practice, etc., is one in which either element of the pair can exercise a decisive role under given conditions

87.   Ibid.
88.   "On Contradiction," p. 109.

. . . the productive forces, practice, and the economic base generally play the principal and decisive role. Whoever denies this is not a materialist. But it must also be admitted that in certain conditions, such aspects as the relations of production, theory, and the superstructure in turn manifest themselves in the principal and decisive role. When it is impossible for the productive forces to develop without a change in relations of production, then the change in the relations of production plays the principal and decisive role. The creation and advocacy of revolutionary theory plays the principal and decisive role in those times of which Lenin said, "Without a revolutionary theory there can be no revolutionary movement."[89]

This dynamic view of the roles of the principal and secondary aspects of a contradiction has been the source of considerable controversy over Mao's own doctrinal soundness and as the next chapter illustrates, it has not found unanimous support in China, either. The point, however, is that at the very best, the parallel between Deng's stress on practice and Mao's ideological preferences of the thirties, has its limitations.[90] The roots of Mao's dogmatism, as manifested in his writings, go down as deep

---

89. Ibid.

90. The identification of "practice as the criterion of truth" with "seeking truth from facts" by Chinese Marxists (Maoist as well as non-Maoist) has always made them vulnerable to the charge of "vulgar empiricism." On the face of it, the slogan "seek truth from facts" is precisely the "bare empiricism," i.e., uncritical belief in facts interpreting themselves for which Engels referred to Newton as an "inductive ass." Nevertheless, one can argue that the populist genre employed by most Chinese Communist writing and the weight of the indigenous ideological tradition make exceedingly culture specific the motifs employed to express ideas. For Mao as well as his successors, "seek truth from facts" was a slogan that needed emphasis because of the deep-rooted Chinese "proclivity for bibliolatry," and its accompanying "epistemological authoritarianism." According to E.R. Hughes, ever since the establishment of state Confucianism in the second century B.C. learning in China has meant the acquisition of knowledge as found in the canon, and the history of Chinese philosophy is replete with evidence of this dogmatic attitude toward the objects of knowledge. See Hughes, "Epistemological Methods in Chinese Philosophy," in Charles Moore ed. *The Chinese Mind* Honolulu: East West Center Press. 1967 p. 93. (For the historical origin of the old saying "seek truth from facts" see Lan Ying, "The New Development of the Ideological Line of Seek Truth From Facts," *Shehui kexue*, no. 4 (1981), pp. 1– 5.)

In the modern context, therefore, seeking truth from facts was not equated with pragmatism or vulgar empiricism but with non-dogmatic, creative empirical theorizing. The resurrection of the slogan "Seek Truth Fom Facts" did not make the post-Mao Chinese

as the pre-Liberation period and there is no clear-cut distinction between a "pragmatic Mao" and a "dogmatic Mao." The Gang of Four's emphasis on theory and consciousness, "their radical ideological reversal of the relationship between theory and practice"[91] seem to have been equally compatible with the writings of the "great revolutionary" of the Yanan period as with the "senile" Mao of the sixties and seventies. And more significantly, the primary concern of Mao and his associates when expounding "On Practice" was not verification as it was for the post-Mao discussions, but to stress the role of revolutionary action (praxis) in transforming one's circumstances (objective reality). Only thus could Mao establish his legitimacy simultaneously as the strategist of the Chinese revolution and its theoretical hegemon.[92]

In contrast, the post-Mao leading coalition preferred to downplay the salience of conflict/contradiction, and deny the decisive role of theory or revolutionary action (identified as voluntarism or leftist errors), which ignored the constraints of objective reality. Deng's advocacy of "seek truth from facts" legitimized a reductionist attitude toward practice to the exclusion of any theoretical validation, whatsoever. Such a trend marked a radical departure not only from Mao, but also from the Leninist position that "facts do not interpret themselves," and spontaneous theorization resulting from a particular practice is not necessarily true of that practice, hence, the need for a vanguard armed with a scientific theory.[93] Indeed, the whole notion of false consciousness and the science/ideology distinction were ignored in post-Mao discussions on practice, and the epistemological position adopted in relation to the relativity of truth, by most theorists, was decidedly pragmatic.

The basic divergence within the practice theorists and among their political patrons foreshadowed the policy and ideological differences that would divide them in the future. The epistemological relativism, which marked the discussion would be a source of satisfaction to those who

theorists and leadership more pragmatic. It was the epistemological position that they adopted in relation to the relativity of truth which made them so.

91.   *JFRB*, 29 June, Commentary above cited.

92.   Frederick Wakemen Jr. *History and Will: Philosophical Perspectives of Mao Tse tung's Thought.* Berkeley: University of California Press.

93.   Collier, "In Defense of Epistemology," pp. 56–57.

envisaged a radical departure from the past. The position staked out at this time would provide the rationale for challenges to the dominance of the Communist Party and demands for institutional and judicial reform, as well as for ideological and political pluralism.

The split within the opponents of "whateverism" was reflected in the exhortation to eliminate dogmatism while upholding the irrefutability of basic Marxist principles. For the incrementalists, epistemological relativism was of little use when the objective was a seal of authority for a *particular interpretation* of the tradition in *opposition* to others. The attempts by Hu Qiaomu and other elders to rein in the discussions stemmed from their realization that the logic of the arguments undermined their selective revision, and instead, allowed rejection of the entire tradition itself.

A combination of factors including economic problems, the embroilment with Vietnam, and the boldly provocative publications and organizational activities of the Democracy Wall activists served to dissolve the consensus on political and ideological relaxation within the leading coalition. In early 1979 while Hu Yaobang inaugurated the theory conference, which brought forth radical critiques of Mao and the Communist political system, Hu Qiaomu and Wu Lengxi prevailed upon Deng Xiaoping to mark a retreat and enunciate the Four Cardinal Principles as the parameters of intellectual discourse. The campaign for a "thorough emancipation of the mind" retained its fetters but would continue to motivate the proponents of institutional and ideological change.

TWO

Revolutionary Practice and
Economic Determinism

The discussions on the criterion of truth employed the term *practice* to demonstrate an essential continuity with the basic principles of Mao's thought. In contrast to Mao, however, the policy preferences of the coalition that emerged victorious at the end of 1978 supported a much more "orthodox" interpretation of historical and dialectical materialism, which stressed the importance of the economic base and productive forces. The role of revolutionary action (praxis) was not denied altogether, but it became the norm to emphasize the significance of objective constraints.

The leadership changes that accompanied the December Third Plenum resulted in Hu Yaobang's appointment as the general secretary of the Central Committee, and Director of the Propaganda Department. His most important responsibility in this capacity was to use his intellectual network to fashion a new ideological consensus that would provide the theoretical basis for the era of reform that the Party was poised to embark upon. The intellectual agenda had two components, (a) to provide a social critique and philosophical refutation of Mao's leftist radicalism, and (b) to furnish an acceptable Marxist rationale for the change of course.

The Theory Conference that convened in early 1979 under Hu's auspices was expected to continue the task of ideological reorientation that had been initiated with the practice-criterion discussions, and facilitate the drafting of a comprehensive historical appraisal of the CCP's record in power and the role of its predominant leader, Mao Zedong. However, differences within the leading coalition surfaced again during the Theory Conference as they had at the onset of the practice-criterion discussions. Intellectuals associated with Hu Yaobang used the media and the first part of the Conference to push for explanations of the phenomena of the Gang of Four and leftist errors from the standpoint of an orthodox sociological determinism. The incrementalists, on the other hand, emphasized epistemology with scholarly debates on the "source of knowledge" and "primacy of matter" with a view to identifying and criticizing the philosophical roots of "voluntarism."

In their speeches at the Conference and in articles published during this time theorists supportive of a sharp break with the past utilized the concept of feudalism to interpret the checkered history of the Party's term in power. The strength of the two thousand-year-old feudal traditions, the lack of a capitalist phase, and the predominance of the peasantry were all attractive explanations for the distortions in Chinese socialism, as well as rationale for new policies of economic liberalization.

From the point of view of China's older generation of leaders such analyses denigrated their traditional constituencies and did little to enhance the prestige and legitimacy of the Party. In the current historical stage it was necessary to stress economic and technological constraints, but to suggest that the CCP had captured power before conditions were "ripe" was reminiscent of charges of "Blanquism" that orthodox Marxists had directed against the Bolsheviks and was, therefore, unacceptable.

The tensions between the two positions failed to be resolved theoretically and through the early 1980s the gap between their ideological preferences widened. While the radical-reformist intellectuals extended their critique to the centralized Leninist bureaucratic system and the alienation it produced, the incrementalists within the leading coalition dug in their heels to oppose bourgeois liberalism and resist sweeping repudiations of the Communist system and its sacrosanct leaders like Lenin and Mao.

Discussions on Feudalism and the Critique of Leftism

The arrest of Jiang Qing, Yao Wenyuan, Zhang Chunqiao, and Wang Hongwen in October 1976, and their characterization as a Gang of Four, provided the immediate successors of Mao a convenient scapegoat to blame for all past policy failures and mistakes. Glossing over the basic ideological affinity that had existed between the Gang and its mentor, Mao, initial attempts to denigrate the former employed the rhetoric of radical leftism.[1] A media barrage of critical articles labeled the Gang and its followers "sham leftists," "hidden capitalist roaders," and "new bourgeois elements" whose aim was to advocate the "theory of the extinction of class struggle" in order to promote "Liu Shaoqi's rightist opportunist line!"[2]

A direct assault on the real ideological orientation of the Gang was inconsistent with the interests of the Hua Guofeng faction which claimed its legitimacy as Mao's chosen successor. Any systematic criticism of radical leftism would entail a reevaluation of Mao himself, and of events such as the Cultural Revolution, which he had personally initiated.

For precisely the same reasons, however, theorists in Hu Yaobang's camp were eager to promote an ideologically and politically consistent assessment of the Gang and its policies. The legacies of the Anti-Rightist Campaign, the case of Peng Dehuai, and the Cultural Revolution, they believed, had created an ideological mind-set that precluded criticism of any manifestation of leftism as a deviation.[3] What was needed was a frank and forthright public admission of errors in policy and ideological orientation in the past three decades, both on the part of the Chinese Communist Party collectively, and Mao individually as its dominant leader. The denunciation of the Gang and the rejection of Mao's policy preferences had

1. "A Great Historic Victory," *RMRB*, Joint editorial with *JFJB*, *Hongqi*, 25 October 1976.

2. "The Right-Wing Face Beneath the 'Great Cloth,'" *RMRB*, 4 February 1977; "From Historical Counter-Revolutionary to Practising Counter-Revolutionary," *RMRB*, 5 May 1977; "Sham Left Faction, Real Right Faction," *RMRB*, 6 February 1977; *Wenhuibao*, 22 October 1976 in *FBIS*, 27 October 1976, p. G3; Wang Zhe," Pseudo Leftists and Genuine Rightists—Viewing the Counter-Revolutionary Revisionism of the Gang of Four From the Question of Class Struggle," *RMRB*, 12 December 1977; Zhi Jiao, "By Inciting Anarchism, the Gang of Four Aimed at Subverting the Dictatorship of the Proletariat," *Hongqi*, no. 5 (1978).

3. William Joseph, *The Critique of Ultra-Leftism in China, 1958–1981*, Stanford: Stanford University Press, 1984, p. 160. See also Commentator, "Follow the Correct Ideological Line and Eliminate the Ultra Leftist Pernicious Influence," *Wenhuibao*, 4 August 1979; Jin Wen, "Thoroughly Criticise the 'Left' Deviationist Line Viciously Pursued by Lin Biao and the Gang of Four," *GMRB*, 23 January, 1979; Mass Criticism Group of the Shanghai Municipal CCP Committee, "A Counter-Revolutionary Book Under a Revolutionary Disguise—A Criticism of the Gang of Four's Concoction, 'Socialist Political Economy,'" *Hongqi*, no. 4 (1978). Shi Zhu, "The 'Leftist' Line of Lin Biao and the Gang of Four and Its Social and Historical Root Causes," *Hongqi*, no. 4 (1979).

raised a number of serious questions concerning not merely the origins of erroneous policies such as the Great Leap Forward and the Cultural Revolution, but more fundamental ones regarding historical development and the nature of the Chinese revolution as well. Specifically, the issues that now needed to be addressed and explained were

(a) How should the phenomenon of the Gang of Four and Mao's "cult of personality" be analyzed?
(b) What was the origin of the "errors" in party line that appeared in the late 1950s and culminated in the politics of the Cultural Revolution?

As party theoreticians grappled with these issues they found themselves inevitably drawn into discussions of the larger picture, viz.,

(a) Had China been "ripe" for a socialist revolution in the 1940s, or had the repeated tendency of ultraleft deviation in party ranks been responsible for a premature declaration of a socialist state?
(b) After coming to power, could the hegemony of the proletariat be sustained in a country where the development of capitalism had been quite uneven and lagged years behind economically advanced capitalist countries, and where the peasantry and the petty bourgeoisie were a large majority?

The March 1978 issue of *Lishi yanjiu* carried an important article by the reform theorist Li Honglin. Reviewing the entire history of inner-party struggles since the inception of the CCP, Li warned against explanations focusing on individual traits and actions, and instead argued for a more systemic analysis of the phenomenon of the Gang of Four. "No political incident is the action of individuals," he pointed out. "The motives and actions of individuals can only be understood in specific socio-historical contexts."[4]

---

4. Li Honglin, "Exposing and Criticising the Gang of Four constitutes a Decisive Battle of a Historical Nature," *Lishi yanjiu*, no. 3 (1978), pp. 3–15. Li's argument was doctrinally sound. Marx's position on the subject needs no elaboration. Lenin, too, had warned against

By early 1979 when the Theory Conference was convened the reformist-controlled media and the Central Party School and CASS theorists had begun to openly undermine the fine line of distinction between Mao and the Gang, which the Hua Guofeng group and other party elders had been observing. The first half of the Theory Conference, which was dominated by the radical reformers, became the forum for launching devastating critiques of Mao's "cult of personality" and abuse of power and linking them to the cause of fundamental institutional reform.

Wang Ruoshui's speech to the assembled delegates described the Cultural Revolution as a "great catastrophe" and placed the blame for it squarely on Mao.[5] He pointed out that Mao's role could not be separated from the Gang and, therefore, the late Chairman should be held accountable for the "disaster" that befell the Chinese masses in the next decade. Other theorists echoed Wang's critique of Mao's theories of continuous revolution and total dictatorship and charged the "leftist deviation" with having brought the country and the Party to the "verge of destruction."[6] Speeches at the Conference as well as articles in the media now linked the origins of Mao's mistakes to the repression unleashed in the struggle against "rightists," that had silenced all dissent and constructive criticism of shortcomings in official policies and work style and also facilitated the emergence of the Gang's "fascist dictatorship."[7]

Su Shaozhi, Li Shu, Liao Gailong, Zhang Xianyang, Wang Guixiu, and Guo Luoji dismissed Mao's concept of "capitalist roaders" and argued conversely that the absence of a full-fledged capitalist stage in China made

regarding "opportunism" as an "incidental phenomenon" not as the "sin, mistake, or revolt of individuals," but the "social product of an entire historical era." Li's categorization of the Gang and its followers in terms of class and lines was not surprising given the timing of the article. Reform theorists around this time were not averse to accepting the Maoist notion of the possible emergence of a privileged bureaucratic class in postrevolutionary society.

5. Wang Ruoshui, "The Greatest Lesson of the Cultural Revolution Is That the Personality Cult Should be Opposed," Speech at the Theory Conference, 13 February 1979, *Mingbao*, (Hong Kong), no. 2 (1980), pp. 2–15.

6. See Merle Goldman, *Sowing the Seeds of Democracy*, p. 47–61; X.L. Ding, *The Decline of Communism in China*, pp. 91–99.

7. Zhang Xianyang and Wang Guixiu, "On the Nature of the Line of Lin Biao and the Gang of Four," *RMRB*, 28 February 1979, also in *FBIS*, 1 March 1979, p. E7.

the system vulnerable to the reemergence of a feudal exploitative class.[8] A forceful *Lishi yanjiu* article by Wang Xiaoqiang queried:

> Why were those in our revolutionary ranks so susceptible to the work style of the old-time ruling classes? Why could so many millions of Red Guards gather to stage a revolt and seize power? How could such a few swaggering clowns pull off such a big farce? Why couldn't a long war-tested political party like ours prevent that unprecedented disaster?[9]

The explanations favored by radical-reformist writers singled out the strength of the peasantry within the ranks of the revolutionary forces as the cause of "political degeneration."[10] Not only was the CCP surrounded by this enormous petty bourgeois class but the social composition of the Party itself was predominantly peasant in origin. The Wang Xiaoqiang article referred to above pointed out:

> The egalitarian concept inherited by the peasants that there should be "no gaps between privileged and under-privileged and between rich and poor" was fundamentally different from the bourgeois advocation of "equal

8.   Ibid.; Guo Luoji, "Commenting on the So-called Crisis of Faith," *Wenhuibao*, 13 January 1980, p. 3. Liao Gailong, "Historical Experience and Our Road of Development," *Zhonggong yanjiu*, no. 19 (1981), pp. 108–77. At an international conference in Yugoslavia Su Shaozhi reiterated that due to its long history as a feudal, autocratic country, China's "cadres and people had been more deeply influenced by feudalism than by capitalism." Some Questions in China's Socialist Economic Construction," paper delivered at the "Round Table 1980 of Socialism in the World" International Conference held in Cavtat, Yugoslavia, from 22–27 September, 1980 in *Selected Studies on Marxism*, (CASS) 1987.

9.   Wang Xiaoqiang, "The Peasantry and the Struggle Against Feudalism," *Lishi yanjiu*, no. 10 (1979), pp. 3–12.

10.   Su Shaozhi, "On the Principal Contradiction Facing Our Society Today," *Xueshu yuekan*, no. 7 (1979). Xiao Lu, "Is Contradiction Between the Advanced Social System and the Backward Productive Forces a Scientific Issue," *Zhexue yanjiu*, no. 7 (1979), pp. 19–20. Wu Daying and Liu Han, "The Theory and Practice of Class Struggle—To Clear the Confusion Created by the Gang of Four on the Question of Class Struggle," *Xueshu yuekan*, no. 3 (1979); in *FBIS*, no. 22, 9 October 1979, p. 14. Jin Wen, "On Current Classes and Class Struggle in Our Country," *Jiefang ribao*, 23 July,1979. On the other hand, Hua Guofeng in his report to the Second Session of the Fifth NPC had claimed that the system of small-scale production in China had "been transformed through appropriate and reasonable measures."

rights" based on the principle of commodity exchange at equal value, nor had it anything in common with the proletarian conception of equality built on the basis of modern science and mass production and ownership of the means of production by the workers . . . as soon as the small producers took control of political power, no ways could be found to prevent them from unknowingly moving in a direction contrary to the general public's interest, nor could anything be done to stop them from reimposing a feudal autocratic system on the people."

Articles on Russian history at this time commented on the similarity between the Chinese peasant "illusion of a deified emperor," and the less than thorough anti-monarchism of the Russian peasantry which generated "pretenders" who claimed to be the "true" and "good tsar."[11] Comparing the Chinese communes to the Russian mirs, a writer named Xiao Lu pointed out that this type of public ownership could only be characterized as "small peasantry socialism" not scientific socialism.[12] And, referring to the upheavals of the GLF and Cultural Revolution, he continued, "if a social system is unable to prevent large-scale disruptions on the productive forces by its innate elements, can this system be called perfect, or mighty, or superior?"

The aim of such hard-hitting critiques was to make the case for political democratization. Wang Ruoshui warned against the dangers of stifling dissent and criticism while Guo Luoji defended the concept of "inalienable rights" and defended the masses' right to express their opinions on all political issues.[13] Guo went so far as to speak up also for the Democracy Wall activists and the views disseminated in *Beijing Spring*. Yan Jiaqi and Li Honglin called for term appointments and a government chosen by and accountable to the people rather than the party leadership. Yu Guangyuan attacked the Maoist preference for a strengthened dictatorship of the proletariat, and linked it to the phenomena of bureaucratism and the "transformation of the servants of the people" into their masters.

11.   Gilbert Rozman, *The Chinese Debate About Soviet Socialism, 1978–1985*, Princeton: Princeton University Press, 1987, p. 151.

12.   Xiao Lu, "Is Contradiction Between the Advanced Social System and the Backward Productive Forces a Scientific Issue?" *Zhexue yanjiu*, no. 7 (1979), pp. 19–26.

13.   Guo Luoji, "Political Questions Can Be Discussed," *RMRB*, 14 November 1979, p. 3.

Recalling the Marxist theory of "withering away of the state," Yu advocated "weakening" the power of the state apparatus and investing control in more decentralized popular organizations.[14]

The tone of these discussions introduced major dissension within the coalition that had come together to defeat the "whateverists." Hu Yaobang's opening address had encouraged the elimination of "remaining forbidden zones" and "mental shackles" to raise and deal with new questions. The calls for free speech, rule of law, and accountable governmental representatives had been initially supported, although in a qualified way, by Deng Xiaoping and Chen Yun. By March 1979 when the Conference reconvened for the second half, the balance of forces had shifted in favor of Hu Qiaomu and Deng Liqun, who equated the reformist proposals with demands for bourgeois democracy, and were apprehensive of a possible emerging nexus between establishment intellectuals and the Democracy Wall activists, some of whom were now openly advocating systemic change.

The crackdown on the Democracy Wall and the decreasing tolerance of Deng Xiaoping's alliance partners for rigorous questioning of party policies and work style came in response to the broadening of targets of criticism to include Deng and other leaders who were implicated in the decision to launch the anti-rightist persecution in the 1950s. It was also, however, largely a product of their realization that the new focus on leftist errors and the dangers of feudal despotism rather than capitalist restoration threatened the legitimacy of both the Communist Party and the Revolution itself.

Although most of the articles and speeches dealing with feudalism (with the exception of a piece by Su Shaozhi and Feng Lanrui which will be discussed in the next chapter) referred to China as a proletarian or socialist state, the implications of their arguments were not lost upon the veteran leadership. Such reasoning raised anew the question posed early on by critics of the Chinese Revolution: Can a party severed from its urban proletarian roots and based predominantly on the rural peasantry be a bona fide Communist Party?[15] The answer to this could be given in

---

14.   Yu Guangyuan and Hu Jiwei, eds., *The Moment of Sudden Awakening*, Beijing: Zhongwai chuban gongsi, 1989. X.L. Ding, pp. 95–97.

15.   See for instance, Benjamin Schwartz, *Chinese Communism and the Rise of Mao*, Cambridge, MA: Harvard University Press, 1951.

the affirmative by revolutionary Marxists who regard the peasantry or other exploited groups as a "substitute proletariat" possessing most, if not all, of the characteristics ascribed to the industrial working class by Marx and Engels. On the other hand, when one begins to stress the conservative character of the peasantry as inherently unchanging, so long as productive forces remain underdeveloped, it becomes difficult to explain how a country with an overwhelming majority of peasants and a Communist Party based on this social class could be said to have accomplished a "proletarian socialist" revolution. The allusion to the "proletarian" character of the Party after the fall of the Gang would appear to affirm China's socialist character. It is, however, not very convincing, given that the CCP was still "surrounded" by an enormous peasant class and its social composition was not substantially different.[16]

The question of the significance to Chinese socialism of the overwhelming peasant composition of the social base came to be hotly debated in the next few years particularly in the context of the drafting of the Resolution on Party History, and the economic decollectivization policies that were being implemented in the countryside.[17] Radical-reformist intellectuals continued to emphasize the adverse consequences of feudal influences rather than capitalist impulses in a backward country struggling to build socialism but their position on this issue was essentially ambivalent. On the one hand, the problems of bureaucratism, the

16.   The reform leadership's bid to admit intellectuals to the party (rather than workers) would change its orientation all right, but this would hardly make it more representative of the proletariat.

17.   Sha Yexin and Wu Yiye, "Chase Away the Ghost of Feudalism," *Wenhuibao*, 10 July 1980, p. 3. "An Important Issue That Concerns the Overall Situation," *Wenhuibao*, 17 July 1979, p. 1. Li Shaochun, "China's Ancient Feudal Despotism," *Guangming ribao*, 14 August 1979. In an article entitled, "The Class Situation and Principal Contradiction in Mainland China: An Important Theoretical Issue at the Second Session of the Fifth NPC," the Hong Kong writing group Qi Xin pointed out that Mao had accurately perceived the problem of popular resentment against the privileges enjoyed by those in power. However, these individuals could not be called "capitalist roaders." Since their aim was to hinder modernization and economic development they were better described as "people in power who follow a feudal autocratic road." Qi Xin, "The Class Situation and the Principal Contradiction in Mainland China—An Important Theoretical Issue at the Second Session of the Fifth NPC," *Qishi niandai*, August 1979, in *FBIS*, 13 August 1979, pp. U1–U5.

reemergence of "feudal privilege," "cult of personality," and egalitarian ultraleftism were attributed to the influence of the peasant millions and the "force of habit" of small-scale production. On the other hand, the rationale for Zhao Ziyang's economic reforms, particularly in agriculture, was to be sought in the need to satisfy the peasants' private proprietary instincts. Wang Dingyuan, for instance, defended the household responsibility system by referring to the dual character of the peasantry. The Chinese peasants' love of socialism and the party could not be questioned, he claimed, but their recent past as small property owners made them harbor lingering attachments to old forms of production. The error of the Stalinist model had been to place the organization of production and distribution in agriculture on the same basis as industry, i.e., the swift elimination of private ownership. Unlike the working class, the peasantry had a strong sense of private interest. Consequently, the working class and its vanguard needed to appreciate how great a source of motivation dispersed household management and labor would be to their allies.[18]

Unlike the remaining leftists in the economic ministries and the military the moderate reformers or incrementalists with Hu Qiaomu as their major spokesman at this time supported agricultural decollectivization and sectoral adjustment. The incrementalist position was that the critical evaluation of the past and the pace and extent of reform should be commensurate with unity and stability. They were, consequently, deeply disturbed by the implications of the discussions on feudalism for the assessment of Chinese society, and by the moral and political challenge to the Party's authority, which had been mounted by the radical reformers' attacks on Mao's personal character and leadership. The seriousness of the challenge was reinforced by the widespread cynicism and disillusionment within the populace, the deterioration of the law and order situation, and the debacle of the attempt to "teach Vietnam a lesson."

For the dual purpose of distancing themselves from the remaining leftists (who were being charged in unofficial publications with "whitewashing history") and providing a corrective for the radical reformers' "excessively" critical approach, the incrementalists leaned in favor of a

---

18. Wang Dingyuan, "The Spontaneous Character of the Development of Socialist Agricultural Collectivization," *Shehui kexue*, no. 11 (1983), pp. 20–25.

more low-key critique of the philosophical underpinnings of economic voluntarism. The renewed focus on epistemology on the part of intellectuals rallying behind Chen Yun and other moderates was aimed not only at legitimizing certain economic initiatives and deflecting attention away from political issues, but also represented a response to the positions staked out in the practice-criterion campaign.

Economic Determinism Versus Revolutionary Praxis
Tracing the Epistemological Roots of Voluntarism

The debate on the economy had begun as early as 1978 when the national media brought back into circulation the erstwhile notorious and discredited "theory of productive forces." The Maoist position had been that the key to the success of socialist construction lay in rapid continuous change in ownership relations, and consolidation of the proletarian dictatorship was the prerequisite to a complete change of the social base. In contrast, a *RMRB* article published in July 1978 argued that Lenin himself had maintained that one of the prime tasks of the proletarian dictatorship was to develop productive forces in order to accelerate socialist construction.[19] In October, *RMRB* published a long piece by Hu Qiaomu entitled, "Act According to Economic Laws, Speed Up the Four Modernizations." Essentially a critique of economic voluntarism, the article stressed that economic work must be carried out in accordance with the law of planned and proportionate development and with the law of value.[20] The publication of Hu's speech was followed a few weeks later by the rehabilitation of Sun Yefang, who had undergone criticism during the Cultural Revolution period for emphasizing scientific rationality over mass movements, and profits over political criteria in matters of investment and development.

In the months that followed, newspapers and journals carried economic reports that revealed conflict over the new economic policy at different

19. Zheng Yifan, "A Critique of Lenin's So-Called Criticism of 'the Theory of Productive Forces,'" *RMRB*, 19 July 1978.

20. Hu Qiaomu, "Act According to Economic Laws: Speed up the Realization of the Four Modernizations," *RMRB*, 6 October 1978.

levels within the CCP leadership. Some provinces and municipalities continued to uphold the campaign of learning from Daqing and conduct meetings to select and award Daqing-modeled enterprises. Others, notably Sichuan and Anhui, led respectively by Zhao Ziyang and Wan Li, implemented policies that promoted competition, allowed enterprises to invest profits as they deemed fit, stressed individual households and industrial and commercial units as a supplement to the state-planned economy, preferred "expert" over "red," and, finally, with regard to employment argued in favor of appropriate circulation of qualified persons, open recruitment and freedom in choosing jobs.[21]

Opposition to Deng's economic initiatives stemmed at this time primarily from the "restorationists," a group of veteran cadres with bases in the military, and in the economic and public security ministries.[22] Both moderate and radical reformers agreed that in the 1950s the private capitalist and individual economies were eliminated too hastily, in disregard of objective laws and the fact that the productive forces were lagging far behind the relations of production.[23] The disaster of the GLF was the outcome of an ascendant "voluntarist tendency" which led to the exaggeration of the role of politics and subjective initiative.

The debates on the "source of knowledge" and the "mutual decisiveness of matter and spirit," which unfolded in early 1980, thus, closely paralleled

21.   Ren Tao, "Investigation Report: Enterprises in Sichuan Province Acquire Greater Independence," *Social Sciences in China*, no. 1 (1980), pp. 201–15. Xue Muqiao, "Some Opinions on the Reform of the Economic System," *RMRB*, 10 June 1980. Zhao Ziyang, "Study the New Situation, Fully Implement the Direction of Readjustment," *Hongqi*, no. 1 (1980), p. 15–20. Chu Chungyi, "'New Economic Group' vs 'Petroleum Group,'" *Tung Xiang*, no. 24 (1980), pp. 9–11. In *FBIS*, no. 123 (1980), pp. 62–67.

22.   The veteran cadres had supported Deng's rehabilitation but opposed too negative an appraisal of the past and of Mao, and the proposal to abolish their lifetime tenures to promote younger better-educated and professionally competent cadres. Criticism of Mao and revision of his thought rankled also with the PLA. PLA interests were, moreover, threatened by the HRS system which worked to the disadvantage of soldiers on active duty and worked as a disincentive for potential recruits. (See Ellis Joffe, "Party and Military in China: Professionalism in Command?" *Problems of Communism*, September–October 1983, pp. 48–63). Finally, the approximately 18 million party cadres who had joined during the Cultural Revolution were ideologically and politically rallied behind the leftists.

23.   Ibid., p. 77. Lu Zhongjian, "On Assessing Mao," *Zhengming*, no. 35 (1980), pp. 24–31.

the 1950s and early 1960s debates on the identity of thought and existence and "two combine into one." The earlier debates had reflected the policy differences between Ai Siqi, Mao, and Chen Boda, who opted for an accelerated program of collectivization, and Liu Shaoqi, Chen Yun, and Yang Xianzhen, who argued for continuing the policy of an "integrated economic base."[24] In the late 1970s and early 1980s as the strategy of the GLF and its consequences for China's economic development came under renewed criticism, philosophical disputes arose once again on the issue of revolutionary will or the subjective factor versus objective necessity.

A February 1980 *Shehui kexue* article, written under the pseudonym Zeming, initiated the argument that the slogan "practice is the only source of knowledge," derived from Mao's essay "On Practice" and also employed during the criterion of truth discussions, was the cause of the "subjectivism" that led to erroneous policy initiatives.[25] The only source of knowledge was the material world or objective reality external to man's consciousness. When practice, which has a subjective as well as objective character, was substituted for objective reality as the source of knowledge one was led to the "voluntarist" conclusion that "practice can make man's subjective knowledge be transformed into direct reality."

Several other writers concurred with Zeming's view that the question of the source of knowledge was crucial because it was linked to the problem of socialist modernization.[26] Mistakes in socialist construction that had been made in the past were due precisely to the "excessive magnification" of the subjective function in practice and a disregard of objective laws.

---

24.   Hamrin, "Yang Xianzhen," pp. 71–73; Merle Goldman, *China's Intellectuals*, Cambridge: Harvard University Press, 1981, pp. 99– 101. Wang Ruoshui, "Do Thought and Existence Not Have Identity?" *Zhexue yanjiu*, no. 1 (1960). "The Problem of Thought and Existence," *Hongqi*, no. 11 (1960). Guan Feng, "On the Identity of Opposites," *Hongqi*, no. 15 (1960).

25.   Ze Ming, "Refutation of 'Practice is the Only Source of Knowledge,'" *Shehui kexue*, no. 2 (1980), pp. 61–66.

26.   *Wenhuibao* (Shanghai), 13 June 1980. Chu Jingning, "Practice Is the Medium of Rational Knowledge—More on the Objective World Is the Source of Knowledge," *Shehui kexue*, no. 6 (1981), pp. 88–91. Li Junru, "The 'Fountainhead of Knowledge' and the 'Origin of the World,'" *Shehui kexue*, no. 6 (1980), pp. 103–4.

Over 20 years ago, were we not divorced from China's objective reality [when we] produced a "great theory" based on hopes of a "great practice," with the result that we walked out of the door of seeking truth from facts and into the side door toward voluntarism and created two big sabotages in the life of the socialist economy.[27]

While Zeming and his colleagues referred primarily to the GLF and the Cultural Revolution as negative examples, their critiques were directed at the over emphasis on practice by the post-Mao theorists as well. Consequently, a spate of articles took issue with Zeming's position and accused him of confusing the ontological problem with the epistemological one. They compared the latter's point of view to Ludwig Feuerbach's mechanical materialism, which disregarded the mediating role of consciousness and conceived of the cognitive process as a passive mirror like reflection of objective reality.[28] Marx's epistemology, on the other hand, emphasized knowledge as the active reflection of the subject on the object, and the establishment of the relationship between subject and object as the prerequisite to the emergence of knowledge.[29] Anything that existed objectively could not directly become the source of knowledge. Only when social practice took it as its target did it become an object of knowledge in its direct and practical sense.[30] Zeming's contention that the "practice is the sole source" viewpoint inevitably led to voluntarism and idealism was rejected by his opponents on the grounds that it overemphasized the subjective aspect of practice. Inasmuch as practice was conscious activity, it did not lose its objective material nature. Within the boundaries of objective laws people could make the results of practice realize their thought and purpose. Change in material objects was the result of human

27. Li Junru, "The 'Fountainhead of Knowledge' and the 'Origin of the World.'"

28. Zhang Huajin & Ma Jihua, "Scientific Proposition of the Dialectical Materialist Theory of Knowledge—Deliberating with Comrade Ze Ming," *Shehui kexue*, no. 5 (1980), pp. 98–101.

29. Liu Ben, "The Origin of Knowledge and the Criterion of Truth," *Zhexue yanjiu*, no. 9 (1980), pp. 12–19.

30. Yuan Kuiren and Lijin, "Practice Is the Only Source of Knowledge—Deliberating With Comrade Ze Ming," *Shehui kexue*, no. 6 (1980), pp. 105–108. Cui Wenyu, "Discussion on the Question of the Source of Knowledge," *RMRB*, 17 September 1981, p. 5.

intervention, although in the final analysis, it was fixed by internal contradiction and laws contained within the objects themselves.

Both sides in the argument selectively drew their legitimacy from the writings of Marx and Engels, which emphasized both revolutionary critical praxis and a deterministic historical materialism.[31] The dilemma that this dialectical combination posed for Marxists was exhibited repeatedly in the history of the international communist movement and the disputes of Kautsky and Plekhanov with Lenin; Stalin with Bukharin; Mao, Ai Siqi and Wang Ruoshui with Liu Shaoqi, Chen Yun, and Yang Xianzhen.[32] The complexity of the post-Mao debate, as in the earlier ones, lay not only in its philosophical and policy-related aspects but also in politics and personality conflicts.

The position taken by Zeming's opponents would be consistent with Marx's distinction between the spider weaving its web and man working

31.   Alvin Gouldner, *The Two Marxisms; Contradictions and Anomalies in the Development of Theory,* New York: Seabury Press, 1980, p. 34.

32.   Kautsky and Plekhanov looked to history as the unfolding of inexorable, immutable laws and minimized the role of revolutionary action. For Lenin, the working out of historical necessity involved recourse to action, i.e., practice, and so left room for human initiative. In China, the divide between the economic determinist and the "critical praxis" stressing revolutionary emerged early. Mao, Ai Siqi, and Chen Boda subscribed to the view that "revolutionary critical-praxis activity" allowed ideas to become a material force in history, and it was possible for theory to guide men's actions in the transformation of society. Communist cadres, who had their formative work experience in Nationalist-controlled coastal cities and later in the base areas behind Japanese lines in Northern China, followed their leader Liu Shaoqi in adopting a more cautious, gradualist and bureaucratic policy approach. Their epistemology was more mechanical and, in Communist parlance, tended toward environmental and technological determinism, reflecting their training in party schools controlled by Bukharin and like-minded colleagues. See Raymond Wylie, *The Emergence of Maoism: Mao Tse-tung, Chen Po-ta and the Search for Chinese Theory: 1935–1945,* Stanford: Stanford University Press, 1980. Carol Lee Hamrin, "Yang Xianzhen: Upholding Orthodox Leninist Theory," in Hamrin, et al. *China's Establishment Intellectuals,* M.E. Sharpe, 1986, pp. 51–91. Jane Price, *Cadres, Commanders and Commissars: The Training of the Chinese Communist Leadership 1920–1945,* Boulder: Westview Press, 1976, ch. 3.

However, in the pre-liberation phase, such differences were not dwelt upon, given the need of the hour for revolutionary struggle. Joshua Fogel comments on the varying stress that Ai Siqi put on determinism and consciousness at different times. *Ai-Ssu-ch'i's Contribution to the Development of Chinese Marxism,* p. 50.

consciously according to a mental blueprint which was precisely a reference to the role of consciousness in constituting objective reality.[33] In *Dialectic, Logic and the Theory of Knowledge*, Engels, too, had maintained that "it is insofar as man has learnt to change nature that his intelligence has increased." At other times, however, Engels upheld the copy theory of reflection and pointed out that human thought reflects more and more completely a "world which exists independently of man's cognition and practical activity."[34] The arguments of Zeming et al., were in line with this kind of reductive materialism which claimed that the world and everything in it is ultimately matter in motion, and, therefore, human activity can be reduced to or understood as a specific form of motion of a specific form of matter.

In the late 1950s and 1960s Yang Xianzhen and his followers had subscribed to the reductive-materialist outlook, which assigned practice to the status of a derivative phenomenon and stressed economic and technological determinism. At that time the divergence represented by Yang Xianzhen and Ai Siqi had translated into policy differences, and the lack of consensus on the strategy of the Great Leap and its consequences for China's economic development intensified polarization on the issue of revolutionary will, or the subjective factor versus objective necessity.[35] Initially, after their return to power in the immediate post-Mao period, Yang, Chen Yun, and Hu Qiaomu strongly repeated their earlier criticisms of the Leap.[36] However, the trend of the practice criterion and feudalism

33. Karl Marx, *Thesis on Feuerbach*, Moscow: Progress Publishers, 1965. See also *Issues in Marxist Philosphy Volume 2: Materialism*, edited by John Mepham and David-Hillel Ruben. Brighton: Harvester Press, 1977, pp. 5–34.

34. Kolakowski, *Main Currents of Marxism*, vol. 1, p. 397.

35. The philosophical reflection of the policy disputes were the debates on identity of thought and existence, and the phrase "two combine into one." See Fan Ruoyu, "The Origin of the Polemic Against 'Two Combining into One,'" *Hongqi*, (1979), pp. 64–69. Ai Siqi, "Engels had Affirmed the Identity of Thought and Existence," *RMRB*, 21 July 1960. Ai Siqi, "A Rebuttal of Comrade Yang Hsien-chen's 'Composite Economic Foundation Theory,'" *JPRS* 27414, no. 212, 17 November 1964. Donald Munro, "The Yang Hsien-chen Affair," *The China Quarterly*, no. 22 (1965), pp. 75–82. Hamrin, "Yang Xianzhen," p. 62.

36. Yang Xianzhen, "Adhere to the Principle of the Basic Question of Philosophy; Study the Documents of the Central Work Conference," *GMRB*, 2 March 1981 in *FBIS*, 23 March 1981. Ai Hongwu and Lin Qingshan, "One Divides Into Two and Two Combine Into One," *GMRB*, 29 May 1964 p. 5. Goldman, *China's Intellectuals*, p. 95.

discussions and the calls for far-reaching political reform promoted a new sense of caution and preference for a more balanced reevaluation of the past. Any critiques of voluntarism and the role of revolutionary initiative they now understood could, in all logical consistency, be extended to the pre-Liberation phase as well and erode the legitimacy of the Chinese Communist movement. Preempting allegations that the Communist seizure of power had been premature Party elders now inveighed against further criticism of voluntarism and renewed the call for combatting the threat from the right.

Consequently, when Zeming finally published again on the issue in 1982 his comments appeared to be directed more at practice theorists and radical-reformist leaders whose emphasis on the practice criterion ruled out any theoretical validation, whatsoever, and undermined the guiding role of Marxism. Zeming and his supporters now did not deny the importance of revolutionary action but argued that the "unrestrained elevation of practice" promoted the interests of "pragmatists" and "narrow empiricists" and served as a pretext to depreciate rational knowledge to the point of negating the guiding role of theory.[37]

The change in the incrementalist position was best illustrated by the fascinating reversal in the writings of Yao Bomao, an old friend of Yang Xianzhen. In July 1980, Yao had defended Yang's mid-1950s idea of a mixed economy and criticized Mao indirectly for a hasty transition to a unitary economic base and reckless attempt to make a premature leap into communism.[38] Two years later, however, he had toned down his criticism considerably and was arguing that the errors of the GLF and the Cultural Revolution should be attributed to the Party's lack of experience in socialist construction.[39] Mistakes were unavoidable as the new tasks were undertaken and did not imply the disregard of objective laws of development. They stemmed, rather, from the fact that such laws were

37. Ze Ming, "Another Refutation of 'Practice Is the Only Source of Knowledge,'" *Shehui kexue*, no. 1 (1982), pp. 30–35. See also Xu Chongde, "'Practice Is the Source of Knowledge' Is a Twisting of the 'Primacy of Practice,'" *Shehui kexue*, no. 5 (1982), pp. 34–36.

38. Yao Bomao, "Revaluating the Theory of an Integrated Economic Base," *GMRB*, 3 July 1980 also translated in *FBIS*, 24 July 1980, pp. L2–L8.

39. Yao Bomao, "The Source of Knowledge Is Practice, Not Matter," *Shehui kexue*, no. 5 (1982), pp. 30–33.

still in the process of being discovered—through trial and error—by revolutionary practice!

Proponents of the "practice is the source of knowledge," approach included Yang's old rival Wang Ruoshui, who had, as a protégé of Ai Siqi in the late 1950s and early 1960s, written prolifically in favor of revolutionary will and the "transformation of the subjective into the objective." Although several of his colleagues in the radical-reformist camp agreed that it was the exaggerated emphasis on revolutionary will and human initiative that had led to costly blunders,[40] and despite his own extremely harsh critique of Mao and the Cultural Revolution, Wang was not prepared to retract his view of the relationship between consciousness and objective reality. His attraction to the early Marx's writings on humanism and alienation, and his own emphasis in the early 1980s on human beings as the "starting point of Marxism," and as an "end rather than the means" in the socialist revolution ensured his consistent resistance to economic or technological determinism. Wang's critique of the GLF was a muted one focusing on revolutionary impatience and overenthusiasm rather than the philosophical position of identity of thought and existence which Yang Xianzhen termed Hegelian idealism.[41] Wang traced the roots of the Cultural Revolution to Stalin and Mao's neglect of the law of identity of opposites and overemphasis on struggle, i.e, "one divides into two" (*yifen weier*).[42] Although Wang apologized to Yang for the persecution that had been directed against him earlier, he continued to oppose him ideologically and restricted the access of Yang and his associates to newspapers and journals that were under his control.[43]

Like Wang Ruoshui, the philosopher Li Zehou rejected reductionist materialism and the formalization and universalization of human exis-

40. Li Honglin, "Historical Initiative and Historical Limitation," *GMRB*, 3 January 1980. Liu Maoyin, "A New Explanation of 'the Foolish Old Man Who Removed the Mountain,'" *Wenhuibao*, 13 August 1980, p. 3.

41. Wang Ruoshui, "The Greatest Lesson of the Cultural Revolution Is That the Personality Cult Should Be Opposed," Speech at the Theory Conference, 13 February 1979, *Mingbao*, (Hong Kong), no. 2 (1980), pp. 2–15, also in *JPRS*, 12 March 1980, pp. 78–99. See also Brugger and Kelly, *Chinese Marxism in the Post-Mao Era*, pp. 88–93.

42. Wang Ruoshui, "The Maid of Chinese Politics: Mao Zedong and His Philosophy of Struggle," *The Journal of Contemporary China*, no. 10 (Fall 1995), pp. 66–80.

43. Hamrin, "Yang Xianzhen," p. 86.

tence in Stalinist Marxism. Critics of Engels within the Marxist tradition have generally objected to the reduction of human practice to matter in motion because it promotes political attitudes of passivity and quiescence whereas focus on practice gives rise to a practical revolutionary stance which inspires people to try and transform their material environment.[44] However, Li Zehou's emphasis on practice along with his appropriation of Kant's cognitive subjectivity stemmed from the need to affirm the role of self-consciousness and individual choice in constituting the unique nature of individual existence.[45] While defining human subjectivity in the context of social practice (labor and the construction and use of tools were central to Li's conception of practice), and retaining the concept of historical necessity, Li was critical of official Marxism for ignoring the individual as historical subject in the interests of the collective and the state. Within the next decade Li's concept of subjectivity (*zhutixing*) would come to occupy a central place in post-Mao intellectual discourse, but in the late 1970s and early 1980s his de-emphasis of class in favor of the individual was still highly controversial.[46]

Li Zehou also was highly critical of Maoist voluntarism with its exaggerated emphasis on erratic political campaigns and disregard of rational planning and goal-oriented social organization.[47] However, he traced its origins not to Marxian epistemology but dominant strains within the indigenous tradition, particularly the Wang Yangming school of neo-Confucianism. According to Li, the subjectivist orientation of Chinese Confucian thought was manifested both in assumptions regarding the infinite malleability of nature and the transformative power of human will.[48] Mao's personality traits, policy preferences, leadership style, and

44. Maurice Cornforth, *Communism and Philosophy*, p. 53. See also David-Hillel Ruben, *Marx and Materialism: A Study in the Marxist Theory of Knowledge*, Sussex: Harvester Press, 1979.
45. Li Zehou, *A Critique of Critical Philosophy*, Beijing: Renmin chubanshe, 1979, p. 407.
46. For Li's contribution to a new intellectual consensus see Lin Min, "The Search for Modernity: Chinese Intellectual Discourse and Society, 1978–88—the case of Li Zehou," *China Quarterly*, December 1992, no. 32, pp. 969–998. Gu Xin, "Hegelianism and Chinese Intellectual Discourse: A Study of Li Zehou," *The Journal of Contemporary China*, no. 8 (Winter–Spring) 1995, pp. 1–27.
47. Ibid., p. 362.
48. For a detailed discussion see Woei Lien Chong, "Mankind and Nature in Chinese Thought: Li Zehou on the Traditional Roots of Maoist Voluntarism," *China Information*,

their appeal to broad masses of Chinese people could all be traced to these deep-rooted premises of the traditional Chinese outlook. Similarly, ideas of frugality and egalitarianism had roots extending into the traditional feudal agrarian society, and had been espoused by Confucian as well as Mohist philosophers who sought to preserve and maintain the status quo, and avoid unsettling change which could accompany economic growth and expansion. The ultraleftist emphasis on "shared poverty," and moral self-cultivation found easy acceptance because of its resonance with long-held beliefs.[49]

Li's explanation, one can argue, is interesting but leaves a lot unexplained. Mao's world view clearly reflected elements of indigenous thought and philosophy (emphasis on the strong-willed human subject and the malleability of material reality among other things), but his emphasis on conflict and struggle was in stark contrast to the harmonious view of social relationships and indeed the cosmos which is a hallmark of the traditional Chinese outlook. Wang Yangming's philosophy of "knowing and doing" was concerned with the problem of turning ideas into material force and a reaction to contemplative and quietistic modes of thought, and thus did have parallels with the Marxist idea of revolutionary praxis.[50] Mao's continuing attraction to Wang Yangming's notion that one cannot know and not act was not incompatible with his Marxian world-view. On the other hand, the Wang Yangming school was also known for its stress on questioning canonical authority and rejection of blind obedience and neither of these two tenets seem to have found any echo in the politics of the GLF and the Cultural Revolution.

Similarly, the focus on feudal values and the outlook of the small producer/peasant—a favorite whipping boy of all Chinese-reformist intellectuals—as an explanation for the acceptance of egalitarian ideas and frugal lifestyles has significant limitations. According to most reformist analyses, China continued to be a predominantly rural, small-producer economy through the late 1970s and 1980s. Yet, the nation of peasants

vol. XI, nos. 2–3 (Autumn–Winter 1996), pp. 138–175. I am grateful to Professor David Kelly for this reference.

49.   Ibid., pp. 157–78.

50.   See, for instance, Frederick Wakeman Jr., *History and Will: Philosophical Perspectives of Mao Zedong's Thought*, Berkeley: University of California Press, 1973.

seems to have responded equally, if not more enthusiastically to Deng Xiaoping's appeal to "get rich quickly." The materialism and consumerism manifested by the small producers in post-Mao China is hardly consistent with Li Zehou's "sedimented" psycho-cultural constructs attached to frugality and self-restraint. Nevertheless, despite the obvious inconsistencies and shortcomings of Li's analysis, critiques such as his that focused on the traditionalist and nativist strains in Chinese Communism were to become a serious source of concern for a moderate leadership committed to defending the legitimacy of the Party as a genuine agent of change and progress.

Against the background of complex philosophical positions, personality clashes and shifting alliances and policy preferences within the leadership a theoretical and political compromise was forged to bring about a closure. The *Shehui kexue* issue that featured Ze Ming's piece also carried an article by Hu Fuming that attempted to find a middle ground by arguing that both parties in the debate were proclaiming half-truths. Hu argued that the propositions "practice is the sole source of knowledge" and "objective reality is the only source of knowledge" were not contradictory, and, therefore, it was incorrect to oppose and separate them. To accept the latter and reject the former would be a regression to mechanical materialism. To accept the former and reject the latter would sever the Marxist view of practice from the materialist theory of reflection.[51]

Hu Fuming seemed to be deferring to Zeming's political evaluation as he wrote, "since the birth of New China, on the philosophical front [we] have not truly critically inherited the materialist tradition in history in order to oppose idealism." However, in support of the radical-reformist position he could not resist adding that it was the "rampant tide of extreme leftism" that caused idealism to spread unchecked.[52]

51. Hu Fuming, "More on the Source of Knowledge," *Shehui kexue*, no. 1 (1982), pp. 30–33. Hu, it may be remembered, was the philosophy professor from Nanjing whose article "Practice Is the Sole Criterion for Testing Truth"—published under the title Special Commentator—had sparked off the debate of 1978.

52. Hu Fuming, "More on the Source of Knowledge," *Shehui kexue*, no. 1 (1982), pp. 30–33.

The Debate on the Decisiveness of Matter Versus Spirit

Another round of polemics initiated in 1980 centered on the mutual relationship between matter and idea/spirit. A series of scholarly articles that also made their way into *RMRB* and *GMRB* located the philosophical origin of the subjective idealism and voluntarism associated with the Gang of Four and Lin Biao in the thesis that matter, in general, plays the decisive role with regard to spirit, but under certain conditions, the latter can serve the decisive function.[53] Subjective idealism and voluntarism were seen as the explanation (or cause) for errors in policy and could be traced directly to the exaggeration of the function of practice over matter.

The formulation in question had been derived from "On Contradiction," in which Mao distinguished between the principal and secondary aspects of a contradiction, and claimed that with the increase or decrease in the force of each aspect either one could be manifested in the dominant position. He went on to conclude:

> some people think that this is not true of certain contradictions. . . . This is the mechanical materialist conception, not the dialectical materialist conception. True, the productive forces, practice, and the economic base generally play the principal and decisive role; whoever denies this is not a materialist. But it must also be admitted that in certain conditions, such aspects as the relations of production, theory, and the superstructure in turn manifest themselves in the principal and decisive role.[54]

The defenders of this thesis maintained its essential correctness and claimed that it had been distorted and carried out to an extreme by Lin Biao and the Gang. Recognition of the "mutual function" did not imply a denial of the ontologically privileged position of matter. Their argument was that having originated from matter, spirit acquired relative independence, and when man's conscious activity created new material forms the

---

53. Jin Shougeng, "An Important Principle of Dialectical Materialism," *Zhexue yanjiu*, no. 1 (1980), pp. 14–27.
54. Mao Zedong, "On Contradiction."

relationship between spirit and matter became characterized by reciprocal or mutual action.

The critics of this view, Qi Zhenhai, Cui Wenyu, and their colleagues, preferred to term the role of spirit in regard to matter as a "reaction," and argued that it was incorrect to claim that spirit under any circumstances could play a decisive role. Since matter had the primacy of origin, and spirit was derivative and secondary, only matter could determine spirit and not vice versa. The question of the relationship between matter and spirit was the basic question of philosophy, and, therefore, to posit a mutually decisive relationship between the two was to be guilty of dualism.[55]

Such a characterization of the rival group of theorists was essentially inaccurate for they never denied the derivative nature of consciousness as an attribute of material objects organized in a certain way. Engels himself had argued that "mutual function eliminates all absolute primary and secondary character." Inasmuch as those theorists did not conceive of matter and spirit as opposed in the manner of two different substances in a particular genetic relation, their standpoint was a monist one.

Furthermore, the contention of Qi, et al.—that stressing the decisiveness of spirit/consciousness under certain conditions reflected an idealist or metaphysical viewpoint—can hardly be taken seriously. The term "metaphysical" refers to any doctrine about "ultimate substance" or "ultimate cause." Any theory that professes to reveal the ultimate nature of reality and to deduce from philosophical first principles the dependence of one type of thing on another is metaphysical.[56] This is equally true of the doctrine of "dialectical materialism," which posits the dependency of spirit on matter. The notion that being/nature is primary and thinking/spirit is secondary simply accords to "matter" the status of ultimate substance, and the "motions of matter" become the ultimate cause of everything that occurs. Hence, the position of Qi, Cui, and others was no less metaphysical than that of the individuals they criticized.

The central issue then, was not that "under certain conditions" theorists were idealist or metaphysical in their approach, but whether or not their position regarding the occasionally decisive role of spirit/consciousness was

55. Qi Zhenhai and Liu Jiyue, "Marxist Philosophy Versus Voluntarism."
56. Cornforth, *Communism and Philosophy*, p. 49.

defensible in the light of what Marx and Engels said and wrote. In a situation where the authority of the classics continued to be drawn upon (claims about practice being the criterion of truth notwithstanding), one would have to argue that the Maoist acceptance of an asymmetric primacy and the idea of reciprocity between dialectically related pairs was justifiable within the tradition. Engels had maintained:

> cause and effect are conceptions which only hold good in their application to individual cases; but as soon as we consider the individual in their general connection with the universe as a whole, they run into each other . . . . When we contemplate that universal action and reaction in which causes and effects are eternally changing places . . . what is effect here and now will be cause there and then and vice versa.[57]

And, in his famous letter to Bloch, he said:

> The economic situation is the basis, but the various elements of the superstructure . . . also exercise their influence upon the course of the historical struggles and in many cases preponderate in determining their form.[58]

Marx, who set aside questions of the "priority" relation of thinking and being in a general sense, spoke more concretely of "social consciousness" and "social being or existence." In this context, he clearly conceived of consciousness exercising more than a simple reaction on objective reality. In Marx's notion of the transcending of "false consciousness" by "true consciousness" (or the proletarian realization of its true identity and mission) was implied the decisiveness of revolutionary action/praxis, and the role of the subject in history. There are numerous examples in Marx's writings that illustrate and reiterate his conception of the power of "proletarian consciousness" as a practical energy directed against the external objective world.[59]

It was precisely this position of Marx that validated Lenin's "voluntarism" against the orthodox determinism of Kautsky and Plekhanov. On Marx's view, objective conditions by themselves would not create a socialist

57.   David-Hillel Ruben, *Marx and Materialism*, pp. 118.

58.   Karl Marx and Frederick Engels, "Letter to E. Bloch," in *Selected Correspondence*, Moscow: Progress Publishers. 1965, p. 417.

59.   Avineri, *The Social and Political Thought of Karl Marx*, p. 142.

revolution for an ignorant, alienated proletariat. Only when that class became aware of its role and position could it change the world. And from this followed the need for a political movement and an organization.

Thus, the charge leveled at Jin Shougeng and others (and Mao indirectly) by the "being is primary" theorists was one which could quite easily be extended to Lenin and Marx as well. As illustrated earlier in the discussion on the source of knowledge the coexistence of voluntarist and deterministic strands in the writings of Marx and Engels make it difficult to sustain a critique of either one by theorists committed to defending the essential unity and coherence of the received tradition.

Therefore, the debate on the decisiveness of matter versus spirit ended in a manner similar to the one on the source of knowledge. Insofar as the two debates sought to provide a damaging philosophical critique of "voluntarism," the attempt was largely unsuccessful. The arguments of the reductionists were inadequate and unable to isolate theoretical flaws in the epistemological position of their rivals. The ability of the "practice is the source of knowledge" and "mutual decisiveness" theorists to hold their own with arguments resembling those of the 1950s and 1960s demonstrated that Maoist subjectivism and voluntarism was not simply the product of arrogance or personality traits associated with certain individuals but had definite, fairly pervasive intellectual roots.

The Resolution on Party History

The background to the ideological debates on feudalism and voluntarism was the ebb and flow of the tides of liberalization followed by tightening of controls. Deng's speech during the closing of the Theory Conference and the crackdown on the most vociferous critics among the Democracy Wall activists was meant to assuage the concerns of the revolutionary elders and also to ensure the political stability and unity required for pressing ahead on the economic front. Although they had acted swiftly and decisively to silence the extremists among the dissidents, Deng, Chen Yun, and other elders could not afford to ignore either the popular crisis of confidence that the movement signified, or the critical rumblings within the legitimate theoretical and intellectual circles. In late 1979 and early 1980 as preparations were underway for the drafting of the Resolution on Party History both the issues of political reform and the reassessment of Mao Zedong demanded the continued attention of the leadership. The debate on the *baochan daohu* (contracting production to the household) and *baogan daohu* (contracting output to the household) systems in agriculture and on the "integration of plan and market" in industry also gathered force during this time. Consequently, Deng's espousal of political reform with its focus on corruption, rectification, and promotion served the purpose of expanding the purge of leftists to include the "restorationists" who had assumed the mantle of opposition after the neutralization of the Hua group.[60]

In the months preceding the 1981 Sixth Plenum, Deng consistently refuted the approach of ignoring systemic factors and concentrating on subjective explanations. On 27 June 1980, he said:

> Criticizing Comrade Mao's personal mistakes alone will not solve problems. *What is most important is the question of systems and institutions.* Comrade Mao made many correct statements, but the faulty systems and institutions of the past pushed him in the opposite direction (my emphasis).[61]

In subsequent discussions on drafts of the Resolution, Deng reiterated over and over again that "systems and institutions are the decisive factor" and "errors of particular gravity" such as the Cultural Revolution, the activities of Lin Biao and the Gang of Four, and the mistakes of Mao

---

60.   Led by the elderly Marshall Ye Jianying and Li Xiannian, these were veteran cadres in the economic ministries. The political attack on them took the form of a well-orchestrated media exposure of the Bohai No. 2 Incident involving the sinking of an oil rig with large casualties in the Bohai gulf the previous November. The reformist-controlled media railed against the petroleum ministry's "blind leadership by subjective opinion . . . bureaucratic rigidity, lack of emphasis on training and expertise, and disregard for human life." The Petroleum Minister, Song Zhenming, was dismissed and Vice Premier Kang Shien and Yu Qiuli, head of state planning were criticized publicly. At the NPC meeting in September 1980, Li Xiannian was forced to follow the example of Deng Xiaoping and Chen Yun in announcing his retirement. Ye Jianying continued to hold on to his position but the influence of the restorationists was vastly diminished. See Jurgen Domes, *The Government and Politics of the PRC—A Time of Transition*, Boulder: Westview Press, 1985, p. 201.

61.   "Talk With Some Leading Comrades of the Central Committee," *SW*, 27 June 1980, p. 283.

Zedong could not all be attributed to the "personal qualities of particular individuals."[62] To do otherwise would be "non-Marxist and at variance with historical materialism."[63]

The reforms related to the introduction of elections at the local level, strengthening of the NPC and the judicial system, and abolition of life tenures for party and state officials were promoted by Deng as well as Chen Yun and Peng Zhen, and were aimed at redressing the problem of defective institutions. The wariness with which the political leadership continued to view freedom of speech and organization, however, was demonstrated in the refusal to allow victorious Democracy Wall candidates like Hu Ping (editor of *Fertile Soil*) and Chen Ziming (coeditor of *Beijing Spring*) to take their seats and the withdrawal of the "four great freedoms" (putting up wall posters, conducting debates, launching demonstrations, and conducting strikes) at the Third Session of the NPC in September 1980.

Deng's instrumental approach to political change was reflected also in his position on reassessment of past policies and Communist leaders. In a speech at a Central Work Conference in December 1980 he clarified:

> shortcomings and mistakes should be seriously criticized, but we must never paint a picture that is all black. Even when it comes to such serious mistakes as the "Cultural Revolution," which was exploited by counter-revolutionary cliques, the historical episode as a whole should not be summarily dismissed as "counter-revolutionary." . . . Obviously, to exaggerate under the sway of emotion Comrade Mao's mistakes can only mar the image of our party and country, impair the prestige of the Party and the socialist system, and undermine the unity of the Party, the army and our people. . . . [64]

Given this reasoning the stepped up critiques of the radical-reformist intellectuals on the "feudal fascism" of the GLF and the Cultural Revolu-

62. "Speech During the Preparatory Meeting for the Sixth Plenary Session of the Eleventh Central Committee," 22 June 1980. "Talk With Some Leading Comrades of the Central Committee," *SW*, 25 October, 1980, p. 287.
63. "Implement the Policy of Readjustment, Ensure Stability and Unity," Speech at a Central Working Conference, *SW*, 25 December 1980, p. 347.
64. Ibid.

tion, and the alienation produced by the "fascist dictatorship" of a "bureaucratic class" were, not surprisingly, viewed as exceeding the limits of constructive criticism. Even more subversive politically was the flood of exposé or wound literature which addressed the issues of bureaucratic privilege and the victimization and persecution of innocent individuals. Plays like *General, What Is the Matter With You?* and *If I Were Real* brought forth pressure on Hu Yaobang from Deng and other elders to tighten literary policy and warn writers against the use of literature for political purposes and to avoid themes that fostered cynicism towards the socialist system. By early 1981 the media was replete with articles praising Marxism-Leninism–Mao Zedong Thought, the leadership of the party, and socialist construction. The relatively liberal atmosphere that had characterized the preceding year and a half dissipated with the singling out of Bai Hua's *Unrequited Love* for criticism by the Army newspaper *Jiefangjun bao* on 20 April.[65] The campaign against "bourgeois liberalization" thus initiated in literary, theoretical, and journalistic circles proved to be short-lived and contained, but was a major factor affecting the climate that produced the final form of the Resolution on Party History.[66]

On the eve of the Sixth Plenum Deng found himself on the defensive not only on issues of political and ideological liberalization but also economic reform. On the latter front differences had emerged between Chen Yun and the radical reformers led by Zhao Ziyang on the issue of decentralization and the role of the plan. Radical-reformist proposals recommended expansion of reform to the urban economy, and economic decentralization to address the problem of the command economy's inadequate responsiveness to societal needs in production, allocation of resources, and distribution of products.[67] Chen Yun, on the other hand, stressed readjustment over reform which translated into better macro control over the economy, administrative rather than economic decentralization,

65.   Guest Commentator, "The Four Basic Principles Should Not Be Violated—Comment on the Play 'Unrequited Love,'" *Jiefangjun bao*, 20 April 1981.

66.   Hu Qiaomu, "Several Questions on the Current Ideological Line," *Hongqi*, no. 23 (1981), pp. 2–22. Deng Xiaoping and Hu Yaobang speeches on ideology in *FBIS*, 31 August 1981, pp. 1–3.

67.   Wu Jinglian and Zhou Sulian, "Correctly Handle the Relationship Between Readjustment and Reform," *RMRB*, 5 December 1980.

and balanced sectoral development.[68] Higher deficits, lower revenues, and decreasing central control over local investment were causes for concern and indicated the extent of erosion of the plan. To make his case for mandatory planning Chen singled out the self-interested economic actions of the peasantry in terms of their adverse consequences for the overall economy.

In the face of this offensive, Deng's approach was to give in to the incrementalists on political questions and support ideological revision on issues related to the economy. Marking a retreat from his earlier repeated references to "feudal forces" and the need for systemic explanations in his speech at a preparatory meeting for the Sixth Plenum Deng recommended:

> . . . when we analyze the causes of the "Cultural Revolution," should we mention the influence of petty-bourgeois ideology? I think it does no harm to omit that reference. If and when it becomes necessary to counter the influence of petty-bourgeois ideology, we can deal with it in future documents. There is no hurry. That is not the question involved here. What should be criticized here is something else, to wit, the misunderstanding, dogmatic interpretation, and erroneous application of Lenin's statement that small production engenders capitalism and the bourgeoisie daily, hourly, and on a mass scale. In analyzing the causes of the "Cultural Revolution" this time, we need not refer to the petty bourgeoisie, neither need we copy the past formula that every mistake must necessarily have three causes social, ideological, and historical.[69]

The final form of the Resolution was clearly a product of compromise and from the perspective of the reformers less than thorough.[70] The

68. Dong Fureng, "Develop a Socialist Economy of Benefit to the People," *RMRB*, 29 January 1981.

69. Deng Xiaoping, "Remarks on Successive Drafts of the 'Resolution on Certain Questions in the History of Our Party Since the Founding of the People's Republic of China,'" 22 June 1981. *Selected Works of Deng Xiaoping, 1975–1982*, Beijing: Foreign Languages Press 1984.

70. Huang Kecheng's article of 10 April 1981 carried by *Jiefangjun bao* had preempted the Resolution's appraisal of Mao. "On the Appraisal of Chairman Mao and the Attitude Towards Mao Zedong Thought," *Jiefangjun bao*, 10 April 1981. Liao Gailong complained, "In my opinion, we should straightforwardly and clearly point out that . . . Comrade Mao Zedong committed left-deviationist mistakes. At present many comrades are of the same opinion. However, our current draft resolution on historical questions is not written on these lines."

inconsistencies displayed in the Resolution reflected the divergent views of moderate and radical reformers and in the following months, theorists in Hu Qiaomu and Deng Liqun's camp spent a great deal of effort in explaining these discrepancies.[71]

The Chinese Communist Party was credited in the Resolution with "very successfully" leading the whole people in the tasks of socialist revolution and construction. As to Mao himself it was conceded that he had made "gross mistakes" but overall his contributions to the Chinese revolution far outweighed his mistakes, "his merits were primary and his errors secondary."[72] In regard to the GLF, the Cultural Revolution, and the undermining of collective leadership and democratic centralism the Resolution made a fleeting reference to the need to cite social and historical causes:

> From the Marxist viewpoint, this complex phenomenon was the product of given historical conditions. Blaming this on only one person or a handful of persons will not . . . enable it (the Party) to find practical ways to change the situation. In the Communist movement leaders play quite an important role. . . . However, certain grievous deviations which occurred in the history of the international Communist movement owing to the failure to handle the relationship between the Party and its leader correctly, had an adverse

71. Fang Qiao, "On Leftist Mistakes and Their Origin," *Hongqi*, no. 5 (1981), pp. 29–30. Guan Jian, "Comrade Mao Zedong's Position and Role in the History of the Chinese Revolution," *Hongqi*, no. 11 (1981), pp. 11–18. Jin Chunming, "Why Were 'Errors of Line' and 'Two Line Struggle' not Mentioned in the 'Resolution?'" *Hongqi*, no. 18 (1981), pp. 39–41. Ma Qibin, Chen Dengcai, "Why Is it That Mao Zedong Thought Does Not Include the Errors Made by Mao Zedong in his Later Years," *Hongqi*, no. 20 (1981), pp. 36–38; "Outline for the Study of the Resolution on Certain Questions in the History of Our Party Since the Founding of the PRC," *Jiefang ribao*, 8 July 1981. Shao Huaze, "Correctly Analyze and Understand the 'Great Cultural Revolution,'" *Hongqi*, no. 17 (1981), pp. 43–48. Shi Zhongquan, "An Example of Summing up Historical Experience—Studying the Resolution," *Hongqi*, no. 14 (1981). Yang Fengchun, "Why Were the Class Roots of the 'Great Cultural Revolution' not Analyzed in the 'Resolution'?" *Hongqi*, no. 18 (1981), pp. 41–43. Yuan Mu, "Uphold Mao Zedong Thought, Develop Mao Zedong Thought—Studying the 'Resolution on Certain Questions in the History of Our Party Since the Founding of the PRC,'" *Hongqi*, no. 15 (1981), pp. 41–48.

72. "Resolution on Certain Questions in the History of Our Party Since the Founding of the PRC." Adopted by the Sixth Plenary Session of the Eleventh Central Committee of the CCP on 27 June 1981. *Beijing Review*, no. 27 (1981), pp. 10–39.

effect on our Party, too. Feudalism in China has had a very long history. Our party fought in the firmest and most thoroughgoing way against it . . . but it remains difficult to eliminate the evil ideological and political influence of centuries of feudal autocracy. And for various historical reasons we failed to institutionalize and legalize inner-Party democracy. . . . [73]

The factors cited were thus once again subjective or symptoms rather than causes. Needless to say, the analysis simply begged the questions, why had the Party failed to institutionalize inner-Party democracy, and why did it follow the incorrect lead of the international Communist movement on the question of the relationship between the organization and its leader; and, of course, why had such an incorrect relationship emerged within the international Communist movement?

The resort to superstructural explanations was in line with the preferences of the moderate leadership. Residual ideological influences of the feudal autocratic tradition could be affirmed and explained, to some extent, on the grounds of the Marxist concept of "lag." However, it also revealed the inconsistency of Deng's dismissal of the influence of the "force of habit" of small production when it came to implementing the Household Responsibility System. (The Resolution debunked as dogmatic the Leninist notion that small production would continue to engender capitalism and the bourgeoisie daily and hourly even after the basic completion of socialist transformation.) It would be a strange kind of Marxist who would be concerned only with ideological influences of a previous socioeconomic order and complacent about the superstructural reflections of the current economic base and production relations!

The tactical retreats on the questions of voluntarism and epistemology were reflected in the Resolution as well. In marked contrast to the articles on "magnification and exaggeration" of subjective initiative and the role of spirit, which had appeared in 1979 and 1980, the text made a favorable reference to Mao's insistence that full scope be given to man's conscious dynamic role which was based on and in conformity with objective reality. Mao was also credited with having "comprehensively and systematically elaborated the dialectical materialist theory on the *sources* (my emphasis),

73. "Resolution on Party History," 1981.

process, and the purpose of knowledge and on the criterion of truth."[74] The use of a plural form for "source" in the *Beijing Review* translation was consistent with the compromise view relayed in Hu Fuming's article that both objective reality and practice served as sources of knowledge.

Conclusion

The discussions on feudalism and "voluntarism" attempted to provide comprehensive and thoroughgoing explanations of the distortions in Chinese socialism. Both, however, fell short of providing the legitimacy sought by the Party leadership. The focus on China's peasant majority was problematic because of its implications for assessments of the nature of Chinese society and, indeed, for the identity of the Communist Party itself. The critiques of voluntarism and subjectivism also could be sustained only on the basis of epistemic positions, which, logically pursued, would deny the validity of the Communist takeover in the first place. The criticisms that Kautsky and Plekhanov had directed at Lenin's Bolshevik Revolution would be vindicated in China as well. Hence, the epistemological position of economic determinism became a difficult one to support, even though its policy implications for the present would be preferable. And finally, the retreat from a full-scale denunciation of past policies and a watered-down critique of Mao were also the outcome of a shared concern among the remaining leftists and the moderate leadership that the Chinese should avoid doing to Mao what the Soviets had done to Stalin.

Radical-reformist intellectuals who sought guarantees against the recurrence of the Anti-Rightist Campaign and the Cultural Revolution did not shrink from linking the phenomena of Stalinism and Maoism, and expanding the scope of enquiry to a far-reaching critique of all deviations and errors that had characterized the Communist movement since 1917. Su Shaozhi pointed out:

> Khrushchev completely attributed the mistakes and tragedy born in Soviet socialism led by Stalin to his personal character. This contradicts the basic

74. "Resolution," 1981.

principles of historical materialism, therefore it cannot give a rational account of the reasons which brought about the cult of the individual, nor can it correctly evaluate Stalin's historical position, even less can it find the path to reform or guarantee that Soviet socialism will develop along a healthy path.[75]

According to the radical reformers, political corruption, nepotism, and bureaucratism could all be traced to the lack of legal and political control over both the rank and file as well as higher leadership echelons of Communist Party cadres.[76] Wang Ruoshui, Ru Xin, and Zhou Yang addressed the problem in terms of alienation of power, the "turning of servants of society into its masters."[77] In his speech at the conference commemorating Marx's death centennial, Zhou claimed:

> In the past, we did many stupid things in economic construction due to our lack of experience and our lack of understanding of socialist construction—this realm of necessity—and in the end we ate our own bitter fruit; this is alienation in the economic sphere. Due to the fact that democracy and the legal system were not on a sound basis, the people's servants sometimes made indiscriminate use of the power conferred on them by the people, and turned into their masters; this is alienation in the political sphere, also called the alienation of power. As for alienation in the intellectual sphere, the classic example is the personality cult which is similar in some respect to the alienation of religion criticized by Feuerbach.[78]

The response of the moderate reformers to such critiques was not unpredictable.[79] Hu Qiaomu dismissed the assertion that alienation was

75.   Su Shaozhi, "Uphold and Develop Mao Zedong Thought," *Makesezhuyi yanjiu*, no. 1 (1984), p. 23.

76.   Su Shaozhi, "Develop Marxism Under Contemporary Conditions—In Commemoration of the Centenary of the Death of Karl Marx," *Selected Studies on Marxism*, CASS 1988, p. 6.

77.   Wang Ruoshui, "On the Problem of Alienation," *Xinwen zhanxian*, no. 8 (1980). Ru Xin, "Is Humanism Revisionism?" *RMRB*, 14 August 1980.

78.   Zhou Yang, "A Probe Into Some Theoretical Problems of Marxism," *RMRB*, 16 March 1983, pp. 4–5. For Zhou's earlier views see Donald Munro, "The Chinese View of Alienation," *The China Quarterly*, no. 59 (1979), pp. 580–582.

79.   See Wang Zhen, "Guard Against and Remove Spiritual Pollution on the Ideological Front, Raise High the Banner of Marxism and Socialism," *RMRB*, 25 October 1983, p. 1.

an objectively existing, supra-historical category which could be used to analyze any society, socialist as well as capitalist.[80] Taking Wang Ruoshui's definition of alienation as a phenomenon appearing when "a subject by its own activity creates and hence becomes an external, alien force, turning around to oppose and control the subject himself," Hu maintained that the attempt to put forward a "theory" of alienation or elevate the phenomenon of alienation to the status of a universal law was incorrect.

> An account of socialist alienation either refers to the many residual phenomena of the old society and their effects as alienation—which contracts the definition; or, in accordance with the definition, it is believed that socialism, as it develops, will inevitably give birth to an alien force that turns around and controls it.

Then, picking on Wang and Zhou's claims that alienation could be overcome by working through the socialist system itself, Hu proceeded to prove his point.

> Laws cannot be overcome by man; what can be overcome by men is not a law. Or perhaps they may agree: "People must simply discover the laws of alienation and then on the basis of these laws, they can overcome their effects."

The attempt to explain the need for the current reforms in terms of intellectual alienation, alienated power, and so forth, were similarly rejected by Hu as a caricature of Feuerbach's ideas and a misguided overemphasis on Marx's earlier works. Hu argued, as Xing Fensi had, earlier in November, that while these works were critical to understanding the course of Marx's intellectual development, they could not be considered representative of his mature thought, thus, neither alienation nor socialist humanism could be substituted for the central truth of Marxist thought—the dialectical-materialist conception of history.

Hu's position was a reassertion of the "orthodox" or "official" Marxist position that alienation belongs to a subjective, social and historical cate-

---

80.   Hu Qiaomu, "On the Question of Humanism and Alienation," *Hongqi*, no. 2 (1984), pp. 2–28. Also *Renmin ribao*, 27 January 1984, pp. 1–5. Stuart Schram, *Ideology and Politics Since the Third Plenum*, p. 51.

gory, revealing the antagonistic relationship between labor and capital. According to this view, alienation is a phenomenon that emerges when human society develops to a certain stage and obtains a complete sense in capitalist society. It is bound to be sublated by social and economic development and leave the stage of history in communist society. The realization of communism is the "active sublation of the self-alienation of men."

For Wang or Zhou to perceive residual alienation in a society still "constructing socialism" was neither a violation of Marxism nor necessarily an enunciation of a law of alienation as Hu contended. His response was essentially the same as it had been in regard to the discussions on feudalism. To accept that alienation, in any form, had existed in Chinese society at some point or another since "socialist transformation," or was in existence at the present time, was to cast aspersions on the legitimacy of Chinese socialism. But, Hu and his colleagues were clearly on the defensive. Reflecting, no doubt, the broad appeal of ideas of democracy and ideological pluralism, it is significant that Hu chose to identify the issue not so much as one of ideological deviation or violation of official doctrine in academic or public discourse as that of social effect.[81]

> If our theory is incorrect in its basic orientation, this will almost unavoidably lead to bad social consequences. Such consequences are difficult to predict completely but no Communist Party member can fail to reflect seriously about them beforehand.[82]

After a brief hiatus during the Anti-Spiritual Pollution Campaign, therefore, the quest for answers and satisfactory explanations on the part of the radical reformers continued with a renewed interest in Western and Eastern European works on the phenomenon of Stalinism, as well as in theorists of the Second International who had provided the earliest indictments of the Bolshevik Revolution. The sensitivity of the issues and the divisions among the leadership prevented the official endorsement of any specific explanation but in the increasingly tolerant atmosphere of the

81. Zhou Yang apologized for the "shortcomings and mistakes" in his March report because they could be utilized by enemies of socialism and undermine the morale of those building a Communist society. *Beijing Review*, no. 50 (1983), pp. 11–12.
82. Hu, "On the Question of Humanism and Alienation."

1980s decade radical-reformist intellectuals applied themselves zealously to the study of the critiques of official Marxism offered by "bourgeois" Marxists such as Althusser and the theorists of the Frankfurt School and the New Left while redoubling their efforts to come up with their own distinctly Chinese answers.

THREE

Stages of Socialism

In the late 1970s the political and philosophical repudiation of radical left-ism was the prelude to a major reappraisal of China's strategy of economic development. The move away from Maoist preferences focused attention on flaws in existing economic institutions and processes and the remedies for them. Differences among the moderate reformers and their radical cohorts became accentuated in the following decade as their analyses and prescriptions diverged on the issues of structural and systemic reform. Moderates affirmed the essential correctness of the Soviet-Stalinist social-ist model and sought appropriate modifications in its application to the Chinese context. Radical reformers, on the other hand, emphasized both the national and historical limitations of the Soviet model and focused their theoretical efforts on promoting the legitimacy of a specific Chinese-socialist economic variant. A key area of contention centered on the defi-nition of the current stage of Chinese development which, in turn, would validate policies related to ownership patterns, norms of distribution, and the respective scopes of plan and market.

The Concept of "Undeveloped Socialism"

The need to delineate stages of development arose in the context of the initiatives taken at the December 1978 Third Plenum to approve agricul-tural collectivization on the grounds of its compatibility with the level of Chinese productive forces. Maoist "egalitarianism" and opposition to "dis-tribution according to work" were castigated as a "tendency to effect the transition from socialism to communism prematurely." Mao's assertion that the contradiction between the proletariat and the bourgeoisie continued to be the principal contradiction in China, and, hence, the possibility of capitalist restoration existed throughout the socialist period reflected a misunderstanding of the nature and requirements of the new stage of development that the Chinese revolution had entered by the mid-fifties.[1] On the question of class struggle and on the alleviation of socioeconomic inequality, the fault of Mao's leadership lay in implementing policies which, although not incorrect in themselves, were inappropriate for the period in question. It followed that, if further mistakes were to be avoided, it was essential to grasp and understand the precise nature of the current historical period.

In this climate of questioning the appropriateness of leftist policies for a specific phase, Su Shaozhi and Feng Lanrui struck a new note by proffering the argument that a retreat in economic policy was necessitated by the fact that China had not yet completed its transition to socialism. Su's presentation at the Theory Conference and the publication of their coauthored article around the same time sparked off a long and simmering controversy over the interpretation of the phrase "transition from capitalist society to communist society," which had been employed by Marx and Engels.[2] Since both Marx and Lenin had referred to lower and higher stages of communism, the disagreement centered firstly on whether the term "transition from capitalism to communism" referred to the higher stage of communism or the lower and secondly, into how many and what stages could the period intervening between the proletarian seizure of power and full communism be divided.

Referring to Lenin's introduction of a transitional stage between the seizure of power and the lower stage of communism and comparing China's backward productive forces and the low degree of socialization of production to the Russian situation, Su and Feng pointed out that the

---

1. "Resolution on Certain Questions in the History of Our Party Since the Founding of the PRC," adopted by the Sixth Plenary Session of the Eleventh Central Committee of the Chinese Communist Party on 27 June 1981, *Beijing Review*, no. 27 (1981), pp. 10–39. Zhu Yuanshi, "The Causes of the Outbreak of the 'Great Cultural Revolution' and its Lessons," *Hongqi*, no. 16 (1981), pp. 43–48. Wang Menggui, "Exploring the Road of Our Country's Socialist Construction," *Hongqi*, no. 15 (1981), pp. 33–40

2. Su Shaozhi and Feng Lanrui, "The Question of the Stages of Social Development After the Seizure of Power by the Proletariat," *Jingji yanjiu*, no. 5 (1979), pp. 14–19.

stage of transition in China would be a long one. More importantly, however, the two authors maintained that the transition was still in progress and therefore the following stages could be delineated in the Chinese context: I. The stage of transition from capitalism to socialism subdivided into (a) transitional period (from the seizure of power by the proletariat to the basic completion of socialist transformation) and (b) "undeveloped" socialism. II. Developed socialism, i.e., the kind of socialist society envisaged by Marx and Lenin.[3] III. Communism.

Describing the transitional stage (Ia) as characterized by the existence of many different economic forms, various classes, and fierce class struggle, Su and Feng located China in the transitional stage of "undeveloped socialism."

> The characteristics of undeveloped socialism are the existence of two forms of public ownership, commodity production and commodity exchange, capitalists have already been basically eliminated as a class but there still remain capitalist and bourgeois remnants, even feudal remnants, there also exist quite a few small producers, class differences among workers, and peasants . . . the force of habit of small production; the productive forces are still not very highly developed. There is not an abundance of products. At this time large-scale turbulent mass class struggles are over, but there still is class struggle, there still is need for a dictatorship of the proletariat, therefore the transitional stage toward socialism has still not been completed.

According to this reasoning, a society that did not entirely resemble the socialist society envisaged by Marx and Engels could not be termed "completely socialist." However, to the extent that it was a society that was a product of a proletarian revolution and one in which the means of production had been brought under public ownership, it could be described as socialist, albeit "undeveloped." The justification for the use of the term socialist in describing China was sought from Lenin's comments in the Soviet context.

3.   This used to be the term for the later stage of Soviet socialism but none of the Chinese writers made any reference to the Soviet position or made any comparisons. Su and Feng, however, did point out that Lenin had used the term "developed" socialist society and Mao had referred to undeveloped and comparatively developed socialist society, hence the concept of "undeveloped" socialism was not a new one.

No one, I think, in studying the question of the economic system of Russia, has denied its transitional character. Nor, I think, has any Communist denied that the term Socialist Soviet Republic implies the determination of Soviet power to achieve the transition to socialism, and not that the new economic system is recognized as a social order. . . . Is it not clear that from the material economic and productive point of view, we are not yet on the "threshold" of socialism?[4]

From the point of view of Su and his colleague, the location of China in a pre-socialist stage of development obviated the need for justification of NEP-like policies such as the responsibility system in agriculture in terms of its compatibility with socialism. In a related article in which he criticized the commune system as inappropriate to the level of development of productive forces in China, Su Shaozhi also rejected as incorrect the formulation included in the Resolution of the Eighth Congress in 1956, which identified the principal contradiction as that between an advanced social system and backward social productive forces.[5] Such a formulation, he argued, was doctrinally unsound because it conveyed the impression that a society can produce an advanced system that transcends the requirements of the productive forces, i.e., that relations of production can be created according to subjective will before there is demand for them by the productive forces.

The most significant aspect of China's economic base, according to Su and other writers elaborating on this theme, was the predominance of the peasantry and small-scale production. This stress on the peasantry along with the low level of economic development also justified the position that China was not quite ready for the kind of socialist relations—exemplified by the commune—that had been established in the 1950s. Su Shaozhi consequently rejected the notion that the system that came about in the wake of socialist transformation was an advanced one.

The social system mainly consists of the relations of production. Whether a relation of production is advanced or not is determined by just one crite-

4. Ibid.
5. Su Shaozhi, "On the Principal Contradiction Facing Our Society Today," *Xueshu yuekan*, no. 7 (1979).

rion, notably contingent on whether or not it can meet the demands of the expanded productive forces and facilitate their development. Although some types of relations of production such as the system of ownership by the rural commune may be superior to the system of ownership by the production team in terms of the level of development, in rural China today where manual labor remains predominant, the one type of production relations capable of measuring up to the standards of the productive forces and speeding up their development would be the system of ownership by the production team . . . rather than the commune. If the basic level is circumvented and the system of ownership by the commune is adopted instead, it would damage the development of the productive forces.[6]

Although Su's critique of the Liuist formulation of the principal contradiction was generally acceptable,[7] his position that China was still not completely socialist and hence could only be judged to be in transition to that lofty goal was countered strongly by the moderate leadership. The thesis of "undeveloped socialism" fitted in with the tone of the discussions on feudalism and undermined the accomplishments of the Chinese Communist Revolution. Su's emphasis on China's backwardness was taken even more seriously in the light of Wang Xiaoqiang and other researchers' denigration of "petty bourgeois" or "agrarian" socialism. Taken together the thrust of these reformist writings was eroding the legitimacy of those very glories—the overthrow of feudalism and capitalism, and the establishment of socialism—on which the Party based its right to lead the country. Hu Qiaomu and Deng Liqun assailed Su in official circles although their call for public criticism of him was rejected almost unanimously by Su's colleagues at CASS.[8] In the wake of the student demonstrations of 1986, however, Su came under renewed criticism as a representative of the rightist trend that contributed to the youths' cynicism and "crisis of faith," and lost his directorship of the Marxism-Leninism Institute of CASS.

6. Ibid.

7. In his March 1979 speech, Deng Xiaoping refrained from using the Liuist formulation and referred instead to the contradiction between the needs of the people and the backwardness of the economic base.

8. Interview with Su Shaozhi, 20 April 1990.

The intellectual rebuttal of Su's thesis was led by Zhu Shuxian and Feng Wenbin. Their argument distinguished between societies characterized by a variety of economic forms and others in which a particular form was decisive.[9] While the former could be labeled transitional the latter would be identified on the basis of the dominant mode of production. With the socialist transformation of the means of production in China, the transition was deemed complete and henceforth China became a socialist society.

The contention of Su and Feng that the existence of two kinds of public ownership distinguished the present Chinese situation from the socialism envisaged by Marx, Engels, and Lenin was rejected on the grounds that state ownership and collective ownership differed only in terms of levels. The transition period, on the other hand, had been characterized by the coexistence of two fundamentally different forms of ownership: public and private. Hence, the distinction between the transitional stage and the stage which Su and Feng termed "undeveloped socialism" was a qualitative one and not one of mere degree.

As his rationale for the argument that China was already socialist, Feng Wenbin claimed that in the late 1940s the "absolute political superiority of the Chinese proletariat" and the highly concentrated nature of modern industry in the hands of bureaucrat capitalists facilitated its nationalization and conversion into the leading component of the whole national economy.[10] Refuting criticism that the Chinese Communists may have attempted a premature establishment of socialism, Feng argued that Marx and Engels had not ruled out the possibility of socialist revolutions for countries in which capitalism was insufficiently developed, nor had they specified that socialism could only be practiced on the basis of a high proportion of large-scale socialized production.

The obvious flaw in Feng's argument was the equation of the proletarian seizure of power with the establishment of socialism. The comments

---

9. Zhu Shuxian, "Also Discussing the Question of Stages of Social Development After the Seizure of Power by the Proletariat," *Jingji yanjiu*, no. 8 (1979). Lin Yuhua, "The General Character of the Transition Period and Its Specific Pattern," *Shehui kexue*, no. 1 (1980). Ma Jihua, "Is Socialist Society a Transitional Period," *Shehui kexue*, no. 2 (1980).

10. Feng Wenbin, "Consciously Implement the Line of the Third Plenary Session of the Eleventh CCP Central Committee and Firmly Advance Along the Track of Scientific Socialism," *Hongqi*, no. 10 (1981), pp. 2–12.

of Marx and Engels quoted ad infinitum by Chinese theorists were made on the assumption of a world socialist revolution where the backwardness of certain nations would be neutralized by the economic development of the more advanced countries. They were not made in the context of socialism in individual countries and hence did not "prove" the possibility of the establishment of socialism in underdeveloped areas where the proletariat was able to seize power for one reason or another.

The three-stage periodization adhered to by Su and his detractors finds little support in Marx's writings. In the *Critique of the Gotha Programme*, Marx had mentioned that "between capitalist and communist society" there lay a "period of the revolutionary transformation of one into the other."[11] Discussing the norm of distribution "in the first phase of communist society as it is when it has just emerged after prolonged birth pangs from capitalist society," Marx made it clear that the period of transition *was* the period of socialism. The need for an intermediate period between the destruction of the old system and the establishment of the new—wherein the foundations of material abundance would be perfected and all old vestiges eliminated—was the rationale for Marx's distinction between two successive phases of communism. Moreover, given Marx's assumption of a proletarian revolution in a mature capitalist society when the conditions for socialism had already matured in the "womb" of capitalism, any intervening period between the proletarian seizure of power and the advent of full communism would tend to be fairly short, thus precluding the necessity for an additional stage of transition interposed between the overthrow of the capitalist system and the lower stage of communism.

It was Lenin who labeled the earlier phase "socialism" and the later "communism."[12] Originally these were the only two phases that he seems to have considered with the tasks of the socialist state (under the dictatorship of the proletariat) to bring about nationalization of industry, central economic planning, and collectivization of agriculture. Rational allocation of resources and higher productivity would eliminate unemployment

11. Karl Marx, *Critique of the Gotha Programme*, The Marxist-Leninist Library, vol. 15, London: Lawrence and Wishart Ltd., 1943.

12. V.I. Lenin, "The State and Revolution" in *Selected Works*, vol. II, Moscow: Foreign Languages Publishing House, 1947, pp. 141–225.

and waste, but in this stage group differences would remain, and the inability of the socialist system to fully satisfy the needs of its members would determine the distribution principle of remuneration according to work. Like Marx, Lenin in his earlier writings such as *State and Revolution* assumed more or less rapid progress from socialism to communism.

The circumstances of the October Revolution, particularly its failure to spark off revolution in Western Europe, brought a change in Lenin's thinking. In *The Marxist Theory of the State* he added a transitional stage between capitalism and socialism. During War Communism (1919) he described Russia not as a socialist society but as one struggling to reach that stage, i.e., one trying "to solve the problems of the *transition* from capitalism to socialism." In other words, given Russia's stage of development, the period could only be that of "building the basis" for socialism.[13] For Lenin and other Bolshevik leaders of the time, nationalization of the means of production was an event that marked progress toward socialism but it was not to be identified with that state. In his article, "Cooperation," written between January and February 1923, Lenin wrote:

> Indeed, the power of the state over all large-scale means of production, state power in the hands of the proletariat, the alliance of this proletariat with the many millions of small and very small peasants, the guaranteed leadership of the proletariat in relation to the peasantry etc.,—is this not all that is necessary for constructing a fully socialist society out of the coop-

13.   Nevertheless, Zhu Shuxian, a theorist in the Hu Qiaomu, Deng Liqun camp, sought legitimization with a quote from one of Lenin's last works to demonstrate that China had completed its transition and had become a socialist society with the collectivization of agriculture. See Zhu Shuxian, "Also Discussing the Question of Stages." The quote, "a system of civilized cooperators is the system of socialism," came from a set of five articles that Lenin wrote a few months before he died and which were referred to by Bukharin as Lenin's legacy reflecting the change in his attitude toward the NEP ("Pages From a Diary," "On Cooperation," "Our Revolution," "How We Should Organize," and "Better Fewer, But Better"). Without going into the controversy over Lenin's last political testament, the point to be emphasized is that even if Lenin changed his understanding of NEP, the significance of the change lay in his perception of the means for bringing about socialism, i.e., the question of whether NEP would lead to socialism, not that NEP Russia was socialist, just as earlier he had never claimed that state capitalism was socialism. Nor did Bukharin ever make that claim for him.

eratives . . . ? *This is not yet the construction of socialism*, but it is all that is necessary and sufficient. (my emphasis) [14]

It was in the Stalinist perspective that the most important element in the process of development of socialism came to be identified with the quantitative extent of nationalization and collectivization. The economy was considered transitional so long as the nationalization and collectivization of the means of production were not exclusive or predominant. According to official Soviet historiography the three phases between the seizure of power and the higher stage of communism were: I. Transition from capitalism to socialism (1917–1936). II. Building of developed socialist society (1936–late 1960s). III. Stage of developed or mature socialism (1971 onward).[15]

However, even in this conception the level of development of productive forces was not completely overlooked. And it was for this reason that Soviet writers maintained that in the USSR approximately two decades were required to complete the transition from capitalism to socialism with the year 1936 marking "the construction of socialism in the main." Eastern European countries, which were at a much higher level of development compared to China, were said to have completed their construction of socialism by the late 1950s or the early 1960s; China, not surprisingly, was included among those countries that had not yet established "socialism in the main."[16] It would appear, then, that according to Soviet doctrine, in addition to transfer of public property into state or collective hands, the proclamation of socialism would also await a level of industrialization commensurate with the requirements of socialism.[17]

14. Stephen Cohen, *Bukharin and the Bolshevik Revolution*, New York: Alfred Knopf, 1973, p. 137.

15. Alfred B. Evans, Jr., "Developed Socialism in Soviet Ideology," *Soviet Studies*, no. 29 (1977), pp. 409–428.

16. Ibid.

17. The periodization of the East European countries themselves approximated fairly closely the Soviet one. The Hungarian Communist Party, for instance, declared at its Eighth Congress in November 1962, that with the completion of socialization the foundations of a socialist society had been laid. The next stage in Hungary was understood to be that of the "complete construction of socialism." See Janos Kadar, "Lenin—The Theoretician and Organiser of Socialist Construction," in *For a Socialist Hungary*, Budapest: Corvina Press, 1974.

In contrast to this, Chinese critics of Su's thesis claimed on behalf of the Soviets, "three years after the capitalist class had been overthrown, Russia having adopted the most elementary steps made the transition from capitalism to socialism, i.e., the lower stage of communism."[18] In the case of China, a *GMRB* Staff Special Commentator article reiterated that "the first seven years after the establishment of the PRC in 1949–1956 were those of basically completing socialist transformation."[19] The discussions preceding the 1981 Resolution on Party History compared Chinese statistics on steel production and other industrial output during this period with the performance of capitalist countries in Marx's time to "prove" that the level of productive forces in China in the mid-1950s was consistent with that conceived by Marx and Engels for establishing socialist production relations.[20] At Hu Qiaomu's insistence the official position was spelled out by the Resolution adopted by the Sixth Plenum.

> Although our socialist system is in its early phase of development, China has undoubtedly established a socialist system and entered the stage of socialist society. Any view denying this basic fact is wrong.[21]

The defeat of Su Shaozhi's thesis at this time was primarily a political one. Su's assertion that China was still in a transitional stage was not only closer to Lenin's view but also consistent with the classical Marxian notion that "scientific socialism" is to be distinguished from "utopian socialism" precisely on the grounds that no socialist socioeconomic form is conceivable

18.   Lin Yuhua, "The General Character of the Transition Period," *Shehui kexue*, no. 1 (1980).

19.   Staff Special Commentator, "On the Characteristics of Chinese Society at the Present Stage," *GMRB*, 14 May 1981, p. 1. Huang Wenzhuan, "Correctly Understand the Social Characteristics of Our Country During the Present Stage—Also Commenting on a Certain Unhealthy Style of Study," *RMRB*, 12 May 1981. Shi Zhongquan, "How Should China's Socialist Society Be Assessed?" *Hongqi*, no. 11 (1981), pp. 2–10. Wen Yanmao, "On the Question of Our Country's Transition From New Democracy to Socialism," *Hongqi*, no. 18 (1981), pp. 32–38. Xu Chengqing, "Why Can Economically Backward Countries Enter Socialism First?" *Hongqi*, no. 10 (1983), pp. 12–17. Lu Zhichao, "Assess Socialist Society With the Theory of Development of Dialectical Materialism," *Hongqi*, no. 14 (1983), pp. 13–17.

20.   Explanatory notes to the Resolution, pp. 501–516.

21.   Resolution (1981).

without the attainment of a certain level of development of the productive forces. The official position associated with Hu Qiaomu and others not only stretched the Stalinist definition but also finds little support among other analyses within the Marxist tradition. For instance, Yugoslavian Communism, which was attracting the attention of Chinese reformers at this time, incorporated a much more dynamic conception of socialization of the means of production, treating it as a process rather than a once and for all act.[22] For the SKJ socialization was neither identical with nor limited to the transfer of productive property into the hands of the proletarian state.

The process of socialization began with the seizure of power by the proletariat, the establishment of state ownership, and the institution of planning. This phase, which the Yugoslavs termed "statist," was essential for all countries, the developed and the less developed. For the latter, the statist phase was more significant and of a longer duration because of the special responsibilities for laying the material foundations for socialism. The Yugoslav formulation differed from the Soviet in including the "statist phase" in the concept of the transition period. This was because for the SKJ state ownership was "indirect" social ownership and hence an inferior form of social ownership. Disposition over the means of production being representative rather than direct state ownership was exercised by associated producers through an agency acting in their name, i.e., the state.[23] The fact that the state now represented the entire society rather than a minority of proprietors did not, however, mean that it had become identical with society. The category "transitional" implied progress from indirect social ownership to "more and more direct social ownership, under the more and more fully direct disposition of the liberated and associated working people," i.e., self-management.[24]

The unqualified identification of state ownership with socialism was likewise rejected by a wide spectrum of Marxist writers from Paul Sweezy, George Bettelheim, and the entire range of state-capitalist theorists like Tony Cliff to East European dissidents like Pavel Campeanu, all of whom have agreed that in Soviet-type societies ownership of the means of pro-

22. Wlodzimiercz Brus, *Socialist Ownership and Political Systems*, London: Routledge & Kegan Paul, 1975, p. 63.

23. Ibid., p. 64.

24. Ibid.

duction being no longer in the hands of private capitalists did not imply that ownership was already socialist.

The essence of socialist relations, according to Paul Sweezy and George Bettelheim, was "domination by the producers over their conditions of existence—over the means of production and the products of their work." "Decisions" made at the "top" by a revolutionary state power (read: nationalization and state control) could not immediately eliminate old social relations.[25] Departing from both the Soviet and Yugoslav formulations the "unofficial" Marxist tradition also ruled out the existence of commodity production in a socialist society.[26] Ernest Mandel linked the disappearance of commodity production to the elimination of scarcity of consumer goods and all private ownership of products in circulation.[27] Mandel also maintained that the mere substitution of the "employer-state" for private employers did not bring about a change in production relations.[28] Such change could come about only when workers acquired real day-to-day say, as opposed to "formal and juridical," in management and planning. Hence, he concluded that any society characterized by the "continued existence of social inequality," "alienation of labor," and a "level of development of productive forces" lower than the "most advanced capitalist country" could not be considered a fully socialist society.[29]

Given the increasing exposure of Chinese theorists to such alternative formulations Su's thesis found considerable support among his colleagues. In the late 1970s and early 1980s, radical reformers still shared the assumptions of their moderate colleagues on the essential tenets of a socialist economy. As they pressed for expansion of commodity relations and a more restricted role for planning they were on the ideological defensive for they did look upon these measures as a tactical retreat from socialist norms. The attraction of Su's thesis was that it entailed far less ideological

25. Paul Sweezy, Charles Bettelheim, *On the Transition to Socialism*, New York: Monthly Review Press, 1971, p. 43, 65–66.

26. Ibid., p. 54.

27. Ernest Mandel, *Marxist Economic Theory*, London: Merlin Press, 1962, pp. 564–565.

28. Ibid., p. 644.

29. Moreover, for Bettelheim, Sweezy, Mandel, and others, all contemporary societies which had experienced proletarian revolutions were transitional societies, the forward development of which in the direction of socialism was, by no means, a foregone conclusion.

revision than would be the case in trying to accommodate the "invisible hand" of the market and individual ownership within the framework of socialism. However, given even Deng Xiaoping's reluctance to compromise on the issue, reformist intellectuals like Xue Muqiao and Yu Guangyuan opted instead for eliciting support for less controversial formulations such as "lower" or "early" stages of socialism which would mollify critics as well as "prevent a premature application of certain principles attributed to the original stage of socialism by Marx."[30]

In 1981–82 moderate reformers were in a relatively stronger position. The controversy over stages was settled in their favor with the definition of socialism as public ownership of the means of production and distribution according to work accepted as the most fundamental description of socialist society. For the moderates, public ownership was synonymous with socialist ownership. Of the two levels—ownership by the whole people or state ownership and group or collective ownership— the former was superior and the latter a more inferior form of social ownership. Hence, the definition of socialism centered primarily on the extent of nationalization.[31]

As economic reform gained momentum in the mid- and late 1980s, however, the reality of economic liberalization could not but become inconsistent with such a statist conception of the socialist economy. The ideological developments related to "structural" reform and the radical-reformist search for alternatives to the Soviet model could not fail to undermine the theoretical assumptions according to which China was deemed a socialist society.

The Primary Stage of Socialism

The Twelfth Congress that convened in September 1982 endorsed Chen Yun's emphasis on readjustment and the elimination of sectoral imbalances

30. Xue Muqiao, *China's Socialist Economy*, Beijing: Foreign Languages Press, 1981, p. 15.
31. Su Shaozhi continued to give a more detailed definition of socialism as elimination of exploitation, public ownership of the means of production, payment according to work, planned development of the state economy, state power of the working class and laboring people, high development of productive forces and spiritual culture. "On Distinguishing Criteria of Socialist Structures," *Guangming ribao*, 21 October 1985, p. 3.

(heavy/light industry, consumption/investment, revenue/expenditure, people's livelihood/production) by more efficient and rational macro-control mechanisms.[32] However, in the immediate aftermath of the Congress Hu Yaobang and Zhao Ziyang stepped up their urging of reformist intellectuals to provide a "theoretical basis" for the expansion of reform into the urban-industrial economy.[33]

The following year being the centennial marking Marx's death, economists associated with the CASS Economic Research Institute utilized the General Secretary's call for developing Marxism to distinguish between a "fixed" foreign socialist economic model, i.e., the Soviet centrally planned command economy, and other variants such as the Yugoslav and Chinese ones.[34] The purpose of this distinction was to invalidate the identification of the Soviet model with a classical socialist model, and simultaneously legitimize the departure of the Chinese variant from the "borrowed" and "dated" Soviet one.[35] The slogan "build socialism with Chinese characteristics" marked the launching of a major ideological offensive by the reformers to raise questions about the "essential" nature of planning and, more importantly, the principle of state ownership.[36] Justification for

---

32.   Hu Yaobang, "Usher in An All-Round New Situation in Socialist in Socialist Modernization," Report to the Twelfth Party Congress, *Hongqi*, no. 18 (1982), pp. 6–32.

33.   Hu Yaobang, "The Radiance of the Great Truth of Marxism Lights Our Way Forward," *Beijing Review*, vol. 26, no. 12 (1983), pp. I–XV; in *Zheng Ming*, 1 November 1984, pp. 6–9, in *FBIS*, 6 November 1984; in *Zheng Ming*, 1 December 1984, pp. 6–9, in *FBIS*, 3 December 1984.

34.   Liu Guoguang, "Several Problems in Current Economic Reform and Readjustment," *Xinhua wenzhai*, no. 6 (1984), pp. 46–48. see also Contributing Commentator articles, "On Rethinking" and "Deepen Theoretical Understanding of Reform," in *Hongqi*, no. 12 (1984), pp. 2–8, 38–40.

35.   Yu Guangyuan, "Perceive the Reform of the Period of Socialist Construction From the Viewpoint of World and Chinese History," *Zhongguo shehui kexue*, no. 1 (1985), pp. 53–68, in Renda *Fuyin*, no. 1 (1985), pp.1–18. "Actively Promote Marxism as the Science of Socialist Construction," *Renmin ribao*, 5 August 1985, p. 5, also in Renda *Fuyin*, no. 8 (1985), pp. 7–8. "Develop Marxism as a Science for Socialist Construction," *Zhongguo shehui kexue*, no. 4 (1983), pp. 3–12. Liao Gailong, "Advance Along the Road of All-Round Socialist Construction: Commemorating the 100th Anniversary of Marx's Death," *Jiaoxue yu yanjiu*, no. 2 (1983), pp. 6–15 in Renda *Fuyin*, no. 4 (1983).

36.   Chen Daisun, "Study Modern Economies of the West and Socialist Economic Modernization of Our Country," *RMRB*, 16 November 1983. Huang Fanzhang, "Take a Correct

continued decentralization of economic decision making and enterprise autonomy was now centered on the reconceptualization of public ownership and the distinction between ownership and management.

In mid-1984, in the context of drafting a resolution on urban reform, discussions heated up over the issue of planned management of state enterprises. Moderates regarded the devolution of control over production decisions, pricing, and profits to enterprises as "erosion" of the plan and "weakening" of public ownership. Reformers, on the other hand, legitimized separation of ownership and management in terms of efficiency and by shifting the weight of socialization to the plane of democratization.[37] As early as 1979–80, Dong Fureng and CASS vice president Yu Guangyuan had recommended reappraisal of the concept of public ownership with the latter arguing that the principle in itself did not imply that in every socialist society "laborers are complete masters."[38] In their articles commemorating Marx's death centennial in 1983, Liao Gailong and Su Shaozhi pointed out that the extensive nationalization, excessive centralization, and state domination over collectives associated with the Soviet model stifled the creative enthusiasm of producers and precluded their taking any real initiative in the economic realm. The main

Approach Toward the Contemporary Bourgeois Economic Theories," *GMRB*, 20 November 1983. Ma Hong, "Marxism and China's Socialist Economic Construction—Written to Commemorate the Centenary of Marx's Death," *Social Sciences in China*, no. 3 (1983).

37.   Su Shaozhi, "In the Midst of Overall Reform Develop Marxism and Construct Socialism with Chinese Characteristics," *RMRB*, 11 March 1983, p. 5. The inspiration for this can be traced to the Polish economist, Wlodzimiercz Brus, who was an advocate of East European reform. According to Brus, both the Soviet etatist model and the Yugoslav self-management model were simply two different paths to achieving socialism, the test for which lay in the degree of control that the working class actually possesses in any system, i.e., the degree of democratization in decision making. In the etatist model, "society is deprived of the prerequisites for disposition over the means of production directly in the economic sphere and retains only the possibility of control or influence by means of political instruments. The test of socialization for the etatist model, then, turns on whether the political system ensures subordination of the state to the will of society — both as regards to setting out the directions of policy and as regards to control over their implementation." See Wlodzimiercz Brus' *Socialist Ownership and Political Systems*, p. 41.

38.   Dong Fureng, "On the Form of Socialist Ownership in Our Country," *Jingji yanjiu*, no. 1 (1979). Yu Guangyuan, "The Basic Attitude Toward Socialist Ownership," *Xinhua yuebao*, no. 9 (1980), pp. 7–14.

reason why the economy lacked vitality, enterprises lacked flexibility, and laborers lacked a sense of responsibility could be traced to the "backwardness of the management system, in laborers not being masters of the state and enterprises," in other words, " a lack of correspondence with the advanced-ownership system of the means of production."[39]

Such critiques, while understandable from the radical-reformist viewpoint, undermined the official assessment of the stage of China's development. For the moderates, laborers being masters of the enterprises or the state *was* the ownership system.[40] The question of a lack of correspondence with an "advanced ownership system" could only arise if one took the position that the form lacked the essence. But, in that case, how could China be pronounced a socialist society? Acceptance of the reformist viewpoint on this issue would lead to the conclusion that the claim of the CCP to establish a socialist society was based on mere legality. The notion of "laborers not being masters" was essentially an admission that control over production and productive property was more significant than the legal aspects of ownership. Interestingly enough, with this concession the radical reformers found themselves in concurrence with the ultra-leftist position on "authority over production," which had been denounced bitterly in 1977–78, in the context of the debate on bourgeois right.[41] Not surprisingly, the Anti-Spiritual Pollution campaign, launched in the wake of the centennial celebrations, came down heavily on the ideas of political and economic alienation, and renewed the attack on the thesis of "undeveloped socialism."

Deng's intervention on behalf of the reformers reined in the moderate ideological backlash and facilitated the incorporation of the principles of "a planned commodity economy" and "separation between state ownership

39. Liao Gailong, "Commemorating the 100th Anniversary of Marx's Death," *Jiaoxue yu yanjiu*, no. 2 (1983), pp. 6–15.

40. Feng Wenbin asserted that "a fundamental characteristic of socialist society is that the people have become masters of their own affairs. . . . Following the establishment of the socialist public ownership, the working people have become owners of the means of production and masters of their country and society. See "Consciously Implement the Line of the Third Plenary Session of the Eleventh CCP Central Committee and Firmly Advance Along the Track of Scientific Socialism," *Hongqi*, no. 10 (1981), pp. 2–12.

41. Jin Jian, "Repudiation of the Theory of Focal Points," *Lilun xuexi*, no. 4 (1978), pp. 19–26.

and management" into the Resolution on Economic Structural Reform passed in October 1984.[42] These paved the way for the contract responsibility and lease systems in industry and the implementation of managerial control over production decisions, above quota goods, and profits.

Contrary to the expectations of its initiators urban reform in 1984–85 produced a host of adverse consequences that belied theoretical assumptions about the integration of plan and market and the behavior of enterprises as economic units.[43] The problems of speculation, corruption, inflation, artificial shortages, and imperfect commodity circulation reflected the inherent contradictions of halfway reform, and leaders like Chen Yun and Peng Zhen were quick to reassert the need for mandatory planning and curtailment of investment and expenditure along with the affirmation of collective interests over that of individual producers and enterprises.[44]

Zhao Ziyang's followers, on the other hand, used the negative developments to press for further expansion and deepening of the reform process. While one set of economists identified the dual pricing system and administrative constraints on the free operation of market forces as the root of the problems,[45] others like Li Yining focused on the link between ownership and economic rationality.[46] The irrational behavior of enterprises and the pursuit of short-term gain by managers and workers could be alleviated, they argued, by providing stakes in the form of joint stock ownership or "relative" property rights.

The emergence of these opinions reflected the evolution underway in the perspective on public ownership and, in particular, the erosion of the consensus on the superiority of state ownership. Since the early 1980s, CASS economists had begun to assert that the question as to which level

42. "Decision of the Central Committee of the Communist Party of China on Reform of the Economic Structure," 20 October 1984; in *FBIS*, 22 October 1984, pp. K1–K19.

43. Harry Harding, *China's Second Revolution*, p. 73, 120–121.

44. Chen Yun, "Speech Delivered at the National Conference," *FBIS*, 23 September 1985, pp. K13–K16.

45. Wu Jinglian, "Again Discussing the Maintenance of a Beneficial Environment for Economic Reform," *Jingji yanjiu*, no. 5 (1985). "Some Thoughts on the Choice of Reform Strategies," *Jingji yanjiu*, no. 2 (1987), pp. 3–14.

46. "Proposal for the Reform of the Ownership System of Our Country," *RMRB*, 26 September 1986.

of ownership—state, collective, or individual—was superior to the others depended entirely on the level of productive forces in any sector of the economy.[47] The "dogmatism" of the Stalinist model, according to the radical reformers, was that the criteria of *da* (big) and *gong* (public) were always employed for assessing the superiority of any type of ownership system. However, it was incorrect to view the evolution of ownership as progressive from a "lower" to "higher" level because the question of whether collective ownership would grow into state ownership or whether there would evolve a third type of ownership was completely open. To characterize "small economy" or "small-scale economy," which were still significant even in the most developed countries, as inferior and "large-scale" economy as advanced when the trend of development of socialist economic organization was not clear was inaccurate.

The novelty of this position was quite striking in terms of the doctrinal tradition from Marx, who often spoke of a nation as "a vast association of producers," and Trotsky, who stressed that "in order to become social, private property must inevitably pass through the state stage as the caterpillar in order to become a butterfly," to Yugoslav socialist theory, which regarded state ownership as indirect and embryonic social ownership, but nonetheless an essential stage.

Thus, reformist writings during the period 1980–87 had created a considerable amount of ideological confusion and ambiguity around the concept of public ownership.[48] On the eve of the Thirteenth Party Congress, however, among radical-reformist leaders and their intellectual followers a new consensus was being fashioned around the notion that whatever pattern of ownership contributed to economic growth and efficiency was

47. Yu Guangyuan, "The Basic Attitude Toward Socialist Ownership," *Xinhua yuebao*, no. 9 (1980), pp. 7–14.

48. During this time Chinese economists extensively discussed the concept of ownership with reference to the Hungarian and Yugoslav economies. Despite a general expression of admiration for the functioning of the latter, they stopped short of accepting self-management as the model for economic democracy, as well as the thesis that state ownership should be replaced by more direct social ownership. In this regard, they claimed that the Hungarian model was more suited to China, without, however, giving up the position that the issue of "higher" and "lower" among different kinds of ownership systems had neither been sufficiently researched nor resolved in current practice.

superior to those that performed less effectively on these two counts.[49] This perspective was not shared by the moderates who raised concerns about the "economic disequilibrium" and emerging social polarization. Their inability to prevail at this time, however, was due in no small measure to the political acumen displayed by radical-reformist intellectuals with their inversion of the moderate argument to promote their own policy preferences. Having compromised with the moderates on the thesis that China had become a socialist society by 1956, Yu Guangyuan, Xue Muqiao, and other researchers went on to argue (in the spirit of seeking truth from facts, one might add) that the existence of a commodity economy and diverse modes of production at the present time implied that these were an inherent feature of socialism. Lenin's definition of socialism as public ownership of the means of production and distribution according to work thus had to be revised to accommodate this. Indeed, commodity economy and diverse property arrangements were not only "special characteristics of the first stage of communism, i.e., socialism, they were also the *basic defining characteristics* of this stage." [my emphasis][50]

By the mid-1980s, Yu Guangyuan was using the same inverted logic to boldly assert that socialism was also "state capitalism."[51] On the one hand, Yu argued that Lenin's vision had been impaired by the limitation of the period of transition, and thus he could not have perceived—as the Chinese reformers ostensibly did—that "in the period of socialist construction the

49.   Gao Hongfan, "Theoretical Abstraction of the Profound Changes in the Countryside—Reading *Economic Reform in Rural China*," *RMRB*, 30 January 1986.

50.   Yu Guangyuan, "Ownership, Socialism, Socialist Ownership," *Shehui kexue yuekan*, no. 3 (1981), pp. 38–51. Yu's claim that this was his own or a Chinese innovation can hardly be taken seriously, since both the Soviet bloc countries and Yugoslavia had affirmed the existence of commodity production under socialism. See, for example, Stalin, *Economic Problems of Socialism in the USSR*. While the Soviets were apologetic about the same, Yugoslav theory affirmed the importance of commodity relations between collectively run independent enterprises by defining the socialist economy simply as a commodity economy. See IX Congress of the SKJ, also Brus, *Socialist Ownership and Political Systems*, p. 76. The positive Hungarian attitude toward commodity economy was reported by Su Shaozhi in his article, "Some Theoretical Questions on Hungary's Economic Structural Reform," *Xinhua yuebao wenzhaiban*, no. 7 (1980), pp. 66–70.

51.   Yu Guangyuan, "Reform Is Also a Philosophical Revolution," *Xuexi yu yanjiu*, no. 10 (1984), p. 9–11.

existence of state capitalism is possible." On the other hand, to justify state capitalism and understate the socioeconomic consequences of the introduction of capitalist features into the Chinese economy Yu utilized Lenin's positive comments in the context of the transitional Soviet society of 1918.[52]

> . . . Let us first of all take the most concrete example of state capitalism. Everybody knows what that example is. It is Germany. Here we have "the last word" in modern large-scale capitalist engineering and planned organization, subordinate to Junker-bourgeois imperialism. Cross out the words in italics, and in place of the militarist, Junker-bourgeois imperialist state put also a state, but of a different social type, of a different class content— a Soviet state, that is, a proletarian state, and you have the sum total of the conditions necessary for socialism.[53]

Hence, contrary to his emphasis elsewhere on democratization, in this context Yu found it expedient to uphold the myth of the state form of the dictatorship of the proletariat in order to distinguish the socialist state from the capitalist one.

It was in this climate of ideological flux and pressing need to provide a theoretical basis for further ownership and enterprise reform that Zhao Ziyang's intellectual supporters found it useful to resurrect Su's thesis of "undeveloped socialism." The essential arguments outlined by Su and others like Xue Muqiao, who had also suggested subdividing the socialist stage into lower and higher phases, had all been incorporated in reformist proposals by this time, and as Zhao Ziyang prepared to unveil the third phase of reform at the Thirteenth Party Congress in 1987, his intellectual establishment refashioned the original theses into the more positive-sounding "primary stage of socialism."

Zhao's speech at the Congress introducing the new formulation reaffirmed the socialist nature of Chinese society and presented the theoretical explanation for the receding horizon of communism.

> How do things stand in China, now that socialism has been developing here for more than three decades? On the one hand, a socialist economic

52. Ibid.
53. Quoted in "Reform Is Also a Philosophical Revolution."

system based on public ownership . . . a socialist political system of people's democratic dictatorship (have) been established, and the guiding role of Marxism . . . affirmed. The system of exploitation and the exploiting classes have been abolished. . . . On the other hand, (China's) per capita GNP still ranks among the lowest in the world. Some modern industries coexist with many industries that are several decades or even a century behind present-day standards. Some fairly developed areas coexist with vast areas that are underdeveloped and impoverished. . . . The backwardness of the productive forces determines the following aspects of the relations of production: socialization of production, which is essential for expanded socialist public ownership, is still at a very low level; the commodity economy and domestic market are only beginning to develop; the natural economy and semi-natural economy constitute a considerable proportion of the whole; and the socialist economic system is not yet mature and well-developed.[54]

Given how far its productive forces lagged behind those of the developed capitalist countries, China's primary stage was destined to span almost a century and a half. During this stage China would accomplish industrialization and the commercialization, socialization, and modernization of production, which many other countries had achieved under capitalist conditions.

The staggering picture of underdevelopment drawn by Zhao raises the question as to what role, if any, was played by the transitional stage in China's socialist development since the legal change in ownership could have been effected basically at any time after the seizure of power by the Communists (and, in fact, the schedule for socialist transformation was changed a number of times). The whole purpose of the transition period in the Leninist conception was, after all, for the economy to overcome its immaturity. The moderate distinction between a transitional stage characterized by the existence of both public and private-property relations, and a socialist one with only state and collective ownership had also been rendered moot by this time with the proliferating "individual economy."

The assertion that China had accomplished its transition served the purpose of accommodating Marx's notion of stubborn resistance on the

54. Zhao Ziyang, "Advance Along the Road of Socialism with Chinese Characteristics," report delivered at the 13th National Congress of the Communist Party of China on 5 October 1987, *Beijing Review*, 9–15 November 1987, pp. 23–49.

part of old exploiting classes and Lenin's idea of sharpening class struggle under the dictatorship of the proletariat, but relegating the two to a period gone by. The affirmation of the socialist nature of Chinese society turned the question of class struggle into a secondary contradiction. With the decisiveness of the socialist mode of production thus established, "capitalist factors" could be reintroduced without posing any problem because there no longer existed any basis for the formation of a class that could thrive on them. Like Bukharin, the CCP could now consider the possibility of a peaceful competition between capitalism and socialism under the dictatorship of the proletariat—the difference being that Bukharin's comments were addressed to a society that he still believed to be transitional.

The threat of capitalist restoration passed with the period of transition and now, with the victory of socialism and forward progress assured, private enterprise and "unavoidable exploitation" had an "irreplaceable function" and could only "serve as useful supplements to the socialist economy."[55] On this score, too, the position adopted broke new ground in the "official" Marxist tradition because according to the Soviet theory of stages it was not until the end of Stage II (building of developed socialist society 1936–late 60s) that socialism was deemed to have attained "not only a complete, but a final victory," removing any threat of capitalist restoration.

The original concept of "undeveloped socialism," found favor eventually in a modified form in the hope of countering an expanding group of critics like Fang Lizhi, Gan Yang, Liu Xiaobo, and others who now openly rejected socialism. By emphasizing that shortcomings and imperfections—to say nothing of "serious mistakes"—resulted from the immaturity of the socialist society the new formulation sought to avoid the "debasement" of socialism by awkward comparisons with contemporary capitalism.[56] The thesis that "China is now in the primary stage of socialism," thus, aimed at clarifying the nature of both "right" and "left" mistakes. On the one hand, it exposed the "mechanistic position of those

55. Yu Guangyuan, "Ownership, Socialism, Socialist Ownership," also "View Reform of the Socialist Construction Period From the Perspective of World and Chinese History," *Zhongguo shehui kexue*, no. 1, (1985), pp. 53–68.

56. Liao Gailong, "Concerning the Question of the Superiority of the Socialist System," *Zhexue yanjiu*, no. 6 (1979), pp. 7–14.

who believed that China could not take the socialist road without going through the stage of fully developed capitalism." On the other hand, it made obvious the necessity for avoiding skipping over stages and attempting to implement policies suited to a much higher level of development, "which [was] to take a utopian view" and [was] therefore the "major cognitive root of left mistakes." Armed with a "correct understanding" of the current stage, the radical-reformist leadership could formulate and implement appropriate policies, for the building of "Socialism With Chinese Characteristics."

The claims of its authors notwithstanding, the final form of the thesis on the primary stage of socialism fell far short of its goal of providing the ideological justification required by the leadership. The new formulation lacked the theoretical cohesiveness and ideological persuasiveness of the original thesis because developments related to structural reform, and theoretical inconsistencies in the positions put forward by authoritative individuals had by the late 1980s rendered the definition of socialism either ambiguous or a truism.

The admission of reform theorists that within the international Communist movement and in China the meaning of basic concepts such as socialism, public ownership, and "laborers being masters," had never been quite clear, undermined the credibility of their claim that China was engaged in "socialist" construction or was in any stage, primary or otherwise, of socialism. The belief of many within reformist circles that the Communist leadership had erred in cutting short the period of New Democracy, i.e., the period of transition (which had been propagated extensively in independent writings around this time) by a premature declaration of socialism simply highlighted the fact that China's "socialist transformation" was in essence an administrative decree and not in any way a reflection of objective reality.

Radical-reformist intellectuals' attacks on state ownership, their publicization of East European views on "etatization," and their acknowledgement that nationalization was not tantamount to socialization, had fundamentally undermined the validity of the official position.[57] In the

---

57. Su Shaozhi, "Earnestly Study the New Situation in the New Period and Advance Marxism," *Xuexi yu tansuo*, no. 1 (1983), pp. 17–22.

aftermath of the Congress the advocacy that ownership forms be evaluated according to the criterion of growth and efficiency produced its logical consequence. In 1988 and 1989, in the face of an exploding economic crisis, rampant cadre corruption, and the unwillingness of Premier Li Peng and Vice Premier Yao Yilin to support Zhao Ziyang's proposal for eliminating price controls altogether and establish a full-fledged market economy, a section of the radical-reformist intellectuals openly advocated the abolition of public ownership and the institution of private-property rights.[58] This group, which included prominent members of Zhao's think tanks such as Wu Jiaxiang, Yan Jiaqi, Wang Xiaoqiang, and Chen Yizi, as well as other influential voices like Wang Juntao and Chen Ziming brought the argument full circle by now asserting, ironically enough, the incompatibility of public ownership with a market economy.[59] And, as in the case of the "laborers not being masters" contention put forward to justify enterprise reform in the early 1980s, the criticisms of Yan Jiaqi, et al., now echoed Mao's view that Chinese socialism had created a "power-based economy" in which cadre control over production was more significant than the legal ownership of the whole people. As a fulfillment of Mao's prophecy that such a state of affairs would eventually lead to "capitalist restoration" some of the most vocal of Chinese reformers now insistently pressed for the substitution of public ownership with private-property relations.

Conclusion

The controversy over stages of socialism was settled in favor of the Stalinist conception of socialism, which identified nationalization of productive property with its socialization.[60] Su Shaozhi's identification of China as a

---

58. Wang Jiuying, "A Brief Analysis of the Causes of Inequities in Social Distribution in Our Country," *GMRB*, 15 October 1988.

59. Chen Yize, Wang Xiaoqiang, and Li Jun, "The Deep-Seated Questions and the Strategic Choice China's Reform Faces," *Zhongguo: Fazhan yu gaige*, no. 4 (1989), pp. 3–9; Yan Jiaqi, "Democracy and Social Equity: A Comparative Analysis of the Role of the Government," *GMRB*, 7 July 1988.

60. CCP Central Party School Research and Writing Group on Scientific Socialism, "The Basic Characteristics of Socialist Society," *GMRB*, 3 October 1983, p. 3.

transitional society reflected not simply a modification of the Stalinist position, but also a willingness to accept the validity of other analyses within the Marxist tradition, such as the Yugoslav conception of socialism or the positions adopted by Western Marxists like Bettelheim, Sweezy, Mandel, etc. The contrast between the socialism described, however sketchily, by Marx, Engels, Lenin, and the state of present-day Chinese society could not be glossed over even by Su's critics. For reformist leaders like Zhao Ziyang and Hu Yaobang the attraction of Su's thesis as a theoretical justification for bold and unorthodox economic policies was enhanced by its potential value for countering cynics who found Chinese socialism wanting in comparison with developed capitalist societies. Hence, in its resurrection as "the primary stage of socialism" the original thesis was expected to serve the purpose of evading the "debasement or lowering of the socialist ideal" by acknowledging that there still remained problems and shortcomings but these would be overcome en route to developed socialism.

However, the context in which the new formulation was adopted differed vastly from the one in which Su initially presented his thesis. In the late 1970s a major concern of intellectuals like Su was that the practice of Chinese socialism did not measure up to Marx's theory. After a decade of theoretical innovation and practical experimentation with readjustment and reform for many in the radical-reformist camp the emphasis had shifted from deficiencies in Chinese reality to questioning the adequacy of theory. The thesis of "the primary stage of socialism" was meant to counter Zhao Ziyang's critics on the left and the right but fell short on both counts. From the moderate perspective ideological revision and practical innovation had undermined the coherence and validity of the basic tenets of doctrine which had served traditionally to legitimize the system and generate support for the goals of the leadership. In the eyes of the right, however, Zhao's approach did not go far enough. This newly emerging liberal opposition from the ranks of the old reformist coalition had completed the transition from revision to renunciation of the socialist project. Zhao's formulation offered too much and too little.

FOUR

The Problem of Class in Socialist Society

The last years of Mao's life had witnessed an intense polarization between the supporters of Zhou Enlai and Deng Xiaoping, and the ultraleftist Shanghai radicals led by Jiang Qing.[1] A basic cleavage between the two groups centered on their experience in the Cultural Revolution and attitudes towards its legacy. The latter group upheld the Cultural Revolution's emphasis on the struggle between the proletariat and the bourgeoisie in socialist society, and the attendant vigilance against capitalist restoration. The radicals policy preferences centered on indigenously generated economic and technological development, high levels of collectivization, normative incentives and an open education system stressing work-study curricula and political criteria. The preferences of the former harked back to pre-Cultural Revolution educational and industrial-agricultural policies and were reflected in the orientation of the Fourth NPC and the Hu Yaobang–Hu Qiaomu sponsored "Report Outline" and "Twenty Articles." Evaluating socioeconomic policies in terms of developmental imperatives and efficiency they perceived the ultraleftist preoccupation with class and class conflict as antithetical to their goals.

Mao's approach at this time consisted of tacit support to the dominance of the moderates in the economic realm and a simultaneous encouragement of ultraleftist rhetorical denunciation of moderate economic policies. The use of his political presence to underscore rather than bridge differences served the purpose of tolerating, on the one hand, wage grade systems and material incentives to rejuvenate the economy and, on

---

1.   Michel Oksenberg and Steven Goldstein, "The Chinese Political Spectrum," *Problems of Communism*, March–April, 1974. Kenneth Lieberthal, "China in 1975: The Internal Political Scene," *Problems of Communism*, May–June, 1975, pp. 1–11.

the other, unleashing media campaigns to contain the political and ideological fallout of those policies. The twin campaigns to Restrict Bourgeois Right and Strengthen the Dictatorship of the Proletariat that dominated the Chinese media in 1975–76 aimed specifically at undermining the legitimacy of moderate economic intiatives and labeling them ideologically suspect tactical expedients.

Consequently, a major objective of the Deng Xiaoping–Chen Yun leadership in the late 1970s was to remove the ideological stigma attached to rightist policies by repudiating the themes of continuous revolution and capitalist restoration. The discussions on class and class struggle, which began in 1978, went beyond the debates on practice and stages of socialist development to justify changes in policy as well as legitimize the *agents* of change—political leaders and the professional intelligentsia—who had been designated an incipient new class by the Maoists and condemned as "capitalist roaders," and the "stinking ninth category."

Symbolized by slogans such as "get rich quickly," "give full play to experts," and "what does it matter if one is a little white and expert," the new policies aimed (a) at linking income directly to output, skill, and expertise, and (b) reversing Cultural Revolutionary educational policies to encourage high-level scientific and technological research and selectively promote talent through the reinstitution of key-point schools, examinations, and academic-achievement oriented curricula.[2] In other words, they promoted both the social inequality and empowerment of specific social groups that the Maoists had argued would lead to revisionism and capitalist restoration. Hence, the anomaly between prevailing doctrine and changing Party practice needed to be removed by refuting Mao's thesis that a socialist society can revert to capitalism due to

(a) socioeconomic policies, which, over a period of time, reproduce relations characteristic of class societies,

---

2.   The Three Documents on which the new policies were based were: "Some Problems in Speeding Up Industrial Development," translated in *Issues and Studies*, July 1977; "Several Questions on the Work in Science and Technology," translated in *SPRCM*, no. 926; "On the General Program for All Work of the Whole Party and the Whole Country," translated in *SPRCM*, no. 921. Originally cited in Goldman, *China's Intellectuals*, p. 215–220.

(b) superstructural legacies of the old overthrown order, i.e., institutions, ideological cultural influences, etc., not suited to the present system, which may be borne either by surviving members of old exploiting classes or reflected in the consciousness of the working class and the peasantry.

(c) the emergence of a technocratic/bureaucratic elite or class.

The ultraleft, it was now argued, had distorted and obscured the meaning of basic Marxist conceptual categories such as class and class conflict, and, consequently, a major theoretical effort needed to be directed toward redefining and elucidating them to clear away popular misconceptions regarding their role in a postrevolutionary society.

The Campaign in Favor of Bourgeois Right

On 5 May 1978, *Renmin ribao* published a Contributing Commentator article (written by Hu Qiaomu and the Office of Research on Political Affairs under the State Council) entitled, "Implement the Socialist Principle of 'to Each According to His Work.'"[3] This article, which had received the prior approval of Deng Xiaoping, was the first in a concerted media effort to present the prevailing norm of distribution in a positive light and to clarify how its application was related to the resolution of current practical problems.

The need for such clarification stemmed from the negative portrayal of bourgeois right[4] during 1975–76 when in a series of articles (stamped with

3. Contributing Commentator, "Implement the Socialist Principle of 'To Each According to His Work,'" *RMRB*, 5 May 1978.

4. The term *bourgeois right* was used by Marx and Engels in their *Critique of the Gotha Programme* in the context of discussing remuneration policy during the transitional stage from capitalism to communism. In an "exchange of equal values"—similar to a capitalist economy, hence the use of the term *bourgeois*—payment would be according to work. The equality in this system lay in that the same or "equal" standard, i.e., quantity of labor would be applied in determining wages and salaries. However, differences in individual abilities, productive capacities, and needs (for example, differing family obligations), would not be recognized in distribution, hence inequality would not be eliminated at this stage.

the legitimacy of terse directives and quotations from Mao) the ultraleftists had revived a GLF theme that commodity production and exchange along with reliance on material incentives and wage differentials to increase productivity perpetuated inequalities that could become the basis for the reemergence of exploitative and antagonistic class relations.[5] The successor leadership's use of the term, "distribution according to work," instead of bourgeois right presented the norm of distribution as a positive socialist one because in recognizing the material interests of the individual and differences in ability and contributions it fostered enthusiasm in the workforce and stimulated the development of productive forces. In previous years, leveled income, stress on egalitarianism, and equal rewards for unequal work had caused tremendous losses to industrial and agricultural production and prevented improvement in the people's livelihood. In contrast to Mao, Deng Xiaoping emphasized that unequal remuneration for laborers with unequal productive capacities and labor contributions would lead not to social polarization but "common prosperity."[6] In defense of "legitimate disparities" the reformers argued, conversely, that the undermining of distribution according to work resulted in the exploitation of hardworking laborers by lazy ones.[7]

Although the campaign against bourgeois right had been waged long and hard in the months preceding Mao's death there were inherent weaknesses in the ultraleftist position that made it relatively easy for Hu Qiaomu, Xu Dixin, Li Honglin, and others to discredit it.[8] In his Directive of February

5. During the GLF Mao had argued, "the concept of bourgeois right must definitely be eliminated . . . the emphasis on qualification, the emphasis on grade levels, the failure to see the benefit of the supply system . . . the grade system is the father, son relationship, the cat-mouse relationship. It must be destroyed all the time." Mao Zedong, "Speech at the First Zhengzhou Conference," *WS 1969*, pp. 247–251; "Comments on a Reply to Comrades A.V. Sanina and V.G. Venzher," *JPRS*, 61269, 20 February 1974, pp. 129–132.

6. This position was outlined in the "Resolution on Economic Structural Reform," 1984.

7. Li Mingsan, "Why Common Prosperity Does Not Mean Concurrent Prosperity?" *Hongqi*, no. 15 (1984), pp. 46–47. Zhang Luxiong, "Will Letting Some People Get Rich First Cause Social Polarization?" *Hongqi*, no. 17 (1984), pp. 38–39.

8. Ibid; Xue Muqiao, *China's Socialist Economy*, Beijing: Foreign Languages Press, 1981. Li Honglin, "The 'Theory of Bourgeois Rights' of the 'Gang of Four' Must Be Criticized," *Zhexue yanjiu*, no. 7 (1978), pp. 30–38. Jin Jian, "Repudiation of the 'Theory of Focal Points,'" *Lilun xuexi*, No. 4 (1978), pp. 19–26; Xu Dixin, "Chairman Mao's Development

1975, which served as the opening shot of the campaign to restrict bourgeois right, Mao had claimed, "our country at present practices a commodity system and the wage system is unequal, too . . . *the only difference is that the ownership system has changed* [my emphasis]."[9] By phrasing it thus, Mao left himself open to indictment, for Marx himself had emphasized that bourgeois right, although a right of inequality, was appropriate to a society which had "just emerged from the womb of capitalism." And Marx went on to say

> . . . it [is] in general incorrect to make a fuss about so-called distribution and put the principal stress on it. . . . Vulgar socialism has taken over from the bourgeois economists the consideration and treatment of distribution as independent of the mode of production and hence the presentation of socialism as turning principally on distribution.[10]

Zhang Chunqiao and Yao Wenyuan's contention that it is "incorrect to attach no importance to whether the issue of the system of ownership has been resolved in form or in reality"[11] had been shared by radical writing groups such as Ma Yanwen, but given Mao's reluctance to conclude that ownership relations in China were not socialist, his overemphasis on distribution was delegitimized as vulgar socialism.

However, if the Maoist critique of bourgeois right could be discredited by summoning the authority of the classics the actual implementation of distribution according to work by his successors was not entirely justifiable either. In defense of their preferred pattern of distribution Chinese theorists and political leaders employed the Stalinist formula, "payment

of Marxism on the Question of Changing the Relations of Production and Developing the Productive Forces," *Jingji yanjiu*, no. 1 (1978), pp. 7–20. "Integrating Moral Encouragement With Material Reward," editorial, *RMRB*, 9 April 1978, in *Peking Review*, 21 April 1978, pp. 6–7.

9. "Directives on Strengthening the Dictatorship Over the Bourgeoisie," in *Peking Review* 9 February, no. 7 (1975), p. 4; no. 9 (1975), p. 5.

10. Karl Marx, *The Critique of the Gotha Programme*, London: Lawrence and Wishart, Ltd., 1943.

11. However, even Zhang, in deference to Mao, settled for the position that such a gap between form and essence had existed before the Cultural Revolution and at the present time, China's ownership system was primarily socialist. Zhang Chunqiao, "On Exercising All-Round Dictatorship Over the Bourgeoisie," *Hongqi*, no. 4 (1975), pp. 3–12.

according to quantity and *quality* [my emphasis] of labor."[12] This formulation had first come into use in 1932, when an apologia was needed for the sharp increase in inequality in the USSR and found no mention either in the writings of Lenin, Bukharin, or early Soviet textbooks on political economy.[13] In fact, in *The Critique of the Gotha Programme*, Marx made it clear that workers must be paid only in accordance with the quantity of labor performed. Engels, in *Anti-Duhring*, clarified that the criterion of quality made sense so long as "the costs of acquiring skills are met by private persons" as for instance in capitalist society, but where these costs had been socialized there was no reason why professors, architects, etc., should get "a little extra" compared with "porters." And, in *The German Ideology*, Marx and Engels both argued that "differences in the *head*, in intellectual abilities do not determine at all any differences in the *stomach* and physical *needs*, hence *differences* in activity do not confer any right to *inequality*, to any privilege in ownership or consumption."[14]

In contrast to this, economists like Xue Muqiao argued:

> Since society is still unable to provide its members with a free supply of all necessary means of subsistence, it can only pay each labourer on the basis of the quantity and quality of labour he performs . . . the division between mental and physical labour continues to exist in a socialist society, while the needs of highly educated mental workers in their work and daily life call for special attention. . . . Under the system of "to each according to his work," higher intellectuals should receive higher pay and enjoy a better standard than the workers and peasants, the manual labourers. . . . Mental labor is a more complex type of labour. Our modernization program calls for building a powerful contingent of specialists with a high standard of scientific and technological expertise and managerial skill, who will make

12.   Deng Xiaoping "Adhere to the Principle of 'To Each According to His Work,'" *Selected Works*. Feng Wenbin, "Consciously Implement the Line of the Third Plenary Session of the Eleventh CCP Central Committee and Firmly Advance Along the Track of Scientific Socialism," *Hongqi*, no. 10 (1981), pp.2–12.

13.   Mandel, *Marxist Economic Theory*, London: Merlin Press, 1962, p. 725; O.I. Shkaratakan, "Sources of Social Differentiation of the Working Class in Soviet Society," in Murray Yanowitch and Wesley Fischer, eds., *Social Stratification and Mobility in the USSR*, White Plains: International Arts and Sciences Press, 1973, p. 13.

14.   Quoted in E. Mandel, *Marxist Economic Theory*, London: Merlin Press, 1962, p. 725.

greater contributions to the nation by performing highly intensive and creative labour. Thus it is reasonable and necessary to give them a higher pay and provide them with better living conditions than the average ones.[15]

In justifying unequal rewards for those who hold different occupational positions reformist leaders and intellectuals, in the manner of their Soviet colleagues, were introducing what Ralph Dahrendorf has termed "an additional act of evaluation," which transforms social differentiation into social stratification.[16] According to the Trotskyte economist Mandel, judging the "quality" of labor in "accordance with its social utility" is for "theoreticians calling themselves Marxists," a "180-degree turn" and "a final break with the labor theory of value."[17] Interestingly enough, in this instance, even the radical reformers preferred the Stalinist formulation, with all its "specificity," over the original prescriptions of Marx and Engels.

On the long-term impact of such policies, Chinese-reformist writings, in general, were much less forthcoming than those of their East European colleagues. The Hungarian theorist Sandor Lakos had noted, for instance, that the differences in wages that come about as a result of distribution according to work over a period of time turn into property differences as they become "embodied in movable goods and personal property of varying size. If we accept the differentiating principle of distribution according to work, we must logically accept the differences resultant in the amount of property."[18] Needless to say, in the case of unearned incomes from profit making or speculative activities, the resultant property differentials would be even greater.

The problem, as Lakos identified it, was that just as one cannot deny the workers the right to enjoy the fruits of labor, one must also accept as "humanly justified" the "right of inheritance," for most people "save and invest part of their income . . . for their descendants." And yet, he pointed

15.   Xue Muqiao, *China's Socialist Economy*, p. 69 and 279.

16.   Yanowitch, *Social Stratification and Mobility in the USSR*, p. XXV.

17.   Mandel, p. 725.

18.   Sandor Lakos, "Questions of Social Equality," in *Modern Hungary: Readings From the New Hungarian Quarterly*, ed. by Denis Sinor, Bloomington: Indiana University Press, 1977, pp. 122–123.

out, "it is also just that the children of all working people should start life with equal chances, and, viewed from this angle, inheritance must not have a determining role." In the Chinese case, the problem of inheritance has been even more complicated by the widespread practice of offspring "inheriting" their parents' jobs or positions. In this instance, decisive differences in starting points are re-created not simply through income differentials but much more seriously, through a perpetuating division of labor. In the post-Mao discussions the wrangling over terminology—the socialist principle of distribution according to work as opposed to bourgeois right—was not without significance. The Maoists had employed the latter term to emphasize Marx's view that distribution in a society that had "just emerged from the womb of capitalism" was "stigmatized" by a bourgeois limitation."[19] This was consistent with Lenin's acceptance of wage differentials in the "transitional phase between capitalism and socialism,"[20] and his insistence that this practice marked a "departure" from the labor theory of value and hence was a "constant source of corruption, demoralization, and bureaucratization." For Lenin and Mao, "payment according to work" was "the exchange of equal values" which prevailed in a capitalist economy, its presence in the postrevolutionary society would be eliminated in due course, but until then measures were necessary to undermine the perpetuation of norms that could result in the erosion of proletarian consciousness.[21]

The dangers of extolling the principle of distribution according to work as a positive socialist principle and consolidating and expanding it as Deng Xiaoping and the reformist coalition were to do was fairly accurately predicted by Yao Wenyuan:

19.   According to Marx, *"It is therefore a right of inequality in its content, like every right. . . . But these defects are inevitable in the first phase of Communist society as it is when it has just emerged . . . from capitalist society. Right can never be higher than the economic structure of society and the cultural development thereby determined."*

20.   The issues raised in the discussions on bourgeois right became intertwined with the debate on whether or not China had completed her transition to socialism which is also why Hu Qiaomu and Deng Xiaoping insisted on calling the principle of "to each according to his work" a socialist one. By describing it thus the post-Mao leadership aimed both at refuting the Maoist conception of it as a "capitalist factor," as well as the notion that its implementation implied that China was not yet fully socialist.

21.   Ibid., p.726.

. . . a small number of people will in the course of distribution acquire increasing amounts of commodities and money through certain legal channels and numerous illegal ones; capitalist ideas of amassing fortunes and craving for personal fame and gain, stimulated by such "material incentives" will spread unchecked; phenomena such as the turning of public property into private property, speculation, graft and corruption, theft, and bribery will increase; the capitalist principle of the exchange of commodities will make its way into political and even into Party life, undermining the socialist planned economy; acts of capitalist exploitation such as the conversion of commodities and money into capital, and labor power will occur. . . . As a result, a small number of new bourgeois elements and upstarts . . . will emerge from among Party members, workers, well-to-do peasants, and personnel in state organs. When the economic strength of the bourgeoisie has grown to a certain extent, its agents will demand political rule, demand the overthrow of the dictatorship of the proletariat and the socialist system, demand a complete changeover from socialist ownership, and openly restore and develop the capitalist system.[22]

In essence, the dispute over patterns of distribution illustrated the difference between the revolutionary outlook of Mao and his followers, who linked the transformative "means" of socialism to the "end" of a classless Communist society, and the evolutionary approach of the successor leadership, who entrusted the emergence of new-production relations to the progressive development of productive forces. In the former perspective the concern over norms of distribution was informed by considerations of equity and social justice. The outlook of the radical reformers and the liberals, who became increasingly vocal in the late 1980s, evaluated distribution principles in terms of efficiency and growth. Not surprisingly, their definition came to center eventually on the "equality of opportunity" and the "rationality and fairness" of distribution by the market economy.

For Mao, who asked his revolutionary colleagues "Have you ever carefully thought about how socialism is going to graduate into communism?,"[23] it was necessary to ascertain precisely how widening socioeconomic

22. Yao Wenyuan, "On the Social Basis of the Lin Biao Clique," *Hongqi*, no. 4 (1975), pp. 20–29.
23. Quoted in Kraus, *Class Conflict in Chinese Socialism*, p. 181–182.

disparities could give way to a stateless, classless society. For his reformist colleagues, ideological clichés came in handy for deferring such awkward questions.

> From a long-term point of view, the distinction between mental and manual labor will gradually diminish. But in a given period and in given circumstances, such a distinction may even grow for a time. Recognition and preservation of the distinction between mental and manual labor are precisely a measure to create the conditions for the final elimination of such a distinction. This conforms to the dialectics of history.[24]

In post-Mao China the "long term" appeared more like a receding horizon. By the late 1980s the question of distribution turned into a tautological argument. The reformers started out defending their characterization of distribution according to work as a socialist principle because it was implemented in a society characterized by public ownership. However, as the nature of public ownership itself came under question, the definition of socialism came to be based essentially on the principle of distribution according to work. Mao's successors proved to be as concerned with norms of distribution as the leftists they had criticized and, hence, no less guilty of vulgar socialism.

Redefining Class

Discussions on "distribution according to work" were accompanied by a short-lived attempt to discredit the Maoist use of ideological and political criteria for distinguishing between classes.[25] Emphasis on economic factors in 1977–78 legitimized the reinstatement of leading cadres and the removal of labels that had been slapped on them, and countless others in the general public, during the Anti-Rightist Movement and the Cultural

24. Xue Muqiao, *China's Socialist Economy*, p. 280.
25. Commentator, "Correctly Understand the Fundamental Changes in China's Class Situation," *JFRB*, 19 July 1979. Su Shaozhi, "Tentative Views on the Class Situation and Class Struggle in China at the Present Stage," in *Selected Studies on Marxism*, Beijing: Institute of Marxism, Leninism, Mao Zedong Thought, CASS, no. 6, February 1981. Li Xiulin, Zheng Hangsheng, "Class Struggle Without Exploiting Classes," *RMRB*, 31 October 1979.

Revolution. It also facilitated a change of focus from themes of conflict and struggle to stability and peaceful economic construction.[26]

The new orthodoxy linked the concept of class firmly to modes of production and the place occupied by different groups within the social division of labor.[27] In his March 1979 speech on the Four Cardinal Principles, Deng Xiaoping ruled out the existence of a bourgeoisie within the party as well as the possibilty of new exploiting classes emerging in socialist society after the conditions of exploitation had been eliminated.[28]

Exclusive emphasis on economic determinants broke new ground in the Chinese Communist conception of class. Since the early 1920s when leaders like Chen Duxiu ascribed the qualities of the proletariat to the Chinese nation as a whole, political and attitudinal criteria had always played an important role in defining the class status of individuals.[29] In his *Elements of Sociology,* Li Da discussed the phenomena of classes not in the section on Economy, but in the section entitled "The Political Structure of Society."[30] Given Li Da's preeminent status as sociologist, economist, and the first systematic exponent of Marxism in China, one can assume that his exposition would become a commonly accepted one. Li's understanding of class as a political concept was indeed shared by others like Li Dazhao, who had, at the very outset, criticized economic determinism as too narrow an explanation of social change.[31]

For individuals who had been victims of Anti-Rightist and Cultural Revolutionary excesses and persecution, the need to criticize arbitrary applications of class designation for political and other ends during the Maoist era was entirely understandable. However, the attempt to make a theoretical case for arbitrariness or idealism in the Maoist view of

---

26. "On Current Classes and Class Struggle in Our Country," *JFRB*, 23 July 1979, in *FBIS*, no. 22, 9 October 1979, pp. 1–10.

27. Hu Fuming, "Politics and Ideology Cannot Serve as the Basis for Identifying Class," *Beijing ribao*, 10 August 1979, p. 3. in *FBIS*, 17 October 1979, p. 27.

28. Deng Xiaoping, "Uphold the Four Cardinal Principles," *SW*, pp. 166–191.

29. Chen Duxiu, "On the Discussion of Socialism," *Shehui zhuyi taolunji*, Guangzhou: New Youth Press, 1922, pp. 32–73.

30. *Li Da wenji*, Beijing: Renmin chubanshe, vol. II, p. 465.

31. Li Dazhao, "My Marxism" in *Li Dazhao wenji*, Beijing: Renmin chubanshe, 1962.

class was difficult to sustain against the weight of the Marxist tradition.[32]

The economic criterion had indeed occupied an important place in the Marxian conception of class. Class structure was perceived as a broader form of the division of labor which in turn was derived from the arrangements within which a particular society organized itself to carry out productive activities. However, similar to his understanding of the relationship between base and superstructure, matter and spirit, Marx's definition did not sustain economic reductionism. With his distinction between a "class in itself" and "class for itself" Marx restricted the scope of the economic determinant by a political and psychological criterion.[33] Moreover, in his writings Marx often used the expression without particular reference to the position of a group in the mode of production. He referred to the intelligentsia as "ideological classes" and even described finance capitalists and industrial capitalists as "two distinct classes."[34]

Lenin's definition penned in "A Great Beginning," in June 1919, stressed the economic element, but the thrust of his other writings and, indeed, his revolutionary practice implied a rejection of any simplistic "one-way determinism" on the question of class.[35] The need for "symbolic and behavioral determinants" to supplement the identification of classes at the productive level was accepted by theoreticians from Bukharin to Nicolas Poulantzas and Guglielmo Carchedi.[36]

32.   Li Shichao, "Commenting on Kang Sheng's Historical Idealist Viewpoint of Determining Class Status According to Political and Ideological Criteria," *RMRB*, 4 August 1980.

33.   Marx and Engels, *Selected Works*, New York: International Publishers, 1968, pp. 171–172.

34.   David McClellan, *The Thought of Karl Marx*, New York: Harper and Row, 1971, p. 154. According to Alan Swingewood, such divergence in Marx's usage suggests that his theory of class was a complex rather than unidimensional one, so that class was "never a single homogeneous structure" but rather a cluster of "contradictory elements." Alan Swingewood, *Marx and Modern Social Theory*, London: MacMillan, 1975, p. 118.

35.   Lenin, "A Great Beginning," June 1919, *SW*, Moscow: Foreign Languages Publishing House, 1950.

36.   N. Poulantzas, *Classes in Contemporary Capitalism*, London: New Left Books, 1975. In "On the Economic Identification of the New Middle Class." Carchedi argued that "certain strata of the working class which, from the point of view of production relations, belong to the proletariat . . . become part of the petty bourgeoisie on political and ideological grounds." *Economy and Society*, vol. 4, no. 1 (1975), pp. 1–86. For some Marxists the differ-

Within the Marxian tradition, both official and unofficial, the political identification of class was derivative of the economy most clearly for those groups with a specific relationship to capital and or productive property, either in terms of ownership or dependence. Groups with no clear relationship to the means of production belonged to one class or another depending on time and circumstances.[37] Most theoreticians made a distinction between productive and unproductive labor in that the former created value and the latter did not. The incomes of intellectuals, managers and state employees were considered therefore an exchange against revenue or "taxes" siphoned off from the wages of productive workers. The services such groups performed being essential to an organized society, their remuneration from revenue or "the collective fund" was legitimate, but when the sum involved was much in excess of what the average worker received, it constituted a type of exploitation. Hence, the possibility existed of such strata not only not sharing the consciousness of the working class but also of acquiring the values of the exploiting classes. In his *Classes in Contemporary Capitalism,* Poulantzas, therefore, consigned "unproductive wage laborers" to the ranks of a new petty bourgeoisie and pointed to their concealed conflict of interest with productive workers since the former were in a sense parasitic in relation to those who create value.

Mao's distrust of intellectuals, Party members, state functionaries, college students, children of cadres, etc., thus finds strong support in Marxian analysis. The identification of certain individuals as capitalist roaders or bourgeoisie was theoretically consistent since the class status of "social groups" with no determinate relationship to the means of production could only be inferred from their ideological and political allegiances.

ence between "class in itself" and "for itself" is not merely a question of consciousness, "but a division between essence and phenomenon, potential and actual and so not simply a dichotomy of the objective and subjective." The stress on the economic factor and a corresponding downplay of the political and ideological aspect would, according to this interpretation, imply a failure to comprehend the Marxian idea of class dynamically and dialectically. See Hillel Ticktin, "The Political Economy of Class in the Transitional Epoch," *Critique,* nos. 20–21 (1987), p. 8.

37.   In *The Eighteenth Brumaire of Louis Napoleon* and *The Class Struggles in France,* for example, Marx listed vagrants, lumpens, etc. (precisely the composition of Mao's own red army during the days of the Jiangxi Soviet), as comprising the class that they served.

Similarly, Mao's stress on behavior and ideological manifestation of class (particularly for members of the old bourgeoisie and landlords), rather than being unorthodox was justifiable within the Marxist conception of "lag,"—a dysfunctional relationship that arises when the institutional and ideological superstructure lags behind the development of the productive apparatus and exerts a drag on social progress.[38]

The post-Mao attempt to come up with a lucid and acceptable definition of class to prevent arbitrary and opportunistic manipulations as had occurred in the past, floundered in the face of changing needs and policy priorities of the different groups who influenced the new intellectual discourse. In the first phase when both moderate and radical reformers joined together against the "whateverists" and other leftists to bring about a "reversal of verdicts" on victims of the Anti-Rightist Campaign and the Cultural Revolution they emphasized the economic determinants of class.[39] However, intellectual critiques of the Cultural Revolution and demands for systemic reform during the Theory Conference along with the Democracy Wall activists' castigation of "new exploiters" and the "ruling class" prompted a partial retreat on the part of Deng Xiaoping, Hu Qiaomu, and others. This was reflected in the 1981 Resolution on Party History that traced the roots of dictatorships, corruption, and bureaucratization to residual ideological influences of the feudal and semi-colonial past. Theorists within the radical-reformist camp were not averse to singling out bureaucrats as a new exploiting class but, as will be explained in more detail in the next chapter, they were sensitive to the nexus that the Maoists had claimed between bourgeois elements in society and bureaucrats that could bring about a restoration to capitalism.

With the consolidation of the rural-responsibility system and the radical-reformist push for its expansion into the urban-industrial economy the situation changed. Application of the economic criterion alone now

---

38.   Alfred Meyer, *Marxism: The Unity of Theory and Practice*, Ann Arbor: University of Michigan Press, 1969, pp. 62–63.

39.   Jiang Nandong, Li Shaogeng, and Yang Pishan, "Have China's Exploiters Been Eliminated as a Class?" *Hongqi,* no. 2 (1980), pp. 35–39. Xu Kun, "Class Conditions and Class Struggle in Our Country at the Present Stage," *Shehui kexue,* no. 3 (1979). Xiao Yougen, "Strive to Eliminate the Evil Influence of Inflating Class Struggle," *Nanfang ribao,* 6 November 1979, p. 2, and in *FBIS,* 21 December 1979, pp. 27–31.

pointed to the reemergence of stratification and exploiting classes as a consequence of deregulation, strengthening of commodity exchange, and privatization of the economy.

At the outset the most obvious area of contention was in the rural areas with the erosion of the collective economy, and the emergence of the 10,000 *yuan* specialized households. Moderate reformers applying the economic criterion objected to the widening disparities and found themselves raising anew the concerns regarding "peaceful evolution to capitalism," which they had attempted to dispense with earlier.[40] Radical reformers, on the other hand, denied that the new agricultural policies constituted a return to capitalism because the land continued to be collectively owned, even though leases and user rights were inheritable and also transferable for consolidation within a few rich households.[41] Their arguments resembled Bukharin's stance on NEP, viz., economic liberalization would bring about social differentiation but this would be structurally limited.[42]

Other forms of property considered vital means of production in the rural economy (animals, agricultural implements, tractors, etc.) were

40. Reformist articles complained frequently of "remnant leftist thinking," which failed to understand the significance of the supplemental economy. Xue Mou, "How to Correctly Understand Small Production After Socialist Transformation Has Been Basically Completed," *Hongqi*, no. 21 (1981). He Jianzhang, "Actively Support, Appropriately Develop Individual Economy in Cities and Towns," *Hongqi*, no. 24 (1981). Yun Xiliang, "The Interests of the State, Enterprises and Individuals," *Hongqi*, no. 16 (1983), pp. 7–12. He Rongfei, "Does Prosperity Necessarily Mean 'Revisionism'?" *Hongqi*, no. 3 (1980), pp. 45–48. Li Guangyuan, "Socialism and the Personal Interest of Workers," *Hongqi*, no. 3 (1979), pp. 66–69.

41. Xue Muqiao, "Postscript to 'A Study of Questions Concerning China's Economy,' " *Hongqi*, no. 21 (1981), pp. 23–30. Du Runsheng, "The Agricultural Responsibility System and the Reform of the Rural Economic System," *Hongqi*, no. 19 (1981), pp. 17–25. Hua Shi, "An Inexorable Historical Development—A Discussion on Several Questions Concerning the Socialist Transformation of Agriculture in Our Country," *Hongqi*, no. 24 (1981), pp. 25–30. However, it was commonly accepted by Marx and other contemporaries that private ownership of land constituted a hindrance to the development of capitalist agriculture because of the land rent appropriated by a nonproductive class of landowners.

42. Xue Muqiao, "The New Trend in Economic Development in China," speech at a symposium in Hong Kong. Excerpts in *Shijie jingji daobao*, 30 October 1980. Also Xue Muqiao and Du Runsheng above cited articles. Ma Hong, "Marxism and China's Socialist Construction—Written to Commemorate the Centenary of Marx's Death," *Social Sciences in China*, no. 3 (1983).

defended as both permissible and compatible with socialism.[43] Character-izing the extension of rural markets and commodity exchange as useful supplements to the socialist economy[44] radical reformers stretched the principle of distribution according to work to include rural entrepreneurs, commodity traders, and prosperous farmers who made a "legitimate return on capital invested."[45] Profits, interests, and inheritance (an instance of past labor dominating present labor) even when accumulated as substantial capital holdings were classified as "earned" income by the radical reform-ers. Such "rewards for private investment" Du Runsheng conceded was not "distribution according to work in its purest form." "However, since it pro-vides that those who do more work and put in more can get more, and since what is put in is still the material manifestation of one's labor" it was "not contrary to the principle of distribution according to work."[46]

Thus, the crucial question of appropriation of surplus was glossed over by advocates of radical reform during this phase. The future evolution of an intermediate class and its graduation to the status of a rural bourgeoisie along with the possibility of a conflict of interest between this group and hired laborers was similarly evaded.[47] Wan Li contended that the individ-ual economy could be effectively managed by legislative and administrative means as well as economic measures such as pricing and taxation.[48] The dangers of encouraging a taste for profit and private property among an ideologically suspect peasantry were admitted in passing, but reform

43. Yu Guangyuan, "Ownership System, Socialism, Socialist Ownership System," *She-hui kexue jikan*, no. 3 (1981), pp. 38–51. Also in Renda *Fuyin*, no. 6 (1981).

44. Ibid. Xue Mu, "How Should We Correctly View Small-Scale Production After the Basic Completion of Socialist Transformation?" *Hongqi*, no. 21 (1981), pp. 41–43. Xue Muqiao, "Reform the Economic Structure and Economic System," *Hongqi*, no. 14 (1980), pp. 6–15. Xiong Fu, "The Yugoslav People Are Advancing Along the Socialist Road," *Hongqi*, no. 18 (1981), pp. 19–24. He Jianzhang, "Actively Support and Appropriately Develop Individual Economy in Cities and Towns," *Hongqi*, No. 24 (1981), pp. 13–16. Su Shaozhi, "Tentative Views on the Reform of the Economic Mechanism in Hungary," *Selected Studies on Marxism*, Beijing: CASS, 1988.

45. W. Hinton, "A Trip to Fengyang County," *Monthly Review*, no. 6 (November 1983).

46. Du Runsheng, *RMRB*, 7 March 1983, also in *SWB/FE*, 7288 BII/11.

47. K. Lieberthal, "The Political Implications of Document No. 1, 1984," *The China Quarterly*, no. 101 (1985).

48. *RMRB*, 23 December 1982.

theorists chose to emphasize the "new" agricultural producer who was equally attracted to socialist cooperation.[49] The novelty of this position was quite striking, especially compared to Bukharin's views during the NEP where he simply claimed that the nationalized nature of land would prevent too pronounced a stratification and *not* that it would preclude the creation of a new class of prosperous peasants.

The introduction of urban-industrial reform in late 1984 raised further questions about the implications of the new developments. The expansion of the non-state manufacturing sector and capital and labor markets prompted a more comprehensive effort to address the discrepancies between theory and reality. Until the mid-1980s radical reformers defended the rising sectoral, regional, and individual disparities by distinguishing between the inequalities in a capitalist society, which stemmed from ownership rights, and a socialist one, which came about as a consequence of varying human abilities and labor contributions. The focus on ownership and exploitation based on access to or control over productive property meant that medium or large-scale individual or private firms and enterprises were listed as collectives in which laborers were both owners and producers while workshops with no more than seven workers were "socialist" or noncapitalist private enterprises.[50] Thus, the number of "new exploiters," it was claimed, was still an insignificant percentage and a distinction needed to be made between the greedy, well-to-do elements, and the hardworking entrepreneurs who also happened to employ some laborers.

By the late 1980s, however, enterprise-related ownership and management reform, the issuing of stock shares, and the burgeoning growth of private entrepreneurial activity, which now accounted for about half the national output, had exposed the inadequacy of previous formulations.[51] The principle of distribution according to work could scarcely apply to income from bonds, dividends, stocks, and ownership, while the implementation of the

49.   Du Runsheng, *RMRB*, 7 March 1983.

50.   Dorothy Solinger, "Urban Entrepreneurs and the State: The Merger of State and Society," in Arthur L. Rosenbaum, ed., *State and Society in China*, Boulder: Westview Press, 1992, pp. 121–141.

51.   Nicholas Lardy, "Is China Different? The Fate of Its Economic Reform," in Daniel Chirot, ed., *The Crisis of Leninism and the Decline of the Left*, Seattle: University of Washington Press, 1991, pp. 147–162.

contract responsibility and leased-management systems, which encouraged capital investment jointly by the state and lessees, made ownership patterns of even state firms blurry. Widespread public discontent at ever-rising levels of material differentiation, cadre corruption, and the flaunting lifestyles of the new rich revived discussion on social equity and fairness. Moderates deplored the substitution of socialist ethics by market-based distribution with its attendant values of self-interest, competition, and efficiency.[52] The radicals distinguished between "unfair inequality," which followed from the unscrupulous activities of a few greedy speculators and embezzlers, and the "fair inequality" or "genuine equality" that they associated with the "equality of opportunity" and efficiency espoused by the market economy.[53] The "multiplicity" and "diversity" of ownership forms in both rural and urban areas, now undeniable, the radical reformers drew attention to the formal "political and class equality" under socialism (although they did not clarify how this differed from the legal and constitutional equality present in capitalist sytems), state ownership of the "commanding heights of the economy," and the continuing dominance, although no longer exclusive, of distribution according to work.[54]

Economic reductionism on the issue of class throughout this period made the supporters of market socialism vulnerable to moderate accusations that the new policies were contributing to the reemergence of exploitative class relations as well as a new "parasite class" that could live off speculation on capital markets.[55] This promoted a reassessment of political and behavioral criteria as determinants of class. In response to moderate concerns about the economic and political implications of the

52.   Chen Yun, "Speech at the National Conference," *FBIS*, September 23 1985, pp. K13–K16.

53.   Lan Qiuliang and Chen Xilian, "Discussing the Socialist Principle of Equality," *RMRB*, 3 March 1986. Commentator, "Common Prosperity Not 'Concurrent Prosperity,'" *GMRB*, 22 July 1984.

54.   Xue Muqiao, "Continuously Develop the Science of Marxism," *RMRB*, 20 March 1987.

55.   Zuo Mu, "Problems of the Reform of China's Ownership Structure," *Jingji yanjiu*, no. 1. (1986), pp. 6–10. Yang Qixian, "The Nature and Functions of the Stock System Under Socialist Conditions," *RMRB*, 3 July 1987.

rise of a new bourgeoisie,[56] radical-reform theorists, counting on the grateful support of the new rich, concluded that their commitment to "Chinese style socialism" precluded the new groups from becoming a "class for itself." The basis of such reasoning was best illustrated by the following example used by Yu Guangyuan.

> A group of intellectuals get together to publish a book on the merits of socialism. Because the individuals concerned are making rich profits selling the books, should one be suspicious of these new entrepreneurs? No, what is worthy of attention in this situation is the love for socialism exhibited by these intellectuals.[57]

Radical-reformist arguments were again taken to their logical conclusion by the liberal intellectuals.[58] Acceptance of economic rationality and the fairness of distribution within the market economy not only rationalized commodification of labor itself to enhance workers' productivity and "equality of opportunity," but also exploitation of hired labor where it facilitated the growth of productive forces.[59] In the interests of administrative efficiency and economy some (including Zhao Ziyang's advisers) went so far as to suggest that superfluous cadres be allowed to live off income from the stock market.[60] The "equality of starting points" thesis brought forth a new twist to the definition of common ownership as liberal theorists proposed the creation of "social individual ownership" whereby state property could be divided up "freely and equally" to enable all members of society to enjoy the rights of private ownership.[61] Advo-

56. Bukharin also had emphasized the political significance of the new stratification and recommended that government policy guard against the "new rural bourgeoisie" providing the peasant masses with anti-Bolshevik leadership if discontent with official policies should set in."
57. Yu Guangyuan, "Ownership System, Socialism, Socialist Ownership System," *Shehui kexue jikan*, no. 3 (1981), pp. 38–51.
58. Wu Jiaxiang, "Several Options for Property Rights Reforms," *Zhongguo: Fazhan yu gaige*, no. 4 (1988), pp. 45–47. Yong Jian and Fan Hengsan, "On the Opening of Ownership," *Xinhua wenzhai*, no. 4 (1989), pp. 36–39.
59. Hu Peizhao, "A Brief Discussion of Exploitation," *Jingji wenti*, no. 1 (1988).
60. Zhang Zhiqing, "The Market Economy and the Way Out for China's Reform," *Jingji kexue*, no. 2 (1989), p. 72.
61. Liu Huiyong, "We Must Rectify a Misunderstanding of the Marxist Theory of Ownership," *Jingji wenti*, no. 2 (1989). Yang Jianbai, "On Social Individual Ownership," *Shehui kexue*, no. 3 (1988).

cates of this "reconstructed individual ownership" ruled out the possibility of any exploitation in a community where everyone was a property holder. Such theorists provided no explanation for their assumption that this "equality" would remain frozen and not produce future concentrations of wealth and productive property.

These theoretical constructs were not officially adopted and did not go unchallenged.[62] In the period of moderate ascendance preceding and immediately following the 1989 Tiananmen events, the intellectual establishments of the revolutionary elders resonated with references to a new class struggle and the insidious "peaceful restoration of capitalism." However, the reaffirmation of market economics by the Fourteenth Congress of 1992 and Deng's call for "deepening of reform" through the mid-1990s illustrated the decreasing appeal of Marxian class categories within the predominant intellectual discourse.[63] Class as a concept was being stripped of its meaning and de-emphasized, or even abandoned, precisely when the increasing differentiation and stratification within Chinese society made its application more salient.

From Class Struggle to Social Struggle

The reconceptualization of class in the late 1970s was linked to the reassessment of the issue of class struggle in postrevolutionary society. Mao's emphasis on "class struggle as the key link," now regarded as a major misconception, was traced to the leftist failure to understand both the nature of social contradictions in socialist society and the motive force for forward development.[64]

---

62. Wang Zhiliang, "Economic Reform Must Adhere to a Socialist Direction," *GMRB*, 9 September 1989. Wu Jianguo, "Fully Realize the Flaws of Bourgeois Liberalization: Correctly Understand the Intrinsic Unity of the Two Basic Points," *GMRB*, 6 July 1989. Wang Zhennping, "A Brief Analysis of Socilism Is the 'Reconstruction of Individual Ownership,'" *GMRB*, 13 September 1989.

63. Jiang Zemin, "Report to the Fourteenth Party Congress," *RMRB* 12 October 1992.

64. The de-emphasis of class and class struggle raised a new philosophical question to be addressed: What accounts for the forward movement of society after the struggle between antagonistic classes is over? See Liu Feng and Zhang Zhuanfang, "The 'Struggle' of Contra-

In the initial phase of emphasizing the economic definition of class it was argued that the criterion for determining the elimination of particular classes should also be economic. Since class divisions are rooted in private property, the socialist transformation in 1956, according to Liao Gailong and Hu Fuming, marked the elimination of landlords, rich peasants, and capitalists. However, no explicit declaration to such effect was made by the Eighth Party Congress and this omission gave rise to "ideological mistakes in the guiding line," and the exaggeration and magnification of class struggle in the next two decades.[65]

diction Is the Dynamic of the Development of Things," *Zhexue yanjiu*, no. 8 (1979); Lu Guoying, "A Probe Into the Classification and Solution of Contradictions," *Zhexue yanjiu*, no. 2 (1980); Liu Xinyu, "What Is the Principal Contradiction in Our Society at the Present Stage?" *Shehui kexue*, no. 3 (1979) pp. 16–20; Lin Yuhua, "Some Problems Concerning the Principal Contradiction at the Present Stage," *Shehui kexue*, no. 3 (1979), pp. 21–26. Soviet theorists had offered varying candidates for new contradictions—the contrast between the growing needs of the population and the inadequate level of development, the contradiction between laborers being rewarded according to work while they work according to their ability, the contradiction between all workers having the same relationship to the means of production but receiving dissimilar rewards, etc (Scanlan, p. 254). In China during the late 50s, Liu Shaoqi had put forward the contradiction between the advanced superstructure and the backward economic base, while Chen Yun emphasized the contradiction between the growing needs of the population and the low level of economic development.

In the post-Mao period, Su Shaozhi's castigation of the Liuist formulation as ideologically indefensible (for it implied that a socialist system could be established before there was a demand for it by the economic base) and his resurrection of the Chen Yun thesis was accepted by leaders like Deng as well. See Su Shaozhi, "On the Principal Contradiction Facing Our Society Today," *Xueshu yuekan*, no. 7 (1979), pp. 14–15; Yu Guangyuan, on the other hand, appeared to be arguing at times that contradictions in the current stage could be at the level of knowledge and would be resolved as one's knowledge increased. See Yu "Reform Is Also a Philosophical Revolution," *Xuexu yu yanjiu*, no. 10 (1984), pp. 9–11, also in *Renda Fuyin*, no. 22 (1984). The new line on contradictions restored the Maoist position of 1956–57 that socialist modernization was a stage of peaceful development that did not require fierce and violent class struggle—all contradictions, basic, principal, and secondary were manifested as contradictions among the people.

65. Chen Zhongli, "When Were the Exploiting Classes in China Eliminated?" *Beijing Review*, no. 22 (1980), p. 25. Li Xiulin, Zheng Hangsheng, "Is Class Really a General Social Formation?" *RMRB*, 24 January 1980. Zhang Yunyi, "Dialogue on the Existence of Class Struggle After the Abolition of Exploiting Classes," *Guangming ribao*, 31 October 1983. For a view closer to that of Mao, see Wang Zhengping, "What Is the Basis for Determining Whether the Exploiting Classes Have Been Eliminated," *Beijing Review*, no. 22 (1980), p. 24.

This simplistic view of the elimination of classes was hard to justify theoretically. The idea that class continues to be relevant for a period of time after the transfer of private property into public ownership was explicit in Marx's concept of the dictatorship of the proletariat and was developed by Lenin in 1919.

> The abolition of classes, is the work of long, difficult, stubborn class struggle, which even *after* the overthrow of the power of capital, *after* the destruction of the bourgeois state, after the creation of the dictatorship of the proletariat, does not disappear . . . but merely changes its forms and becomes still more violent in many respects. The dictatorship of the proletariat is not the end of class struggle, but its continuation in new forms. . . . [It] *is* the class struggle of the proletariat after it has won a victory and taken political power in its own hands, against a defeated but not annihilated, not vanquished bourgeoisie, which has not ceased to offer its resistance, but has strengthened its resistance.[66]

The necessity of a proletarian dictatorship stemmed also from the "spontaneous tendency" toward capitalism that existed in a transitional society according to Lenin.

> Take the economic front, and ask whether capitalism can be restored economically in Russia. We have combated the Sukharevka black market. . . . The old Sukharevka market in Sukharevskaya Square has been closed down, an act that presented no difficulty. The sinister thing is the "Sukharevka" that resides in the heart of every petty proprietor. . . . That "sukharevka" is the basis of capitalism. While it exists, the capitalists may return to Russia and may grow stronger than we are. . . . While we live in a small peasant country, there is a firmer economic base for capitalism in Russia than communism.[67]

Lenin's notion that during the transitional period the "psychological heritage of capitalism" remained within members of the old exploiting class as well as the revolutionary classes was not reflected in post-Mao

---

66. Lenin, "Greetings to Hungarian Workers," *CW*, vol. 24, p. 315.
67. Joseph Esherick, "On the 'Restoration of Capitalism'—Mao and Marxist Theory," *Modern China*, vol. 5, no. 1 (1979), p. 45.

analyses, which emphasized that "to eliminate the exploitative system is to eliminate the exploitative class as a class."[68] However, the Communique of the Third Plenum pointed out:

> In our country there still exist a small number of counter revolutionaries and criminal offenders who are hostile to and try to sabotage our socialist modernization. We must never relax the class struggle against them or weaken the dictatorship of the proletariat.[69]

Such a formulation simply begged the question that if the bourgeoisie no longer existed as a class, and the proletariat "owned" the means of production, what was the justification in continuing to use the term "proletariat" to refer to the working class, or to stress the class character of the state, which represented itself as the dictatorship of the proletariat? Secondly, with the elimination of the erstwhile exploiters as a class, why should any conflict with "remnant exploitative individuals" be termed a class struggle?[70]

The 1936 Soviet constitution had distinguished between workers and peasants on the basis of their dissimilar status with respect to the resources of production. However, the relationship between these two classes being "nonantagonistic," theoretical consistency would demand writing the epitaph on class struggle. In the 1950s, Khrushchev's innovation lay in his assertion that the dictatorship of the proletariat was required in the pre-socialist transition period when the remnants of a hostile class still required suppression by the proletariat. With the legal change in property relations in the mid-1930s the class term proletariat lost its significance. For the new "socialism-cum-communism epoch" that the Soviet Union

---

68.   Hu Fuming, "Politics and Ideology Cannot Serve as the Basis for Identifying Class." Liao Gailong, "Class Struggle and Contradictions Among the People in Socialist Society," Report delivered on 19 December 1981 at a National Forum on Research and Teaching of Party History Convened by the Central Party School, cited in Stuart Schram, *Ideology and Politics Since the Third Plenum, 1978–84*, London: Contemporary China Institute, SOAS, 1984, pp. 27–28.

69.   "Communique of the Third Plenum of the Eleventh Central Committee of the Communist Party of China," *Peking Review*, no. 52, 1978, pp. 6–16.

70.   Commentator, "A Scientific Understanding and Handling of Questions Concerning Class Struggle," *Jiefangjun bao*, 9 October 1982. "Correctly Appraise and Handle the Class Struggle in the Current Stage," *Renmin ribao*, 6 November 1982.

had entered wherein classes had been "eliminated" but distinctions among strata remained (as also differences in the "utilization of property"), the "state of the whole people" replaced the dictatorship of the proletariat.

Mao's dismissal of Khrushchev's formulation as revisionism entailed an about-face on his own part and the abandonment of his theory of New Democracy and the People's Democratic Dictatorship. As Benjamin Schwartz has documented, in the late 1940s and early to mid-1950s, Mao had claimed that the Chinese path to communism would be characterized by a certain amount of class collaboration.[71] In a feudal and semicolonial society where capitalism had been insufficiently developed, the national bourgeoisie retained a progressive character. In speeches like "On the People's Democratic Dictatorship," and "Common Programme," Mao put forward his thesis that in the specific circumstances of China, a peaceful transformation was possible in which capitalist elements would be "educated" and "reformed" into socialism.[72] The Chinese media claimed on Mao's behalf that "none of

---

71. Benjamin Schwartz, *Communism and China: Ideology in Flux*, p. 17.

72. This was in direct contrast to the Stalinist position at the time, viz., socialism could be built only after the establishment of the dictatorship of the proletariat and after a bitter class struggle with the urban and rural bourgeoisie. Stuart Schram has quoted a 1958 speech of Mao's to illustrate Mao's notion that members of the "exploiting classes" can "change their class natures" and so "have their hats removed when they have been genuinely reformed." "Classes, Old and New, in Mao Zedong's Thought, 1949–1976" in James Watson, ed., *Class and Social Stratification in Post-Mao China*, Cambridge: Cambridge University Press, 1984, p. 38. It is important to remember, however, that such "reform" or "transformation" was in the context of a changed environment, hence the subjective element was only being cited *in addition* to the objective one. Donald Munro also argued that, "there is a general tendency in Maoism for the link between man's social nature (thought) and the economic base (so essential in the Marxist definition of social relations constitutive of man's essence) to be sometimes fuzzy, sometimes nonexistent, and never as necessarily linked as in classical Marxism. . . . A bourgeois intellectual can gain a proletarian nature (a labor viewpoint) by working with peasants, and . . . in the case of manual laborers, political education alone, with no change in social relationships, is sufficient to bring about change in social nature (i.e., change in thoughts and class). . . . The official position has been that changes in the individual's class are a product of both political education and participation in the appropriate social practice or social relations." See "The Malleability of Man in Chinese Marxism," *The China Quarterly*, no. 48 (1971), pp. 613–15. In the mid-1950s, the optimism regarding the extent to which class differences stemming from social background could be eliminated through education can be traced

the previous classics of Marxism-Leninism contain this type of theory, and no other state in the world has ever had this experience." [73]

The Hundred Flowers Campaign, the fate of the GLF, and the Lushan Plenum, along with international developments, shattered Mao's complacency about the Chinese bourgeoisie's "love for socialism," and as the Soviet Union under Khrushchev embarked on de-Stalinization, Mao conversely began to stress the persistence of class conflict for "decades or even longer periods after socialist industrialization and agricultural collectivization." [74] The publication of "On the Historic Experience of the Dictatorship of the Proletariat," in April 1956, marked the replacement of the People's Democratic Dictatorship with the more orthodox nomenclature.

In 1979, Deng Xiaoping's emphasis on the proletarian dictatorship and his reluctance to write off class struggle completely was linked to his need to keep dissident opponents in line (Maoists within the Party and the Democracy Wall activists) and maintain law and order. [75] In a speech discussing principles of theoretical work Deng argued:

also to the Chinese Communist acceptance of Pavlovian ideas of the plasticity of the nervous system. Munro maintains that "the Chinese malleability theory" contained an even "deeper and more comprehensive confidence in the changeability of people than found in the Soviet Union." However, in practice, the official belief in malleability was contradicted by the continuation of old-class designations and labels to stigmatize successive generations long after the objective basis for class differences had been eliminated. See Donald Munro, *The Concept of Man in Contemporary China*, Ann Arbor: University of Michigan Press, 1977, pp. 81–82.

73. Schwartz, p. 87.

74. Mao Zedong, "A Proposal Concerning the General Line of the International Communist Movement," 14 June 1963, in Griffith, ed. *Sino-Soviet Rift*, Cambridge: MIT Press 1964, p. 277.

75. For Party veterans the dictatorship of the proletariat was a basic concept the retention of which provided evidence of doctrinal continuity even as new ground was being broken in other areas. Lenin had maintained, "up to now this axiom has never been disputed by socialists, and yet it implies the recognition of the *state* right up to the time when victorious socialism will have grown into complete communism." Lenin, "The Discussion on Self-Determination Summed Up," *CW*, vol. 19. In *The State and Revolution*, he reiterated, "the essence of Marx's teaching on the state has been mastered only by someone who has understood that the dictatorship of a *single* class is necessary not only for every class society in general, not only for the *proletariat*, which has overthrown the bourgeoisie, but also for the entire *historical period* separating capitalism from "society without classes" from Communism.

. . . in our country both the exploiting classes and the conditions for exploitation have already been eliminated. . . . However, we must realize that under socialism, there are still offenders and other evildoers who do harm to our social order and new exploiters like grafters, embezzlers, profiteers, and speculators. These cannot be completely eliminated even over a rather long period of time. The struggle against them is different from the struggle between classes in the past (for they cannot be an overt and complete class), but it is still class struggle in a special form, or a continuation of past class struggle under socialism in a special form. We must exercise dictatorship over these antisocialist elements.[76]

Needless to say, the characterization of incarceration measures against criminals (other writers added rapists, arsonists, and such like to the list) as class struggle—even in a special form—was a considerable stretching of the Marxist definition of class and class conflict, and, when one comes to think of it, not that different from the ghosts and monsters of the Red Guard vintage.[77]

The consolidation of Deng's position and the need for a "peaceful and stable environment" for reform, as well as the specific course of reform itself brought back into vogue the theory of New Democracy and a reappraisal of the principle of the People's Democratic Dictatorship.[78] Following Deng's emphasis on "faulty systems and institutions," in a 1980 speech on the sources of past mistakes, reformist intellectuals linked the issue of political liberalization to a correct understanding of the concept of proletarian dictatorship. Feng Wenbin, who had argued against Su Shaozhi that China was already a socialist society, now contended, as Khrushchev had done, that Marx's concept of the dictatorship of the proletariat was applicable only to the period of transition.[79] In the socialist stage reten-

76.   Deng Xiaoping, "Uphold the Four Cardinal Principles," *Selected Works,* 30 March 1979, pp. 166–91.

77.   Some writers consequently attempted to make respectable the "new concept put forward by Comrade Deng Xiaoping after summing up historical experiences." See Wei Zhongduan and Cui Zhengqi, "Why Do We Say That Class Struggle at the Present Stage in Our Country Is a Special Form of Class Struggle?" *Wenhuibao,* 17 July 1979. Sun Ruiyuan, "Why Is it That Not All Ideological Differences in the Party Reflect Class Struggle in Society?" *Hongqi,* no. 19 (1981), pp. 38–40.

78.   "The Formulation of the People's Democratic Dictatorship Is More Suited to Our National Conditions," *Wenhuibao,* 17 March 1981.

79.   Feng Wenbin, "On the Question of Socialist Democracy," *RMRB,* 24 November 1980.

tion of the term *dictatorship* led to an overestimation of class enemies and a preoccupation with the coercive aspect of the state.

The intensification of Stalinist repression in the Soviet Union after 1936 and Mao's theory of "continuing the revolution under a strengthened dictatorship of the proletariat" in the 1960s were seen by scholars like Liao Gailong, Yan Jiaqi, and Li Honglin as an erroneous exaggeration of the class nature of the socialist state.[80] The overriding concern with the persecution of real and perceived class enemies resulted in the neglect of positive political functions—the development of norms, procedures, and institutions for governing, and enhancing democratic participation of the "people" represented by the socialist state.

In this phase of reorientation de-emphasis of class was directed at undermining the repressive nature of the state and the concentration of power in the hands of individuals who could misuse it opportunistically as illustrated in repeated campaigns against rightists. The concept of class still remained central to the distinction between socialist and capitalist systems and specific political forms. The identification of Democracy Wall activists with bourgeois democratic forms of government—popular elections, parliament, and multiparty sytems—justified their rejection by elite intellectuals who lobbied for a socialist democracy, which they believed was compatible with constitutional limits to authority and freedom of speech and expression.[81]

The partial success of intellectual arguments for political liberalization in the context of a growing conservatism in the ranks of Deng's moderate allies was reflected in the reaffirmation of the People's Democratic Dictatorship. On 21 April 1981, *RMRB* reprinted a contributing commentator's article from *GMRB* entitled "The People's Democratic Dictatorship Is in Essence the Dictatorship of the Proletariat," which restored the early 1950s thesis regarding the "specific historical conditions and circumstances" of

---

80.   Liao Gailong, "Historical Experience and Our Road of Development," *Zhonggong yanjiu*, no. 19 (1981), pp. 108–77. Yan Jiaqi, "Socialist Countries Must Also Properly Resolve the Problem of the 'Political System,'" *GMRB*, 8 December 1980. Li Honglin, "What Kind of Democracy Do We Want," *GMRB*, 11 March 1979.

81.   Zhang Xianyang and Wang Guixiu, "Proletarian Democracy and Bourgeois Democracy," *RMRB*, 6 September 1979.

China's socialist transformation.[82] However, still maintaining distance from Khrushchev's heterodoxy, the official formulation emphasized that the People's Democratic Dictatorship was not only suited to the period of New Democracy but also to the socialist stage.[83]

In the early 1980s discussions on alienation and humanism directed attention again to the lack of popular control as an explanation of malfeasance and abuse of power. Reformist writings during this time expanded their critique of leftism to include arguments that dictatorial tendencies and authoritarianism were a common phenomena of the Leninist-Stalinist political system.[84] The point of departure now became the problems, which emerged soon after the first Communist Party came to power.[85] Su Shaozhi's address on the centennial anniversary of Marx's death dwelt on Lenin's realization that

> despite the great successes of the cause initiated by the October Revolution, it suffered from quite a few defects and inadequacies, and that is why he [Lenin] raised the question of democratizing the organs of the proletarian

82.   A Contributing Commentator article two days later indicated that the consensus on the lack of class struggle was not unanimous. The 23 April article warned that class struggle would not end in the near future. On the contrary, the influence of international imperialism, the Taiwanese system and the infancy of Chinese socialism, might well result in its possible reemergence "rather conspicuously in one issue or another under certain conditions and within a certain period of time." Contributing Commentator, "To Uphold The People's Democratic Dictatorship Is an Unshakeable Principle," *Guangming ribao*, 23 April 1981.

83.   Ibid. CCP Central Party School Research and Writing Group on Scientific Socialism, "The Class Content and Historical Task of the Dictatorship of the Proletariat," *GMRB*, 11 July 1983, p. 3.

84.   *Selected Writings on Studies of Marxism*, Beijing: Institute of Marxism-Leninism and Mao Zedong Thought, CASS, 1981. Liao Gailong, "Historical Experience of the Dictatorship of the Proletariat and Our Road of Development," *Issues and Studies*, October, November, and December 1981. "Answers and Explanations Regarding Some Questions Which Have Been Posed in Connection With the Study of the 'Resolution,'" *Yunnan shehui kexue*, no. 2 (1982). Su Shaozhi, "Some Questions in China's Socialist Economic Construction"; "Some Important Questions for Research on Our Development Strategy," *Shehui kexue zhanxian*, no. 1 (1982), in *Xinhua wenzhai*, no. 6 (1982), pp. 47–49.

85.   Su Shaozhi, "Earnestly Study the New Situation in the New Period and Advance Marxism," *Xuexi yu tansuo*, no. 1 (1983), pp. 17–22. "Marxism Must Study the New Situation in the Contemporary World," *Xinhua wenzhai*, no. 3 (1983), pp. 11–12.

dictatorship and the Soviets, of opposing bureaucratism and over-concentration of powers, and of giving full play to the role of cooperatives. Stalin deviated from Lenin's thinking on these questions, and this led to serious tragedy for the Soviet party and state as well as for Stalin himself.[86]

Two years later Su had extended his criticism to Lenin himself. Discussing Rosa Luxembourg's differences with Lenin on the subject of inner-party democracy, Su maintained that the latter's "emphasis on iron discipline was right in the context of an underground Communist Party; however, when the Communist Party becomes the ruling party, internal democracy must be implemented."[87]

In the mid-1980s, Yu Guangyuan struck a new note by rejecting the need for class dictatorship on the grounds that the struggle between antagonistic classes had given way to a common struggle against nature. Social contradiction in the new phase involved "people's cognition or understanding" and the "struggle between advancing and holding on."

> The progressive is to grasp the inevitable tendency of historical development, clearly understand that one must stand in the forefront of the age, dare to discard historically obsolete things, develop new things, become a force propelling history forward. Thought which is in opposition to this occupies the conservative aspect of the contradiction.[88]

One can note in passing that such a definition provided the rationale for a benevolent view of "progressive" entrepreneurs who propelled history forward and "conservative" workers and other defenders of "egalitarianism" and the "iron rice bowl" of socialism who lacked the courage to discard the old! Yu's stress on attitude and worldview was indeed a reaffirmation of Mao's political and behavioral criteria although for very different ends.

86. Su Shaozhi, "Develop Marxism Under Contemporary Conditions—In Commemoration of the Centenary of the Death of Karl Marx," *Selected Studies on Marxism*, CASS, 1988, p. 6.
87. Gordon Chang, "Interview With Su Shaozhi," December 1985, *Bulletin of Concerned Asian Scholars*, no. 1 (1988), p. 13.
88. Yu Guangyuan, "Reform Is also a Philosophical Revolution," *Xuexi yu yanjiu*, no. 10 (1984), pp. 9–11, also in *Renda Fuyin*, no. 22 (1984).

Other theorists like Liao Gailong did not share Yu's view. "Mankind's struggle with the natural world," Liao argued, "is always conducted through society," and inevitably manifested as contradictions between individuals.[89] But, Liao concluded that the term *class struggle* was ill suited for a society that had overcome class opposition. When antagonistic contradictions had assumed secondary importance, the struggles for material production and scientific experimentation, and conflicts among individuals should be referred to instead as "social struggle."[90] With this novel formulation radical reformers hoped to assuage moderate fears of a new class struggle arising from widening inequalities and reemergence of socioeconomic polarization.

However, Liao also went on to say that nonantagonistic contradictions in socialist society could turn antagonistic if "handled incorrectly." Such an admission was contrary to the unilinear deterministic view of social progress stressed otherwise by the Party leadership and many reformist writers in the early 1980s. The emphasis on "conscious purposive activity" or the Party's "correct handling" shifted attention once again from productive forces and the economy to politics and the superstructure. The retreat vindicated Mao's concern that serious contradictions could come about in socialist society as a consequence of leadership errors, i.e., without formal changes in the political structure or the ownership system.

With the renewed interest in "political structural" reform in 1986 reformist arguments moved closer to the Khrushchev formulation by renouncing the proletarian bias of the socialist state in favor of a state representing "all citizens."[91] De-emphasis on the proletariat as a leading class in the socialist context led to a reassessment of bourgeois democracy as

89.   Liao Gailong, Centennial Speech, earlier cited, also in *Renda Fuyin,* no. 4 (1983).

90.   Liao Gailong, "Again Discussing Mao Zedong Thought and 'Socialism With Chinese Characteristics,' " *Mao Zedong sixiang yanjiu,* no. 2 (1985), pp. 1–7, also in *Renda Fuyin,* no. 3, (1985).

91.   Zhang Weiguo, "Li Honglin on Reunderstanding Socialism," *Shijie jingji daobao,* 11 April 1988, p. 7, also in *FBIS,* 28 April 1988, p. 20. Su Dongbin, "China Is Heading Towards 'New Socialism,'" *GMRB,* 27 March 1989, p. 3, also in *FBIS,* 11 April 1989, p. 22. Wang Ruoshui, "The Cult of the Individual and Intellectual Alienation," *Jingbao,* 1988 April pp. 24–27, and May 1988, pp. 40–44.

well.[92] Just as the commodity economy had been rendered class neutral, democratic processes involving parliamentary procedures, rule of law, checks and balances, elections, and interest groups that had evolved in the course of the bourgeoisie's struggle against feudalism were no longer seen in class terms but rather as progressive elements equally necessary in a socialist society. The advocacy of separation between the Party and the state (stemming from the perception that the current political structure was the main obstacle to the success of economic reform) underscored the new conception of the state as a neutral arbiter standing above class interests.[93]

By the late 1980s the language of rights of citizens and individuals had completely replaced the terminology of class in reformist intellectual discourse. The relegation of the dictatorship of the proletariat to the transitional stage again by theorists like Yu Guangyuan was decidedly at odds with the official adoption of the thesis of the "primary stage of socialism," and the admission of the immaturity of Chinese socialism. The reintroduction of capitalist factors and multiple and diverse forms of ownership was accompanied by radical-reformist assertions that China "no longer required a political system that excluded one or more classes from the socialist community with democratic rights."[94] Class dictatorship, according to Wang Yizhou, produced the alienation of individuals from social and class goals, and the requirement that everyone think and act like a member of the proletarian class deprived individuals of the right to think freely. Thus, the essence of the Marxian notion of class consciousness was now seen as "dehumanization," and the denial of individuality.

The disavowal of class dictatorship was a repudiation of a fundamental tenet of doctrine. The concept of the dictatorship of the proletariat had

92. Hu Jiwei and Chang Dalin, "Exploring China's Theories on Democracy," *RMRB*, 30 December 1988, p. 5. Yu Haocheng, "Protection of Human Rights Is a Just Cause in the Advance of Mankind," *Shijie zhishi*, 1 December 1988, pp. 2–5, also in *JPRS*, 89018, 1 March 1989, p. 1.

93. Yan Jiaqi, "Conversation With Wen Yuankai," in David Bachman and Dali L. Yang, eds. and trans., *Yan Jiaqi and China's Struggle for Democracy*, Armonk, N.Y.: M.E. Sharpe, 1991.

94. Yu Guangyuan, "For the Victory of Reform and Opening and the Cause of Socialist Construction for Modernization," *RMRB*, 28 April 1989.

been claimed by Marx as one of his "essential discoveries."[95] In the *Critique of the Gotha Programme*, he pointed out, "Between capitalism and Communist society lies the period of the revolutionary transformation of the one into the other. There corresponds to this also a political transition period in which the state can be nothing but *the dictatorship of the proletariat*.[96] On the 10th anniversary of the debate on "practice as the criterion of truth," tracing the responsibility for flaws in the socialist system to Marx himself was seen by radical-reformist intellectuals as an essential requirement of the task of "developing Marxism."[97] However, the abandonment of class categories and the rejection of proletarian dictatorship removed the basic premise of Communist Party leadership. The reluctance of Su Shaozhi, Yu Guangyuan, Li Honglin, and others to endorse a move toward a multiparty system at this point reflected only their inability to grasp the full significance of their own arguments.

Commitment to the concept of class dictatorship, for reasons of legitimacy was non-negotiable for the political leadership as a whole — both moderate and radical reformist. The intellectual challenge unfolding in the events of 1989 was interpreted in class terms not only by Party elders but younger leaders like Li Peng as well. In the early 1990s the phrase *dictatorship of the proletariat*, which had been completely eclipsed in political discourse in the preceding years, began cropping up again as the leadership consolidated itself against renewed threats to doctrinal continuity and the authority of the Communist Party.

Conclusion

The early post-Mao discussions on "bourgeois right" grew out of the need to invalidate leftist "egalitarianism," and affirm that China's socialist

95.   Eric Chester, "Revolutionary Socialism and the Dictatorship of the Proletariat," *Critique*, 1986.
96.   *Critique of the Gotha Programme*, appendix.
97.   Yu Guangyuan, "Commemorating the Tenth Anniversary of the Discussion on the Question Regarding the Criterion of Truth," *RMRB*, 6 May 1988, p. 5.

development was not being sabotaged by new socioeconomic policies. The controversy over whether class should be defined in primarily economic terms or according to political and ideological criteria as well was similarly related to the effort to deny the possibility of new exploitative classes emerging in socialist society. For the moderate cadres and intellectuals castigated as capitalist roaders in the past, an emphasis on economic criteria was the only valid one, and their insistence on this eventually brought them into conflict with the reformist trend toward privatization. Radical reformers, though, found political criteria more useful, as time went on, for understating the socioeconomic implications of changed-ownership patterns and the new role of capital in the increasingly market-oriented economy. For very different reasons, Mao's most vociferous critics found themselves in agreement with his position on class status.

Class had never been defined exclusively in economic terms and had consistently been understood as a concept of political economy by Chinese Marxists beginning with Li Dazhao and Chen Duxiu. Such a political definition facilitated the broader coalition against the principal enemy in the pre-liberation era. After the establishment of the "proletarian" state and the nationalization or collectivization of productive property, the political aspect continued to be the more significant, as behavior and standpoint became the measures of class status. The excesses brought about by the application of such criteria evoked a commitment to a stricter economic definition, particularly on the part of victims of the new class struggle. Economic reform in the post-Mao era made it expedient once again, to refer to "reformed" or "patriotic" capitalists and entrepreneurs as those who earned their place in the ranks of the working class by toiling for "socialist modernization."

The discussions on class struggle and determinants of class status illustrated the tenacity of certain aspects of the Chinese-Marxist tradition. The early abhorrence to the disintegrative aspects of class struggle noticed by Levenson, Li Yuming, Arif Dirlik, and others had been muted somewhat by the radicalization of May Fourth intellectuals and the altered vocabulary of discourse at the beginning of the 1920s. The united-front strategy, the "collaboration of four classes," and the concept of a people's democratic dictatorship, however, underscored the preference for social harmony over conflict among the Chinese elite. In this light, Mao's emphasis on violent and disruptive class struggle through the 1960s and 1970s marked a deviant trend that was reversed soon after his passing. The re-adoption of the phrase "people's democratic dictatorship" and the replacement of class struggle by social struggle signified a return to the dominant tradition.

FIVE

Refuting the Theory of a Bureaucrat Class and Affirming Socialist Democracy

In addition to bourgeois right and superstructural remnants of the old order a third source of socioeconomic polarization and capitalist restoration identified by Mao was bureaucratic degeneration and an alliance between party-state functionaries and the liberal and technocratic intelligentsia. The 1950s' events in Eastern Europe that demonstrated the power of students and intellectuals to mobilize people against an unpopular regime, the outcome of the Hundred Flowers Campaign, the "cult of the expert" accepted by Liu Shaoqi, Deng Xiaoping, Peng Zhen, and others in the post-GLF period, their resistance to the Socialist Education Movement and toleration for the liberal intellectuals' critiques of Mao's policies and leadership style heightened the Chairman's apprehensions regarding an emerging "political-literary nexus," which would act as a brake on further revolutionary progress.[1] In the last decade of his life, Mao's major ideological preoccupation was the need to explain the phenomenon of "reaction," i.e., the Communist Party itself becoming the major obstacle to the attainment of a socialist society.

During the Cultural Revolution and through the 1970s a variety of radical-leftist groups attempted to articulate a structural explanation for the rise of a bureaucratic class by identifying the state and its attendant political institutions as the source of inequality and exploitation.[2] Writing

1. Merle Goldman, "Mao's Obsession With the Political Role of Literature and Intellectuals," in Roderick Macfarquhar, Timothy Cheek, and Eugene Wu, eds., *The Secret Speeches of Chairman Mao*, Cambridge: Harvard University Press, 1989, p. 40.

2. Wang Li, Jia Yixue, and Li Xin, "The Dictatorship of the Proletariat and the Great Proletarian Cultural Revolution," *Hongqi*, no. 15 (1966), *Peking Review*, 23 December 1966, p. 20. Whither China?" in Klaus Mehnert, *Peking and the New Left*, Berkeley: University of California Center for Chinese Studies, 1969, p. 99; Writing Group of the Shantung Provincial Committee of the Chinese Communist Party, "Adhere to the Method of Class Analysis, Correctly Understand the Struggle Between the Two Lines," *Hongqi*, no. 13 (1971), in *SCMM*, 23 December 1971, p. 18.

groups of the Philosophy and Social Sciences Department of the Academy of Sciences, Sheng-Wu-lian, and Ma Yanwen placed China in the stage of state capitalism and argued that policies that stressed professionalism, routinization, elitist education, and material inequality as a spur to higher and more efficient production undermined further progress toward communism.[3] Cadres who promoted such policies sought to preserve the current bureaucratic state-capitalist system because it provided themselves and their allies, the intelligentsia, with the privileged position and authority to command and appropriate capital. Just as Lenin had claimed that trade-union economism and parliamentary reformism would not lead to socialism, in the stage of state capitalism, radical-leftist writers pointed out, Mao's theory of continuous revolution emphasized that Communism would not be achieved without a strengthened dictatorship of the proletariat and unrelenting struggle against the class of bureaucrats.

The post-Mao leadership's reversal of Mao's preference for continuous revolution in favor of an elite-guided process of steady economic growth based on rational planning and professional expertise necessitated yet another major theoretical reorientation. Upon his reinstatement, Deng lost little time in restoring the legitimacy of cadres and intellectuals, who had been stigmatized as revisionist in the preceding period.[4] In his speeches on science and education policy he rejected the "two estimates"[5] as falsehoods "peddled by the Gang of Four" and stressed that the overwhelming majority of Chinese intellectuals "served socialism of their own volition."[6] Both scientific researchers and other intellectuals differed from "manual workers only insofar as they perform[ed] different roles in the social division of

3.   For my analysis of Ma Yanwen's position I have drawn from Edward Friedman's summary of the four essays written by this group in 1976. However, Friedman does not comment on the conceptual significance of Ma Yanwen's treatment of the bureaucrat class beyond regarding it as a Marxist idealist position. Edward Friedman, "The Societal Obstacle to China's Socialist Transition," in Nee and Mozingo, ed., *State and Society in Contemporary China*, Ithaca: Cornell University Press, 1983, p. 154–158.

4.   Deng Xiaoping, "Respect Knowledge, Respect Trained Personnel," 24 May 1977, *SW*, pp. 53–54. "Some Comments on Work in Science and Education," 8 August 1977, *SW*, pp. 61–72.

5.   These were (1) in the first 17 years of the PRC the bourgeoisie was predominant in the educational sphere and (2) the world outlook of the vast majority of intellectuals was basically bourgeois.

6.   Deng Xiaoping, "Setting Things Right in Education," 19 September 1977, *SW*, p. 80.

labor." Thus, "everyone who work[ed], whether with his hands or with his brain, (was) part of the working people in a socialist society."[7]

Deng's position was a restatement of the views expressed in his Report to the Eighth Congress in 1956 (and not shared by Mao),[8] which emphasized social roles rather than class origins to conclude that peasants, workers, and office employees or intellectuals could no longer be differentiated on class grounds ("the differences are only a matter of division of labor *within the same class* [my emphasis]").[9] It also reflected the consensus among his reformist colleagues that intellectuals be viewed primarily as carriers and promoters of modern professional values and scientific

7.   Deng Xiaoping, "Speech at the Opening Ceremony of the National Conference on Science," 18 March 1978, *SW*, p. 105.

8.   While Deng maintained that it was no longer necessary to differentiate between peasants, workers, etc., on *class grounds* Mao stressed that although the bourgeoisie could be included in the category of "people," it retained its identity as a separate class. The Contradictions speech reflected Mao's deep sense of satisfaction at having avoided the "leftist excesses" of Soviet collectivization, and betrayed his anxiety over the developments in Hungary and Poland in late 1956. Consequently, while he maintained that Chinese intellectuals, in general, continued to be concerned solely with enhancing their professional capabilities and careers, and sections of the bourgeoisie and petty bourgeoisie continued to "reflect their ideological consciousness," Mao still argued that "debate" and "self-molding" through study rather than coercion was necessary for handling such contradictions among the people. As to the younger generation coming of age in the new society, Mao professed a considerable amount of optimism when he contrasted the events in Poland and Hungary with China. "The sons and daughters of workers and peasants [in Hungary] are big on going on strike, big on demonstrating, listening to the orders of the Petofi Circle. Our [200] sons and daughters of landlords, rich peasants, and capitalists—we don't have a Petofi Circle naturally—love their country. Except for a very few . . . the great majority are patriots [who] approve of socialism and want to make China into a great nation; [and because they] have this kind of ideal, we are better off than Hungary." At this time Mao hoped rather than believed that a Petofi Circle would not emerge in China. Events in Eastern Europe that demonstrated the power of students and intellectuals to mobilize people against an unpopular regime fitted in with Mao's own conception of the political role of literature and intellectuals in general. See "On the Correct Handling of Contradictions Among the People" (Speaking Notes), 27 February 1957, in MacFarquhar, Cheek, Wu, eds., *The Secret Speeches of Chairman Mao*, Harvard: Contemporary China Series, 6 1989.

9.   *Eighth National Congress of the Communist Party of China*, Peking: Foreign Languages Press, 1956, pp. 213–214.

knowledge. In the current context it was crucial that they be co-opted into key administrative and policy positions.

The issue of bureaucracy proved harder to resolve given the varying orientations of the political leaders and intellectuals who comprised the dominant post-Mao coalition. Moderate leaders and their intellectual coterie dismissed outright the idea of a bureaucratic class as anti-Marxist. Their denial of such a class in Chinese society was based on an oversimplified and doctrinaire interpretation of Marx, for they argued that even in pre-socialist systems bureaucrats had only served the interests of another propertied ruling class. Having no independent economic interests they did not constitute a separate class and, at best, made up only a small fragment of the dominant social group.[10] The premise for dismissing the existence of a "bureaucratic class" within the Party was the argument that Communist cadres neither possessed any means of production nor stood in an exploitative relationship vis-á-vis the workers or the peasantry.[11] It was conceded that some "officials assumed bureaucratic airs" and developed "unhealthy practices" such as "seeking privilege" from time to time. Nevertheless, such "bureaucratism" was restricted, its presence was linked to economic backwardness, and its final elimination could come about only with vast increases in productivity.[12]

As the discussions on feudalism and the phenomenon of the Gang of Four revealed the radical reformers were eager to single out bureaucratic privilege and abuse of power as a major problem for Chinese socialism. Writing on the theme of alienation, Wang Ruoshui argued that intellectual, political, and economic alienation could continue to exist where, despite the socialization of the means of production, power continued to be monopolized by a tyrannical leader or an irresponsible bureaucratic elite.[13]

10. Wang Hongchang and Liu Mengyi, "Does a Bureaucratic Class Exist Within the Party," *Zhongguo qingnian bao* 7 February, 1981 and *FBIS*, 23 February, 1981, pp. 27–30.

11. Kong Qian, "Comment on 'Opposing the Bureaucrat Class,'" *Jiefangjun bao*, 9 February 1981.

12. Lin Boye and Shen Che, "Commenting on the So-Called Opposition to the Class of Bureaucrats," *Hongqi*, no. 5 (1981), pp. 12–18. Zhang Yun, "Refuting the Theory of Family Lineage," *RMRB*, 17 May 1978, p. 3. Yu Mingren, "It Is Imperative to Criticize the Theory of the 'Three-Stage Development of the Bourgeoisie,'" *RMRB*, 8 April 1978, p. 2.

13. Wang Ruoshui, "Discussing the Problem of Alienation," *Xinwen zhanxian*, no. 9 (1980), translated in David Kelly, ed., "Wang Ruoshui: Writings on Humanism, Alienation and Philosophy," *Chinese Studies in Philosophy*, Spring 1985, pp. 25–38.

Hu Yaobang and his intellectual followers initially appear to have been in favor of rejecting the notion of capitalist roaders and new bourgeoisie while affirming the idea of a bureaucratic class.[14] Such a distinction between the two categories would serve the dual purpose of absolving reformist leaders of charges of revisionism and capitalist restoration, i.e., legitimizing their economic policies on the one hand, and, on the other, facilitate criticism of residual Maoists for *their* display of "bureaucratism," as well as provide the theoretical rationale for socialist democracy and legality as a check against *any* bureaucratic abuse of authority. Guo Luoji, an ardent spokesman for political democratization, criticized the notion of capitalist roaders as anti-Marxist but in reference to Trotsky's "so-called class of bureaucrats," he pointed out that the "concept of social servants turning into masters" had yet to be understood correctly.[15]

However, given their own orientations, philosophical and policy preferences and limited agenda for change at this time, the critique of bureaucracy as a new *class* was not sustained or developed by intellectual supporters of radical reform. Their reluctance to pursue this line of analysis could not be attributed to the strength of moderate arguments. Deng's refutation of a bureaucratic class, and his denial of the possibility of capitalist restoration in 1979 did not stand scrutiny either in terms of Marx and Engels' own writings or those of their followers (and one might add, facts as well). *The Communist Manifesto*'s assertion that "the executive of the modern state is but a committee for managing the common affairs of the whole bourgeoisie" was polemical, and Marx's conception of the state was not one in which the political was simply derivative of the economic. An insistence on the importance of understanding bureaucracy both historically and functionally characterized all of Marx's works. The "sociological

14.   Li Honglin, "Exposing and Criticizing the 'Gang of Four' Constitutes a Decisive Battle of a Historical Nature," *Lishi yanjiu*, no. 3 (1978), pp. 3–15. Articles stressing the predominance of the petty bourgeoisie in the Chinese Revolution would seem to be referring to Marx's discussion in *The Eighteenth Brumaire of Louis Bonaparte* regarding the conservative French peasantry's support for Napoleon. The term "bureaucratic class" was used specifically by critics like Wang Xizhe. They agreed with Mao that such a class could appear in a socialist system but disagreed on the means to check it.

15.   Guo Luoji, "Commenting on the So-called 'Crisis of Faith,'" *Wenhuibao*, 13 January 1980. Guo's reference to Trotsky is an early example of the reform theorists' search for alternatives to Stalinism and their reappraisal of other heretics like Bukharin at this time.

significance" of Marx's discussion of bureaucracy, according to Schlomo Avineri, lay in his "insistence that bureaucratic structures do not automatically reflect prevailing social-power relations but pervert and disfigure them."[16] In the contexts of both Germany and France, Marx and Engels emphasized the semiautonomous status of the bureaucracy and argued that under conditions of class equilibrium the state could emerge as a completely independent force.[17]

Given his assumption that the concept of class equilibrium was not applicable to a mature capitalist society Marx did not consider the problem of bureaucratization a serious one in the context of a working-class revolution. Even so, in his study of the Paris Commune he did put forward three main preconditions for the success of the workers' state: (1) The salaries of state functionaries should not be higher than those of skilled workers. (Hence individuals would be precluded from seeking office for pecuniary gain.) (2) Functionaries should be elected and subject to recall at any time. (3) There should be no separation of legislative and executive functions. Taken together, these preconditions would both prevent bureaucratization and prepare the way for an eventual withering away of the state.

The complacency about the degeneration of a workers' state dissipated in the light of Soviet reality. For a wide range of opinion from Kautsky

16.   Schlomo Avineri, *The Social and Political Thought of Karl Marx*, Cambridge: Cambridge University Press, 1968, pp. 48–52. Alan Swingewood makes a similar argument in *Marx and Modern Social Theory*, pp. 138–166.

17.   Karl Marx and Frederick Engels, *The German Ideology*, edited by C.J. Arthur, New York: International Publishers, 1976, p. 80. Karl Marx, "The Civil War in France," *The Karl Marx Library: On Revolution*, vol. I edited and translated by Saul Padover, McGraw-Hill, 1971, p. 349. "The Eighteenth Brumaire of Loius Napoleon," ibid., pp. 318–320. In the original draft of *The Civil War in France*, published for the first time in 1934, Marx argued, "This parasitical excrescence [the bureaucratic state] upon civil society, pretending to be its ideal counterpart, grew to its full development under the sway of the first Bonaparte. . . . The governmental power with its standing army, its all directing bureaucracy, its stultifying clergy, and its servile tribunal hierarchy had grown so independent of society itself, that a grotesque mediocre adventurer with a hungry band of desperadoes behind him sufficed to yield it. . . . Humbling under its sway even the interests of the ruling classes, whose parliamentary showwork it supplanted by self-elected Corps Legislatifs and self-paid senates . . . the state power had received its last and supreme expression in the second Empire." This translation is from Schlomo Avineri, pp. 50–51.

and Plekhanov to Lenin, Bukharin, and Trotsky the circumstances of the October Revolution made possible a negation of the revolution and a return to an exploitative system. Marx's discussion of the origins of Bonapartism was more applicable to the Russian situation than his remarks on the Paris Commune for two reasons. In Russia, autocracy and the rudimentary existence of capitalism implied that the weakness of both the bourgeoisie and the working class could more likely result in an "equilibrium" rather than a clear hegemony of one class over another, thus paving the way for a possible emergence of an autonomous state power and bureaucracy. Secondly, economic backwardness and scarcity (rather than the presumed abundance of a society in which mature capitalism is replaced by a working-class revolution) dictated that the working- class state be run not by its own functionaries but by a section of the erstwhile exploiting class, some of whom were recruited on the basis of their desertion of class ranks and acceptance of working-class ideology, and others out of necessity. Even more significantly, the lack of education and culture, which, in the first instance, was responsible for keeping members of the working class out of positions of prominence and authority, could be perpetuated if developmental priorities and scarce resources restricted opportunities to a select few and increased rather than decreased the gap between the technocratic-bureaucratic elite and the working class.

Kautsky's rebuttal of anarchist critics like Mikhail Bakunin and Waclaw Machajski on the possibility of the working class seizing power only to surrender it into the hands of a bureaucracy was premised on an early elimination of the division of labor between administrators and workers. However, in 1919, he reversed his position and used the term *new class* to refer to the system of inequality and privilege that he perceived as emerging in the Bolshevik state. The Menshevik view represented by Plekhanov similarly maintained that the level of development of productive forces in Russia suggested the possibility only of a bourgeois state, and any attempt "to build socialism before economic conditions were ripe for it would result in a new form of despotism."[18]

Initially concerned only about the "spontaneous tendency toward capitalism," nearing the end of his life Lenin became increasingly apprehensive

---

18. Kolakowski, vol. 3, pp. 162–163; Tariq Ali, ed., *The Stalinist Legacy*, Penguin Books, 1984.

about the growing distance between the bureaucracy and the proletariat.[19] In *The State and Revolution* he had maintained that the phenomenon of "civil servants, the 'servants of society'" becoming "transformed into *masters* of society" so characteristic of the capitalist system could never be found in the workers' state. By December 1922, Lenin was conceding that "that which we call our apparatus is still completely alien to us; it represents a bourgeois, tsarist mechanism."[20] In his speech to the Fourth Comintern Congress Lenin said:

> Let us take Moscow, with its 4,700 responsible Communists, and that weighty bureaucratic machine—who is running it? I greatly doubt whether one can say that Communists are running that heavy thing. To tell the truth, it is not they who are running it, it runs them. Something has happened here that is similar to what they used to tell us about history in our childhood. . . . Sometimes it happens, that one people conquers another people, and then the people who conquered are the conquerors, and the conquered ones are the defeated. . . . If the people who did the conquering are more cultured than the defeated people, then the former will impose their culture on the latter, but if it is the other way around, then . . . the defeated will impose their culture on the conqueror. Has not something similar happened in the capital of the RSFSR; is it not true here that 4,700 Communists . . . turn out to have been subjugated by an alien culture?[21]

The idea of cultural backwardness was also used by Bukharin to reject the gynecological imagery of socialism developing in the womb of capitalism with respect to the maturity of the working class as a "social-organizing force."[22] The bourgeoisie in feudal society had been able to develop its cultured and qualified elite because its base in the cities accorded it independence of the old ruling class, the landlords. The situation of the proletariat was different because in bourgeois society it was deprived economically as well as culturally, i.e., it possessed neither property nor education. Because of this lack of development of administrative skills within the class itself, initially the leaders of the proletarian state

19. Paul Bellis, *Marxism and the USSR*, New Jersey: Humanities Press, 1979, pp. 51–53.

20. Alfred Meyer, *Leninism*, notes p. 214.

21. Meyer, ibid., p. 215.

22. Stephen Cohen, *Bukharin and the Bolshevik Revolution*, New York: Alfred Knopf, 1973, p. 141.

were of necessity drawn from a "hostile class . . . from the bourgeois intelligentsia."[23] The possibility of the emergence of a new class arose from this division of labor and "monopolistic" authority and privilege. Thus, Bukharin's position on the elimination of exploitation and the conditions for the disappearance of classes was similar to Kautsky and Plekhanov. In response to Michels' contention that "social wealth cannot be satisfactorily administered in any other manner than by the creation of an extensive bureaucracy. In this way we are led . . . to the flat denial of the possibility of a state without classes,"[24] Bukharin argued that a new-class alignment could be retarded by (a) the growth of the productive forces and (b) the abolition of the educational monopoly.

Trotsky criticized the Soviet bureaucracy for enjoying its privileges under the form of an abuse of power.[25] He rejected the idea of a class of "state capitalists" on legal grounds but did not deny the exploitative nature of the bureaucracy or the possibility that at some time in the future it could legalize its privileges and become a new possessing class. The most unique aspect of the Soviet bureaucracy was the "degree of independence" that it had achieved from the predominant class. In every other society, particularly the bourgeois, the bureaucracy represented the "possessing" and "educated" class and was controlled by it. In the Soviet system, on the other hand, the bureaucracy had set itself above a class with "no tradition of domination" or control and one which had barely emerged from "destitution and darkness." It had become, therefore, "in the full sense of the

23.   Ibid.

24.   In his book, *Political Parties*, Michels had held that, "social wealth cannot be satisfactorily administered in any other manner than by the creation of an extensive bureaucracy. In this way we are led by an inevitable logic to the flat denial of the possibility of a state without classes. The administration of an immeasurably large capital confers upon the administration influence at least equal to that possessed by the private owner of capital. Consequently the critics in advance of the Marxist social order ask whether the instinct which leads the members of the possessing classes to transmit to their children the wealth which they have amassed, will not exist also in the administrators of the public wealth of the socialist state, and whether the administrators will not utilize their immense influence in order to secure for their children the succession to the offices which they hold," quoted in Bellis, p. 71.

25.   L. Trotsky, "Social Relations in the Soviet Union," in Tariq Ali, ed., *The Stalinist Legacy*. Mandel, "What Is the Bureaucracy?" also in *The Stalinist Legacy*.

word the sole privileged and commanding stratum."[26] Consequently, Trotsky preferred to term the Soviet Union a "contradictory society halfway between capitalism and socialism" rather than one that was "transitional" or "intermediate." The latter definition, he believed, was "capable of producing the mistaken idea that from the present Soviet regime *only* a transition to socialism is possible. In reality a backslide to capitalism is wholly possible."

Thus, the question of legal versus actual control had arisen very early on within the international Communist movement, and there never appears to have been much of a dispute regarding which was more significant.[27] The stress on material privileges of the technocratic-bureaucratic elite and its greater access to the knowledge and skills necessary for its continuing dominance drew attention to the fact that the task of ensuring effective disposition and organization of the economy by immediate producers did not follow automatically with the setting up of the workers' state, and access to authority and privilege over a period of time could facilitate a change in property relations with its attendant implications for the consolidation of new classes.

The link between ownership and effective disposition over productive property emphasised by ultraleftists in China was thus no departure from the views of early Marxist writers or more contemporary new class–state capitalist theorists. Furthermore, their position on this issue was shared by most of the Democracy Wall intellectual activists, as well, despite the latter's

---

26. Trotsky, *The Third International After Lenin.*

27. Marx's definition of class did not even employ the term *legal ownership* and Lenin's formulation left room for ownership relations which may not be "fixed and formulated in laws." In his economic writings which served as basic reading material for many a member of the Russian Communist Party, Bogdanov had maintained all along that a ruling class in any society is the group of individuals who organize the economy, irrespective of actual ownership of productive property. While he came under considerable fire for his theory of empirio criticism, there appears no evidence that Bogdanov's position on ownership was ever challenged. Among contemporary Marxists there are very few theorists who would seriously entertain doubts about ownership being anything but effective disposition over productive property. Even writers like Hillel Ticktin, who denied that the Soviet bureaucracy was a ruling class, did so not on the basis of legality but insufficient control over the labor process. See Hillel Ticktin, "The Political Economy of Class in the Transitional Epoch," *Critique*, nos. 20–21 (1987), p. 18.

bitter denunciations of the Maoists. In the late 1970s and early 1980s, Chen Erjin, Dong Fang (pen name of Wang Yifeng), Zhu Jianbin, Wang Xizhe, Wei Jingsheng, Shi Huasheng, and others also identified an "authentically new exploitative mode of production" with the "unicorporation of the twin powers of political leadership and economic control" in Soviet-type societies. Characterizing Western capitalism as "money capitalism" and Eastern "socialism" as "power capitalism" these writers pointed to the primitive accumulation tasks accomplished by "privilege capital" and linked the coercive monopolization of power by the minority to the emergence of an embryonic ruling class.[28]

What distinguished the Democracy Wall writers from the Maoists was the formers' rejection of a strengthened Dictatorship of the Proletariat as a solution to bureaucratization. Instead, inspired also by Locke and Montesquieu, these writers, who saw themselves not as dissidents but as "natural allies" of the reformist leadership, advocated the undermining of bureaucratic control by full-scale democratization with elections and American-style checks and balances, along with worker control over the economy.[29]

The demand for this fifth modernization on the part of Wall activists and their increasing tendency to extend their critique of CCP elites to include Deng Xiaoping himself elicited strong reaction and the latter's support for Hu Qiaomu's initiatives for clamping down on liberalizing trends.[30] Following Deng's assertion that no exploiting classes, bureaucratic or bourgeois, existed in China, Hu Yaobang reiterated that the highly negative tones of Democracy Wall publications threatened to further erode

28.   Wang Xizhe, "Mao Zedong and the Cultural Revolution," *Chinese Law and Government*, 1985, pp. 1–98. Chen Erjin, *China: Crossroads Socialism*, (translated by Robin Munro), London: Verso, 1984.

29.   Jin Sheng, "Human Rights, Equality and Democracy— Commenting on the Contents of 'Move on the Fifth Modernization," *Tansuo*, 29 January 1979, pp. 4–7, *JPRS*, 73787, 29 June 1979; James Seymour, *The Fifth Modernization: China's Human Rights Movements, 1978–79*, Stanfordville, N.Y.: Human Rights Publishing Group, 1980. James Tong, ed., "Underground Journals in China Part I and II," *Chinese Law and Government*, vol. 13, nos 3–4, (1980) and vol. 14, no. 3 (1981).

30.   Among other things Deng was responding to the Shanghai Democratic Forum's declaration that its task was to "settle accounts with those whom the Gang of Four called capitalist roaders but failed to deal with," Deng Xiaoping, "Uphold the Four Cardinal Principles," 30 March 1979, *SW*, pp. 166–191.

popular confidence in the leadership.[31] Hence, it was necessary to refute new-class theories and to emphasize that the phenomena of high-handedness, privilege seeking, nepotism, sycophancy, etc., were not a product of the socialist system. Rather, as in the case of explanations of the "cult of personality" and the Gang of Four, such problems were to be understood as holdovers from the feudal past. While exploiting classes had been eliminated as a social group in 1956, an ideological "lag" reflecting their values persisted in the superstructure. Better enforcement of party discipline, ideological education, and economic development would eliminate or vastly limit the problem in due course.

Such a diagnosis could scarcely have been theoretically satisfying for Hu's followers. Radical-reformist intellectuals, however, despite their own harshly critical assessments of the Stalinist-Maoist political systems and their receptivity to various strands of hitherto heretic Marxist writings, were reluctant to adopt either the positions of the Democracy Wall publications or the perspectives of Kautsky, Lenin, Bukharin, and other more contemporary new class–state capitalist theorists. Their support for the reformist coalition's new economic and educational policies made difficult their endorsement of critiques like those of Kaustky, et al., which did not distinguish conceptually between the rise of a bureaucrat class and the restoration of capitalism. Theorizing on state capitalism has tended not to clarify whether the new class would restore private property in the classic capitalist form or "within a new mode of production without historical precedent," and the terms *bureaucratic class* and *new bourgeoisie* have been used interchangeably in such analyses. Furthermore, if effective disposition over productive property were used as the criterion for identifying a bureaucratic elite there would be little ground for distinguishing between "good" Dengist cadres and "bad" Maoist ones. Consistency would also demand that managers and various categories of scientists be included in this class as well for their functional expertise conferred on them directly

31. "Preliminary Analysis of Hu Yaobang and China's Future," *Dong xifang*, no. 19, 10 July 1980, pp. 8–12, translated in *JPRS* 76427, 12 September 1980, pp. 17–26. According to Hong Kong sources, Zhao Ziyang made similar remarks in a speech in Sichuan. See Qi Xin, "About Deng Xiaoping's Talks on the Problems of Privileges—and About the Social Background of the Drama 'If I Were the Real One,'" *Qishi niandai*, no. 1 (1980), pp. 74–75, in *JPRS* 75142, 15 February 1980, pp. 83–87.

by the authority to regulate the process of production—command capital, allocate resources, and dispose of commodities.[32] For the radical reformers the link between bureaucrats and capitalist restoration was compounded by the shading of the two categories of Party-state cadres and the intelligentsia in class-based critiques. The conflation of the intellectual and bureaucratic categories was also the premise of the Hungarian sociologists George Konrád and Ivan Szelényi's theory of a new class of intellectuals that exercised "control" over the productive process by virtue of its specialized knowledge.[33]

The identification of intellectuals with the Party-state bureaucracy was especially significant in China for historical and cultural reasons, as well as those related to Leninist assumptions about working-class "trade union consciousness" and the need for an intellectual vanguard.[34] Merle Goldman and others have pointed out that movements such as the Anti-Rightist Campaign or the Cultural Revolution were not directed at intellectuals as a group by an impersonal state-bureaucratic machinery.[35] Rather, they were policies of persecution directed by one set of intellectuals against another. This is equally true of the more recent post-Mao campaigns against "bourgeois liberalization," "spiritual pollution," and the democracy movement, which were contests or power struggles among intellectuals of different persuasions. Tensions between the more bureaucratically oriented Peng Zhen, Hu Qiaomu, and Deng Liqun and such groups as artists and writers or liberal intellectuals in general have led to periodic expulsions and disciplinary action, but the hallmark of the Deng era was its further co-optation of intellectuals into the Party to enlist their services and ensure their political loyalty. During the periods in which anti-intellectual themes

32.   Jaroslav Krejci, *Social Change and Stratification in Postwar Czechoslovakia*, New York: Columbia University Press, 1972, p. 129. Erik Olin Wright, *Class, Crisis and the State*, London: New Left Books, p. 41. Originally cited in Larry Wortzel, *Class in China: Stratification in a Classless Society*, Westport: Greenwood Press, 1987, p. 71.

33.   George Konrád and Ivan Szelényi, *The Intellectuals on the Road to Class Power*, New York: Harcourt Brace Jovanovich, 1979.

34.   V.I. Lenin, "What Is to Be Done? Burning Questions of Our Movement," *CW*, Moscow: Progress Publishers, 1964, vol. 5, pp. 375–376.

35.   Goldman, *China's Intellectuals*, p. 25. See also Ding Xueliang, *The Decline of Communism*, pp. 38–39.

are replaced by moves to give them more influence over policy the symbiotic relationship between the two elites is underscored and their distinctive character becomes more elusive.

In the late 1970s and early 1980s the convergence of interest between Party leaders and intellectuals on education policy also made the application of Bukharinist-Trotskyte views on the origins of a new class problematic. The latters' focus on the education-culture cleavage would validate Mao's approach to education and undermine the legitimacy of the changes brought about since 1977. A basic characteristic of the reformed educational structure was its bifurcated and elitist nature. A small number of keypoint schools and universities funded by the state and under the administration of the Education Commission received the best teachers and resources, while ordinary and vocational schools offered an inferior substitute to a majority.[36] Stanley Rosen argued that the two educational tracks, which afforded increasingly scarce opportunities for crossover, would produce a small elite of highly skilled and educated professionals while the remainder would have to settle for vocational, nonformal education or none at all. The resultant division of labor would confine the majority of the population to agricultural and vocational occupations and guarantee highly paid prestigious urban jobs to a chosen few.[37]

While the early Bolsheviks stressed education as a means to political democratization, and the Maoists aimed at eliminating class and status distinctions through an increasingly accessible education of uniform quality, Dengist educational reforms focused primarily on the achievement of economic modernization. The chronological priority accorded to the development of the productive forces translated into a perceived need for a highly trained technocratic sector at the expense of intergroup, interclass, and interregional mobility. The official claim that intellectuals and state cadres along with manual laborers constituted a single class of workers without antagonistic interests overlooked the fact that the reformed

36.   Elizabeth D. Krup, "The Maoist Influence on Current Educational Policy in China," MA thesis, University of Michigan, 1987, p. 34. I am grateful to Professor Donald Munro for this reference.

37.   Stanley Rosen, "Recentralization, Decentralization and Rationalization: Deng Xiaoping's Bifurcated Education Policy," *Modern China*, vol. 2, no. 3 (1985), pp. 302–303. Also cited in Krup, p. 34.

education system helped to enhance rather than restrict the mental/manual, worker/intellectual, rural/urban distinction. Justifications for higher pay and better living standards for intellectuals only reinforced the traditional view that mental labor was more valuable and prestigious than manual labor.[38]

The significance of differential access to education in systems where the power, position, and privileges enjoyed by the elite cannot be transferred legally to its heirs has been noted by many contemporary scholars, Marxist as well as non-Marxist. Paul Sweezy singled out privileged access to education as "probably the most important way in which the bureaucracy reproduces itself as a class."[39] Consequently, in the managerial-bureaucratic stage, which generally followed the displacement of the mass-mobilizational change strategies of revolutionary elites, it was difficult to sustain any critique of a bureaucratic class without involving the intelligentsia. In the immediate post-Mao period, the vulnerability of both Party cadres and intellectuals to the charge that they were a class information can be identified as an important reason for the increasing preference for a de-emphasis of the concept. However, the post-Mao coalition's rejection of the concept of a new exploiting class was selectively dogmatic. The assumption of working-class "dominance" in China reflected a "fetishism" for legality rather than fact, but it was crucial for the argument that since intellectuals and bureaucrats are not distinctive classes they must either form part of the working class or be considered in its service. Such a theoretical resolution of the class issue still left other basic problems unresolved. Of foremost importance among these was the need perceived by leading intellectuals to ensure that intra-elite differences on ideological and policy-related matters would no longer be settled by recourse to violence and coercive intimidation as in the preceding period. In a reformed socialist society where rationality demanded "experts in command" and the educational system ensured their reproduction as a group, the strengthened position of the intelligentsia required additional assurances against future

---

38. Xue Muqiao, *China's Socialist Economy*, p. 280.
39. Paul Sweezy, "Towards a Programme of Studies on the Transition to Socialism," in Paul Sweezy and Charles Bettelheim, *On the Transition to Socialism*, New York: Monthly Review Press, 1972, pp. 123–135.

reversals of policy, and legal-constitutional safeguards for physical security and professional autonomy.

For individuals like Liu Binyan who saw themselves as the "conscience of the Party" and as representatives of the general interest (both in the tradition of the scholar literati as well as the more modern self-image as the voice of society), the need to reflect the reality of bureaucratic abuse of power was linked to the broader attempt to renew the legitimacy of the ruling elite. These intellectuals rejected the roles assigned to them by political leaders in favor of an "empirical revisionism," which provided a "mirror image" of society rather than camouflaging its dark side. The need to explain bureaucratic excesses and abuse of power, without recourse to class categories, lead to an interest in the norms and structure of feudalism and the discussions on the Asiatic Mode of Production and Oriental Despotism where the link between property relations and bureaucratic authority was less direct and clear-cut. The early Soviet emphasis on cultural backwardness as an explanation for autocracy and political despotism was also echoed in the mid- and late-1980s debates on culture and the renewed popularity of May Fourth themes of Enlightenment values versus the backward traditional culture of China's peasant society.

The focus on themes such as alienation and humanism by intellectuals like Wang Ruoshui, Ru Xin, Gao Ertai, and Zhou Yang stemmed logically from their need to address the problem of bureaucratism theoretically and to probe the significance of their own experiences as well as that of their colleagues without reference to the concept of class. The allure of Marx's early works lay precisely in their philosophical orientation and lack of economic or sociological determinism. In *The Critique of Hegel's Philosophy of Right* Marx extended the concept of alienation and reification to bureaucratic administration but, as Alan Swingewood points out, " . . . at this stage of Marx's development there was no theory of class domination, and bureaucracy is depicted as standing above class interest."[40] In his later writings, Marx retained his concern with alienation as well as his conception of the quasi-independent nature of the bureaucracy but linked them concretely to the domination of private capital and an extended division of labor.

40. Swingewood, *Marx and Modern Social Theory*, p. 152.

Theorists of alienation and humanism chose selectively from Marx those elements that served their own interests and those of their patrons. For Marx, the division of labor was as important a reason for alienation as the existence of commodity relations and private capital. Many reformist intellectuals, on the other hand, basking in the new appreciation of their specialized knowledge, and the claim that intellectual creativity was replacing simple labor and capital as the source of value, were more concerned with intellectual and political alienation while tracing alienation in the economic realm simply to "stupid mistakes in economic construction."[41] It was also significant and telltale that theorists like Wang Ruoshui accepted only two of Marx's three prescriptions for the safeguarding of the workers' state from bureaucratization—the right to elect and recall and the right to supervise. Marx's suggestion that salaries of state functionaries be kept deliberately low to preclude individuals from seeking such positions for pecuniary gain was rejected by Wang. In line with the new preference for material incentives over normative ones and in the spirit of "distribution according to quantity and *quality* of work" Wang stated, ". . . nowadays it is, of course, impractical to require leading cadres to receive the wages of common workers as in the Paris Commune. But we should adopt their spirit and oppose the extension of privilege."[42]

Hu Qiaomu and Deng Liqun understood better than their opponents the implications of the new theorizing and their attempt to rein in such themes during the "anti-spiritual pollution" campaign and in 1987–88 when the debate was resurrected was not surprising.[43] If the writings on alienation aimed at displacing the idea of class, from their perspective, this was not simply a drastic revision of Marxism, but also translated into a repudiation of the role of the Party as the medium of class expression in postcapitalist society. Moderate political leaders were in favor of muting emphasis on class distinctions and conflict but could not support a displacement of

41.   Zhou Yang, "A Probe Into Some Theoretical Problems of Marxism," *RMRB*, 16 March 1983, pp. 4–5.

42.   Quoted in David Kelly, "Wang Ruoshui and Socialist Alienation," in Goldman, et al., ed., *China's Intellectuals and the State*, Cambridge: Harvard Contemporary China Series, 3 1987, p. 167.

43.   *Xin Qimeng*, nos, 1, 2, 4 (1988). Wang Ruoshui, "The Cult of the Individual and Intellectual Alienation," *Jingbao*, April 1988, p. 24–27, and May 1988, pp. 40–44.

the concept of class altogether by an "abstract affirmation" of the individual subject or human being. On the other hand, if the conception of alienation as understood by Wang, et al., encompassed the significance of class divisions, its application to present-day Chinese society implied the continued existence of exploitative relations. Reformist writings were by no means clear on these points. Gao Ertai accused Lin Biao and the Gang of Four for conducting a "campaign of establishing appropriation over property in the name of opposing the concept of private property in a socialist setting."[44] According to Gao, the "Lin Jiang crowd" had "replaced proletarian dictatorship with feudal despotism and substituted feudalism for socialism."[45]

There were striking parallels between the radical reformers' critiques of the alienation of power in socialist societies (as also the late-1980s emphasis on cadre control over public property by Yan Jiaqi and others) with Mao's own attacks on bureaucrats, and one has to recall that for all the fuss about "capitalist roaders" during and after the Cultural Revolution Mao himself remained reluctant to conclude that a bureaucratic class already existed in China.[46] The difference between Mao and the alienation theorists in the early 1980s centered on the means to prevent bureaucratism. Mao's preoccupation with the superstructure and the threat of restoration via a political counterrevolution led to his mass mobilization against the Party and unleashing of the Red Guards. Radical-reformist intellectuals who had witnessed the violence and trauma of the Cultural Revolution, not surprisingly, rejected the "populist and proto-fascist" flavor of ultraleftist "extensive democracy," which had generated fear, distrust, and insecurity at all levels of society, in favor of legal and constitutional checks on abuse of authority.[47]

44. Gao Ertai, "An In-Depth Examination of Alienation," in *"Man Is the Starting Point of Marxism"— A Collection of Articles Discussing Human Nature and Humanism*, Beijing: Renmin chubanshe, 1981, pp. 72–98. Also translated in *Chinese Studies in Philosophy*, Fall 1993, p. 26.
45. Quotes from pp. 7 and 20 of *CSP* translation.
46. David Kelly, however, believes that Hu Qiaomu's comparison of Wang's "public servants turning into masters" with Cultural Revolutionary slogans was misplaced. See *China's Intellectuals and the State*, p. 167. For Brugger and Kelly's views on the comparison between the 1960s and 1980s positions, see also *Chinese Marxism*, pp. 147–159.
47. Cao Siyuan referred to the Cultural Revolution as an example of "anarchic democracy." See "Thoughts on the Reform of the NPC," *FBIS*, 23 November 1984, p. 23.

The demands for a "highly civilized, highly democratized society" voiced by an overwhelming majority of reformist intellectuals drew on Marx's prescription that bureaucratism in a socialist state would be eliminated by political democratization. The need for institutionalization and political reform had been similarly perceived by the Soviet and Eastern European intelligentsia as a guarantee against the Stalinist era. Konrád and Szelényi have pointed out that, unlike the Party leadership whose political hegemony is threatened by democratization intellectuals, as a group the intelligentsia stands to benefit by the extension of civil and political freedoms that release it from the control of the former and permit it to legitimately and directly pursue its group interests.[48] Alvin Gouldner who also has referred to intellectuals as a class rather than a stratum, argues:

> The political and economic interests of the new class then are uniquely dependent on their continuing access to media, particularly mass media, and upon institutional freedoms protecting their right to publish and speak. Impairment of these rights—that is censorship—is a basic liability in the New Class's effort to advance itself. Since its ascendence depends greatly on its access to free communication, its opposition to censorship is one of the main struggles that has *united* it historically, as in the period prior to the French Revolution. Indeed, New Class opposition to censorship cross cuts both East and West. . . . It is here, in its opposition to censorship, that the partisan class interests of the New Class coincide with universal interests in public rationality [emphasis in original].[49]

One does not have to accept Gouldner's definition of intellectuals as a class to appreciate the fact that in the first phase the unwillingness of leading intellectuals to support the Wall writers' demands for full-scale democratization stemmed from their self-identification as a part of the elite, their congruence of interests with the reformist political leaders, and perception of dependency upon the latter. Unlike the "marginal intellectuals" (to use Ding Xueliang's term), who comprised the Wall movement, establishment intellectuals relied upon political patrons for improvements

---

48. Konrad and Szelenyi, *Intellectuals on the Road to Class Power*, p. 231–232.
49. Alvin Gouldner, *The Future of Intellectuals and the Rise of the New Class*, New York: The Seabury Press, 1979, p. 64.

in their material status, protection of their professional autonomy, career advancement, and access to the policy-making process.

By the mid- and late 1980s the recurrent cycles of intellectual relaxation and persecution that resulted from moderate opposition to liberalization and the radical-reformist leadership's priority of economic over political reform, along with the willingness of reformist patrons to sacrifice their intellectual clients in the interests of stability and unity had highlighted the shortcomings of such dependency and "alliances."[50] The vulnerability of the reformist patrons themselves as demonstrated in Hu Yaobang's dismissal in 1986, and the attacks on Zhao Ziyang in 1988 and early 1989, further strengthened intellectual preference for "procedural politics" and formal institutional checks against arbitrary exercise of power.[51]

Disenchantment in the political arena was matched by dissatisfaction with the failed materialization of anticipated improvements in material and economic standing. Hyperinflation in the latter part of the 1980s hit particularly hard those groups with fixed incomes like intellectuals. The 1988 Global Membership discussions in the *World Economic Herald*, which assessed the performance of the Chinese economy within a global context, pointed to the continuing low investment in education, and contrasted the inadequate funds for intellectual salaries and educational infrastructure to the phenomenal rise in official spending on cars, guest houses, and other amenities for party-state cadres.[52] Privileged access to education, moreover, increasingly appeared of little value in the newly emergent partially privatized economy where the incomes of barbers, cab drivers, and hotel waitresses far exceeded those of most intellectuals.

The dissolution of intellectual ties with the bureaucratic elite was assisted by the opportunities for other linkups, which emerged in the

50. Hu Yaobang's inability or reluctance to save Hu Jiwei, Wang Ruoshui, Li Honglin, and Ruan Ming in 1983–84 was repeated in Zhao Ziyang's acquiescence to the disciplining of Liu Binyan, Su Shaozhi, and Zhang Xianyang in 1987, see Ding Xueliang, p. 43.

51. Yan Jiaqi, "From 'Non-Procedural' to Procedural Politics." Su Shaozhi and Wang Yizhou, "Two Historic Tasks of Reform," *RMRB*, 5 March 1988, p. 5. Su Shaozhi, "Some Problems of the Political Reform in China," *China Information*, vol 3, no. 2, Autumn 1988, p. 36.

52. Ding Xueliang, *The Decline of Communism*, pp. 153–154. Also Richard Kraus, "The Lament of Astrophysicist Fang Lizhi: China's Intellectuals in a Global Context," in Dirlik and Meisner, ed., *Marxism and the Chinese Experience*, pp. 294–315.

mid-1980s and expanded later in the decade with increasing administrative and economic decentralization. In his discussion of "institutional parasitism" Ding Xueliang has demonstrated how independent-minded official intellectuals were able to appropriate the resources of government agencies and their own units by both "regular and irregular" means[53] to expand their networks of personal relations, and establish quasi-voluntary associations that boosted the dissemination of their ideas and enhanced their security within a cohort of like-minded associates.[54] New profit-oriented presses contributed to the proliferation of *tongren* (cliquish) journals and book series, which facilitated publication relatively free of bureaucratic intervention and censorship as well as financial independence.

The emergence of a group of successful and ambitious industrial and commercial entrepreneurs also provided intellectuals with a new additional source of funding and sponsorship. Think tanks like The Capital Institute for Research on Legal Systems and Social Development (sponsored by the Capital Steel and Iron Company) and the Stone Institute for Research on Social Development were among the most well-known examples of the link between business and intellectuals, but managers of smaller enterprises (state and nonstate) were also increasingly eager to resort to innovative advertising by offering financial rewards for a favorable mention in publications and reports.[55]

The social and economic problems that surfaced from 1985 onward elicited divergent interpretations from the moderate and radical camps. The former linked them to the growth of commodity relations and the erosion of socialist ethics, while the latter now looked to the concentration of political and economic power as the root cause of the distortions

---

53. For his discussion of "small treasuries" and "falsification of accounts" see *The Decline of Communism*, pp. 72–75.

54. The rising sense of group consciousness and solidarity was evident in the resistance to and non-cooperation with criticism and persecution initiatives against their colleagues during the Anti-Spiritual Pollution and Bourgeois Liberalization Campaigns.

55. Ding, pp. 65–76; Dorothy Solinger, "Urban Entrepreneurs and the State," pp. 121–141; Connie Squire Meaney, "Market Reform in a Leninist System: Some Trends in the Distribution of Power, Strategy and Money in Urban China," *Studies in Comparative Communism*, vol. 22, nos. 2–3 (1989), pp. 203–220.

in the developing-market economy. In the face of a resurgent moderate initiative, which threatened to derail the reform process discussions on bureaucratism, returned to the radical-reformist intellectual agenda with a new sense of urgency from 1986–89.

As witnessed in the discussions related to the proletarian dictatorship in this phase the political superstructure came to be seen as the major obstacle to economic reform. Theorists like Su Shaozhi and Wang Yizhou picked up once again the themes of feudalism and the small-producer economy that had dominated discussions during the Theory Conference and this time around followed through on the logical implications of those arguments. The link between political power and economic control, which had been denied with the rejection of the concept of a "bureaucrat class," now assumed a central role in the explanations for continuing problems within the system.[56]

Falling back again on the base-superstructure relationship stressed within the orthodox Marxist tradition, Su and Wang now argued that the predominance of small-scale production in the traditional economy along with the strength of the small-producer class within the ranks of the victorious CCP brought about a reconstitution of feudal relations within the "form" of a socialist state. The bureaucratic structure of the proletarian dictatorship with its patron-client relations, lack of functioning democracy, cliques, tyrannical cults of personality, attachment to nepotism, and privilege continued the tradition of feudal despotism.[57] The "feudal" socialist superstructure in turn fostered a command economy, which replicated the pattern of a traditional economy by obstructing the commercialization of agriculture (despite concentration of land in collectives), and promoting large-scale industrial production, which continued to be managed in a vertical-feudal mode with detailed decisions on production, marketing, and investment made at the top.

56. Zhang Weiguo, "Whither the State Ownership System?" *Shijie jingji daobao*, 3 April 1989, p. 10, *FBIS*, 25 April 1989, pp. 48–49.

57. Su Shaozhi, " Political Structural Reform and the Opposition to Feudal Influences," *RMRB*, 14 August 1986; Su and Wang Yizhou, "Several Problems Concerning Political Structural Reform," *Baike zhishi*, no. 1 (1987), pp. 2–5; Jiang Siyi, "Eliminating the Evil Legacy of Feudalism Is An Important Task," *RMRB*, 1 August 1986; Tian Jujian, "Feudal Remnants Must Be Analyzed in Depth," *RMRB*, 13 September 1986.

Yan Jiaqi and Zhang Xianyang pointed to the "combination of Party-state economy" as the cause of the total subordination of society to the Party-state. The totalistic structure of the Party-state with its monopolistic control, they pointed out, had created a "stratum" of "bureaucratic privilege" and "special interests," which resisted change that would undermine its dominance.[58]

The discussions on bureaucracy in the late 1980s reversed the positions adopted by reformist leaders in the immediate post-Mao phase when they distinguished between legal ownership rights and control over state property and economy and denied the exploitative character of the bureaucracy. The new assertion of a "bureaucratic stratum" with "total control over society" essentially vindicated the views of ultraleftists as well as Democracy Wall writers like Chen Erjin and Wang Xizhe. However, there was a crucial difference between the radical-reformist intellectual position and that of the other two groups. For the latter the bureaucracy was an obstacle to the attainment of socialism. For radical-reformist intellectuals, on the other hand, the bureaucratic stratum had become the main impediment to the establishment of a capitalist society.

The new class–state capitalist contention that the "bureaucratic class" or "bourgeoisie within the Party" could bring about an authentically new exploitative mode of production was indeed supported by the new analyses, which focused on bureaucratic manipulation of the partially privatized economy.[59] Party-state functionaries' privileged and monopolist access to and control over material resources, capital base, licensing, etc., along with connections and networks put them in a unique position to exploit the opportunities afforded them from economic liberalization. The beneficiaries of halfway economic reform were the bureaucrat capitalists whose new-found channels for amassing wealth would be undermined by a return to the structures, norms, and values of the planned socialist economy, whereas a transition to a complete market, i.e, a full-fledged capitalist restoration would deny them their special inside tracks.

58. Zhang Weiguo, "Whither State Ownership," Yan Jiaqi interview with Wen Yuankai; Zhang Xianyang, "Marxism, Reflection and Transcendence," Su Shaozhi, "Feudal Remnants Block China's Path," *China Daily*, 22 July 1986.

59. Chen Yizi, Wang Xiaoqiang, and Li Jun, "The Deep-Seated Questions and the Strategic Choices China's Reform Faces," *Fazhan yu gaige*, no. 4 (1989), pp. 3–9.

At a symposium on the "crisis of state ownership" Wang Yizhou pointed out, "the privileged treatment for those vested beneficiaries does not come from membership dues, but from the monopoly of state ownership."[60] According to Yan Jiaqi, the monopolization of all resources within state ownership was the root cause of corruption and distortion in a society moving toward the market, and the integration of cadre and capitalist needed to be arrested by the introduction of private property and competition.[61]

For Su Shaozhi, Wang Ruoshui, Zhang Xianyang, and others, the rationale for a "deepening of economic reform" now emerged from their perception of the compatibility of political democracy with commodity relations. The concept of "totalism" was aimed at undermining the validity of Deng's "anti-left in economics and anti-right in politics," which translated into support for economic pluralism and resistance to political liberalization. Their arguments for political leaders like Deng and Zhao Ziyang emphasized the instrumental rationality of political reform in facilitating the emergence of a "genuine" market.[62] Rebutting moderate arguments against privatization and contending that the problem with China was "too much feudalism, not too much capitalism" reformist articles during this period emphasized the accomplishments of a commodity economy over a feudal one. In place of the dependent vertical interaction of feudal economic relations the commodity economy introduced "free exchange of products among equal producers." The "equality of opportunity" within the commodity economy promoted "free movement of labor," "fair exchange of value" as the principle underlying the division of labor and the emergence of independent economic interests. Ideas of equality, fairness, and diverse interests translated in the political sphere into democracy and pluralism.[63]

60. See Zhang Weiguo, "Whither the State Ownership System?" *Shijie jingji daobao,* 3 April 1989, p. 10, *FBIS,* 25 April 1989, pp. 48–49. Also Goldman, p. 273.

61. *Daobao,* 11 November and 4 December 1988.

62. Ding Xueliang, "The Disparity Between Idealistic and Instrumental Chinese Reformers," *Asian Survey,* vol. XXVIII, no. 11 (1988), pp. 1117–39.

63. Su Shaozhi, "Remarks at the *Hongqi* Symposium on 'Building Socialism With Chinese Characteristics,'" *Hongqi,* no. 14 (1986); Liu Shiding, "Political Structural Reform Must Be Coordinated With Economic Structural Reform," *Minzhu yu Fazhi,* no. 8 (1986), pp. 20–21.

The novelty of such arguments at this time was the discussion of commodity relations or the market economy and liberal democracy in terms of the progressive, civilizing influence of the bourgeoisie or middle class in history. Class, as a positive concept, found its way back into the dominant discourse, although in an inversion of the ultraleftist position. In rectifying the bias of official Marxist accounts of capitalist democracy such idealist conceptions went to the other extreme. The new alignment of the intelligentsia with the emerging entrepreneurial class meant that the interests of both groups were articulated as universal interests of public rationality.

Prior to the events of 1989 the solution to rule by the bureaucracy for most radical reformers was elite democracy. Li Honglin, Yu Haocheng, Su Shaozhi, and Hu Jiwei were a minority who extended the application of democratic rights to workers and peasants. Most of their colleagues concentrated on pointing out that in a society that lacked "a middle class and modernizing forces, intellectuals' modern consciousness and values were a priceless source of the modern spirit."[64] Fang Lizhi, who rejected Marxism completely and advocated wholesale Westernization, argued that education, training, and professional skills were the criteria for participation in policy making and politics. Intellectuals, Fang maintained, were an "independent stratum occupying a leading place," while the broad masses of the peasantry were not quite ready for democracy. He invited his audience to

. . . go travel in the villages and look around: I feel those uneducated peasants, living under traditional influence, have a psychological consciousness that is very deficient. It is very difficult to instill a democratic consciousness in them, they still demand an honest and upright official; without an official they are uncomfortable.[65]

One can also note in passing that radical reformers as a group throughout this period did not hesitate to deny their moderate rivals the right to publish and express themselves in journals and newspapers under their control.[66] Ding Xueliang points out that many institutions and

64. Ding, Xuching, *The Decline of Communism in China: Legitimacy Crisis, 1978–1989.* Cambridge: Cambridge University Press, 1994, p. 180.
65. "Conversation of Fang Lizhi With Wen Hui and Ming Lei," *Zhengming*, no. 117 (1987), p. 20. Originally quoted in Kraus, "The Lament of Astrophysicist Fang Lizhi."
66. For complaints by moderate ideologists in this connection see *Hongqi*, no. 3 (1987), pp. 2 and 24.

journals had acquired a cliquish (*tongren*) character, "although still 'public' in name, they were almost closed to people with disparate political preferences."[67]

The new analyses of a totalist state that blocked the emergence of a market-based liberal democratic system along with an exacerbating economic crisis brought on by skyrocketing inflation (unofficially estimated at 50 percent and triggered off by the decontrol of urban food and commodity prices in May 1988) and a renewed inner-party confrontation produced a rift in the radical-reformist camp. Faced with the prospect of an intensified moderate offensive against Zhao Ziyang, Zhao advisers, Wu Jiaxiang (a fellow in the Investigation and Research Division of the General Office of the Party Central Committee), Chen Yizi, Wang Xiaoqiang, and Li Jun (director, deputy director, and fellow at the Institute for Research on the Economic System Reform under the State Council) along with intellectuals like Zhang Bingjiu, Yang Baikui, and Xiao Gongqing put forward a theory of "neo-authoritarianism" as a way out of the decentralization/recentralization, reform/crisis/reform cycle.[68] Against Hu Jiwei, Su Shaozhi, Yan Jiaqi, and Yu Haocheng, who argued for immediate democratization as a solution, Yang and others proposed a "new enlightened despotism" to guide the transition to a full-fledged market economy and political democracy.[69] As a theory "neo-authoritarianism" was claimed by its advocates to be committed to political and economic liberalism, thus the basic difference between themselves and their "rival colleagues" centered not on "whether China

67. Ding, *The Decline of Communism*, p. 66.

68. For a detailed treatment of neo-authoritarianism see Stanley Rosen and Gary Zou. eds., The Chinese Debate on the New Authoritarianism," *Chinese Sociology and Anthropology*, Winter 1990–91, Spring 1991, and Summer 1991. Mark Petracca and Meng Xiong, "The Concept of Chinese Neo-Authoritarianism," *Asian Survey*, vol. XXX, no. 11 (November 1990), pp. 1099–1117; Barry Sautman, "Sirens of the Strongman: Neo-Authoritarianism in Recent Chinese Political Theory," *China Quarterly*, no. 129 (March 1992), pp. 77–102; Ting Gong and Feng Chen, "Neo-Authoritarian Theory in Mainland China," *Issues and Studies*, January 1991, pp. 84–98.

69. Yang Baikui, "Democracy and Authority in the Course of Political Development," in *Chinese Sociology and Anthropology*, (*CSA*), vol. 23, no. 3 (Spring 1991), pp. 67–80; Dai Qing, "From Lin Zexu to Jiang Jingguo," in *CSA*, vol. 23, no. 3 (Spring 1991), pp. 61–66.

should develop a market economy and democracy but on how those goals should be achieved."[70]

Although their individual analyses and specific prescriptions varied, somewhat, all proponents of neo-authoritarianism agreed that pluralist democracy could only be the "result of reform in China, not its precondition."[71] The preference for a market economy stemmed from the perceived weaknesses of the planned economy and consequences for both economics and politics. Neo-authoritarians agreed with other radical reformers that "vague and unclear property-rights relationships" embodied in state ownership prevented the effective utilization of productive property and obscured social responsibilities and the pursuit of individual interests.[72] In theory, the state represented society in possessing and managing the means of production but, in actual practice, public property was carved into "vertical strips and horizontal blocks" and fell under the ownership of departments, units, and localities.[73] More often than not, state ownership tended to degenerate either into "individual bureaucratic ownership" or the "feudal warlords' economy" which turned competition into "civil wars" among governmental departments.[74]

Echoing the "totalist" argument neo-authoritarians also pointed out that the complex macroeconomic regulation required by a planned economy produced an intense concentration of power in the state and a politicization

70. Wu Jiaxiang and Zhang Bingjiu, "Radical Democracy or Stable Democracy?" *GMRB*, 31 March (1989), p. 3; Wu Jiaxiang, "An Outline for Studying the New Authoritarianism," Xiao Gongqin and Zhu Wei, "A Painful Dilemma: A Dialogue on the Theory of 'New Authoritarianism,'" *Wenhuibao*, 17 January (1989), p. 4; Zhang Bingjiu, "The Progress and Coordination Between Economic and Political System Reform," in *The New Authoritarianism*. edited by Liu Jin and Li Lin, Beijing: Beijing Institute of Economics Press, 1989, pp. 1–26.

71. Xiao Gongqin, "On Transformative Authoritarianism; in *The New Authoritarianism*". Yang Baikui, "Democracy and Authority;" Cao Yuanzheng, "The Model of the Market Economy Under a 'Soft Government,'" and "The Model of the Market Economy Under a 'Hard Government,'" in *CSA*, vol. 23, no. 3. (Spring 1991), pp. 24–31 and 32–38.

72. Rong Jian, "Does China Need an Authoritarian Political System in the Course of Modernization?" *CSA*, Winter 1990–91, p. 62.

73. Ibid.

74. Wu Jiaxiang, "The New Authoritarianism: An Express Train Toward Democracy by Building Markets," in *The New Authoritarianism* pp. 39–46.

and bureaucratization of the entire society. The interests and demands of various classes, strata, and groups could be reflected only through a single political channel, and political clout became the "most effective and convenient shortcut" for the pursuit of economic and other interests. The "dualism (separation) of politics and economics" was necessary not only for promoting vitality, competition, and dynamism in the economy, but also for undermining bureaucratic manipulation of "supraeconomic coercion mechanisms" to exercise extraordinary interference in all spheres of society.

The operation of a full-fledged market would "reduce to a minimum the scope of public power and the number of public decisions."[75] The emergence of autonomous and organized economic interests premised on equality, mutual benefit, and contractual relations in a privatized economy would undermine the fusion of politics and economics, and contribute to the "pluralization and contractualization" of the political sphere. For neo-authoritarians the key to success was the sequence of development. Immediate introduction of democracy as suggested by Hu Jiwei, Su Shaozhi, Yan Jiaqi, and others would be inefficient and prolong the transition to market relations. Firstly, in a society characterized by a weak market and imprecise delineation of rights and responsibilities, the "transactional political costs" would go up tremendously as more and more people would seek political power for economic benefit.[76] Secondly, the emergence of a healthy market would be obstructed by the "delinquent behavior" of vested interests. According to Wu Jiaxiang, "The consumer would want to avoid the higher prices of the open commodity and labor-services markets and seek the lower-priced or free-of-charge products and labor services of the internal market." The "laborer would want to avoid the labor market" and become an "imperial worker" with a "guaranteed income regardless of whether there is a drought or a flood, and one who stands on other people's shoulders." The coexistence of a multitrack system of fixed labor, contract labor, and temporary or part-time labor was identified by Wu as a natural result of "market avoidance."[77]

---

75. Yang Baikui, "Democracy and Authority in the Course of Political Development," p. 74.
76. Wu Jiaxiang, "Express Train," p. 40.
77. Ibid.

Such resistance to the market on the part of political constituencies would promote wavering and indecisive leaderships reluctant to use "coercive force" to guide and push the whole society from tradition into modernity. For Yang Baikui, "coercive guidance or propulsion" could only come from a "modernization-oriented social group consisting primarily of the modern industrialist and commercial circles as well as groups of intellectuals who possess the consciousness of modernity." Wang Juntao proposed a cabinet composed of technocrats, elite intellectuals, and political leaders in favor of free enterprise. Wang Xiaoqiang, who in the late 1970s had traced the origins of ultraleftist tyranny to the yearning for a savior or an emperor on the part of the ignorant peasant masses, joined Chen Yizi and Li Jun in supporting the demand for "enlightened despotism" or "elite democracy."[78] Still contemptuous of the "backwardness of the economic and educational standards of the vast majority of the masses" Wang and his colleagues argued in favor of elite politics" in which a "power elite" and an "intellectual elite" would "occupy the positions of leadership, represent the masses," and oversee the transition to a market economy and liberal democracy. Since the foundation of a stable liberal democratic order was a solid middle class of property owners the basic task of the new authority was to create the conditions for the emergence of such a class.

Although the liberal democrats were quick to point out empirical weaknesses and historical inaccuracies in neo-authoritarian arguments there was indeed a remarkable congruence of views between the two groups.[79] The arguments of neo-authoritarianism were a logical culmination of the ideological evolution set in motion with the epistemology debates and the critiques of ultraleftist voluntarism. The emphasis on economic determinism and the role of productive forces in the discussions on the source of knowledge, feudalism, and the concept of "undeveloped

78.   Chen Yizi, Wang Xiaoqiang, and Li Jun, "The Deep-Seated Questions and the Strategic Choice China's Reform Faces," *Fazhan yu gaige*, no. 4 (1989), pp. 3–9.

79.   For liberal democrat rebuttals see Wang Yizhou, "Why We Cannot Agree With the New Authoritarianism," *CSA*, vol. 23, no. 4 (Summer 1991), pp. 56–66; Yu Haocheng, "Does China Need the New Authoritarianism?" Also in *CSA*, pp. 44–55; Qin Xiaoying, "Escaping from a Historical Cycle," also in *CSA*, pp. 7–30; Huang Wansheng, "A Dialogue on the Critiques of the New Authoritarianism," *Wenhuibao*, 22 February 1989.

socialism" continued to be favored by leaders like Deng and Zhao and
was reinforced by the newer analyses that accompanied the expansion of
reform through the next decade. By drawing attention to the issues of
intellectual and political alienation or emphasizing subjectivity theorists
like Wang Ruoshui and Li Zehou tried to maintain a balance between the
economic determinist and voluntarist anthropomorphic strands within
the Marxist tradition even as they abandoned basic tenets such as class
conflict, class dictatorship, and even the common ownership of productive property. The adoption of the "primary stage of socialism" thesis
marked, however, the triumph of economic determinism and by consign-
ing the goal of socialist society to a very distant horizon it paved the way
for theories marginalizing teleological concerns and rationalizing the
immediate and complete transition to a market economy.

Neo-authoritarianism was an attractive theory for incumbent leaderships like those of Zhao Ziyang and Deng Xiaoping with their emphasis
on political control and stability, and instrumental approach to socialism
as well as capitalism. The opposition of intellectuals like Su Shaozhi and
Wang Ruoshui stemmed, in no small measure, from their personal experience of continued persecution in the reformist era and their unwillingness
to continue to settle for the rule of men, no matter how enlightened,
rather than the rule of law. In the decade from 1979 to 1989 Chinese intellectuals—radical and liberal reformers, neo-authoritarians, and democrats—had gone from being allies of a reforming Communist leadership
to champions and spokespersons for themselves as a group, and for
emerging industrial and commercial interests.

During and after the Tiananmen crackdown both neo-authoritarians
and liberal democrats were punished or exiled for advocating a "peaceful
evolution to capitalism." The evolution continued in to the 1990s, nevertheless, on its own momentum and with the support of Deng Xiaoping.
The political agenda of liberal democracy suffered a setback and, ironically, the arguments for shutting the door on political democratization
were reminiscent of Fang Lizhi and his colleagues:

> China should also take into account . . . its people's limited capacity to
> withstand political and psychological strains . . . and their lack of democra-
> tic practice, experience, and habit. . . . When many people are still preoc-

cupied by the daily toil of basic survival, it is impossible to expect from them a high degree of democratic participation.[80]

Conclusion

The discussions on bureaucratism, which began in the early post-Mao era in China, aimed at addressing the issue of arbitrary Party rule, particularly in terms of its consequences for intellectuals as a group. The common categorization of intellectuals and bureaucrats and state cadres within the Marxist tradition made it expedient for both groups to reject the thesis of a new class in socialist societies. Discussions on bureaucracy in the late 1970s and early 1980s, similar to those on bourgeois right and the economic determinants of class, were dominated by a concern to affirm that China's socialist development had not been sabotaged by the emergence of a new privileged elite. The violence of the Cultural Revolution and its legacy had served temporarily to solidify the comfortable notion of progressive linear development and rendered distasteful any cynical theories of regression and restoration, which came disturbingly close to vindicating Mao's theses on continuing revolution in "socialist society."

The renewed focus in the mid-1980s on feudal despotism, totalism, and bureaucratic control over the economy demonstrated that official protestations, notwithstanding, Mao's successors did not really succeed in marginalizing his concerns regarding the reemergence of exploitative groups in postrevolutionary society. The ideological debates on social theory, which began in the late 1970s and continued through the late 1980s, not only revealed the limitations and ambiguities in the moderate and radical-reformist critique of leftism, but also vindicated Mao's preoccupation with bureaucratic degeneration, capitalist restoration, and the disaffection of the intelligentsia. By the mid- and late 1980s not only had the Chinese economy advanced well on the road to privatization, but the radical-reformist intelligentsia had moved aggressively to claim the institutional and politi-

80. Zheng Wen, "China Can Never Copy Wholesale the Western Democratic System," *Jingji ribao*, 18 July 1989, p. 3; *FBIS*, 4 August 1989, p.24; Wang Guofa, "Democracy Should Not Go Beyond Social Development," *Liaowang*, 7 August 1989, p. 17; *FBIS*, 21 August 1989, pp. 32–33.

cal space created by reform and emerged as a counter elite (to use Ding XueLiang's term) with impressive resources and an agenda of its own. The articulation of its own interests and those of the emerging entrepreneurial class dominated intellectual discourse during this time and contributed effectively to undermine the legitimacy of the Party and erode the fragile ideological consensus that Deng Xiaoping had hammered out with a series of opportunistic compromises in the past decade.

SIX

Conclusion

Ideological developments in the immediate post-Mao era were comparable to and reminiscent of developments in the international Communist movement in the wake of the historic Twentieth Congress of the CPSU. Khrushchev's denunciation and exposure of the grim realities of the Stalinist era marked a watershed, but as far as leaderships and political regimes were concerned, de-Stalinization delivered much less than one had been led to expect. For Marxist intellectuals, though, both in the East and the West, it was the beginning of a period of creativity, intellectual liberation, and reconstruction, prompted by critical questioning of orthodoxy and a new interest in other non-Marxist intellectual traditions.[1]

Ideological reorientation in China began with an easing of restrictions on party intellectuals under the sponsorship of the new General Secretary Hu Yaobang. Given Deng Xiaoping's limitations as a theoretician, or his lack of interest in the finer aspects of ideological discourse, the task of revitalization and of charting the premises of the new course devolved entirely on a broad base of theoretical workers. The intellectual pluralism made possible by this was enhanced by the divisions within the leadership on the questions of the extent and direction of further reform and reassessment of previous policies. The precise extent of freedom and autonomy characterizing debate and discussion varied with periods of liberalization, alternating with demands for conformity. Nevertheless, in the decade and a half or so after the return of Deng Xiaoping, the diverse and voluminous amount of theoretical activity that had resulted from the effort to explain the significance of the Chinese experience in constructing socialism was being compared by observers and participants alike in scale and intensity to the May Fourth Movement.

1. Benton, *The Rise and Fall of Structural Marxism*, p. 3.

The attempt to fashion a new ideological consensus within the Party was essentially a failure. The campaign on practice—conceived to validate an entirely new set of priorities and policies early on—exposed the cleavage within the post-Mao coalition between "upholders" and "developers" of Marxism, i.e., those who would attempt a restructuring of the Marxist-Leninist-Stalinist-Maoist legacy without abandoning its basic assumptions, and others who preferred to move on to a new paradigm of relativism for understanding "facts." For the former, relativism was no solution for the need was a "seal of scientific authority" to authenticate their selection of some doctrinal tenets over others. The extent of their commitment to a slogan such as "practice is the sole criterion of truth" was illustrated in the enunciation of the Four Cardinal Principles that established boundaries for debate which could be entirely arbitrary.

The position of the rival group of theorists was, of course, the more interesting and significant, because it signaled an intent to remove the stigma from "revisionism" and make the idea of revision itself a sign of vitality and theoretical creativity. The orthodox definition of Marxism as a science provided the justification for its supersession by new discoveries and innovations. As intellectuals like Jin Guantao understood it, the development of science was not a continuous process of accumulation of knowledge but a discontinuous and revolutionary one in which earlier conceptions and theories were falsified, rejected, and replaced by new theoretical constructs.[2]

The discussions on practice were, in a real sense, a fertile breeding ground for the skepticism and doubts about the validity and relevance of Marxism, which would be emphasized prominently in the coming decade by Fang Lizhi, Liu Zaifu, and others. For these individuals, Marxism had become an epistemological obstacle, an outmoded perspective that needed to be replaced by newer ones. The motivation of the Chinese leadership in espousing a manifestly irrelevant and obsolete theoretical framework when it appeared to be pressing for innovation on other fronts was at first inexplicable, and, then, inherently suspect.

2. Jin Guantao and Liu Qinfeng, *Explore a Method Which Unites Natural Sciences and Social Sciences*, Shanghai: Shanghai Renmin Chubanshe, 1986, pp. 59.

Radical-reformist attempts to extend the terms of debate were dogged at every step by moderate attempts to contract the agenda.[3] The evolving discussions on voluntarism, the source of knowledge, stages of socialism, classes, and class struggle brought home to the latter the significance of Fan Ruoyu's insistence in early 1978 that revision could not be undertaken piecemeal without estimating the consequences for the entire doctrine. The retreat of Yang Xianzhen, Deng Liqun, Hu Qiaomu, et al., on the question of de-Maoification revealed the complexity of the situation where critiques of Maoist voluntarism and subjectivism, the GLF, and the Cultural Revolution could be logically extended to the pre-liberation period and the Communist Party's path to power, and ultimately socialism itself as a system and model of development.

In the early post-Mao period Su Shaozhi and Feng Lanrui's attempt to locate China in a pre-socialist phase and hence obviate the need to justify economic reform in terms of its compatibility with socialism was a significant development. It reflected the spirit of the debate on practice yet retained the Marxist perspective and remained ideologically defensible. The thesis that China was still a transitional society was not simply a modification of the official Chinese position, but also indicated a new willingness to accept the validity of other Marxist analyses such as the Yugoslav conception of socialism, or the positions adopted by Western Marxists like Bettelheim, Sweezy, and Mandel. In the Chinese context it was a novel, yet theoretically consistent analysis that provided an objective and systematic explanation of CCP errors as well as a justification for the "step backward."

A prominent influence on Su seems to have been the Polish economist, Wlodzimiercz Brus, who has emphasised "the aspect of continuity" between capitalism and socialism.[4] According to Brus, the appearance in capitalist societies of trends such as the regulation of the market, various

3.   Editorial Department, "Communist Ideology and Our Practice," *Hongqi*, No. 17 (1982), pp. 2–8; "Our Banner Is Communism," *Hongqi*, no. 10 (1982), pp. 2–6. Hu Qiaomu, "On the Practice of Communist Ideology," *RMRB*, 24 September 1982. Xiong Fu, "Study the Report to the Twelfth CCP Congress From the High Plane of Communist Ideology," *Hongqi*, no. 18 (1982), pp. 31–43.
4.   Wlodzimiercz Brus, *Socialist Ownership and Political Systems,* London: Routledge and Kegan Paul, 1975, p. 12.

forms of planning, a growing public sector, and state intervention in the economy justify the view that socialism is, "a systemic formation placed further along the trend line, and thus . . . does not appear by chance, but rather as a result of definite development processes."[5] In response to those who, like Joan Robinson, would argue that socialism came to be substituted for capitalism by latecomers to industrialization for the purpose of rapid accumulation, Brus maintains that, "socialism can prove economically rational in less-developed countries not because of but in spite of their immaturity, and the 'jumping of stages' involves a number of negative consequences. It is precisely from the changes taking place in the world of mature capitalism that one can derive, amid zigzags and conflicts, with varying strength in different countries, the continuing tendency toward socialism as the stage logically following capitalism."[6] Needless to say, such an analysis was of immense value to reformers like Su. It provided a critique for the Maoist attempt to make the transition to socialism "in conditions of immaturity"; it also validated the introduction of capitalist features, which continue to be of use in the socialist stage, and asserted a linear progression of history in which backward countries such as China were actually a step ahead, having undergone a proletarian revolution.[7]

Similarly, Wang Ruoshui, Gao Ertai, Ru Xin, and Zhou Yang's explanation of dictatorship and authoritarianism in terms of "alienation of power" in a society "still constructing socialism" was, at the time, neither a violation of Marxism nor necessarily an enunciation of a law of alienation as Hu Qiaomu and Wang Zhen contended.[8] The moderate adherence to Stalinist tenets, however, meant that nationalization was identified with socialization, and alienation was interpreted as a subjective, social, and

---

5. Ibid., p. 11.

6. Ibid., p. 13.

7. For instance, Liao Gailong, unlike Su Shaozhi, continued to assert that China became a socialist society after an accelerated capitalist stage. See "Advance Along the Path of All-Round Construction of Socialism," *Jiaoxue yu yanjiu*, no. 2 (1983), pp. 6–15.

8. Wang Ruoshui, "On the Problem of Alienation," *Xinwen zhanxian*, no. 8 (1980). Ru Xin, "Is Humanism Revisionism?" *RMRB*, 14 August 1980. Zhou Yang, "A Probe Into Some Theoretical Problems of Marxism," *RMRB*, 16 March 1983, pp. 4–5. For Zhou's earlier views see Donald Munro, "The Chinese View of Alienation," *The China Quarterly*, no. 59 (1979), pp. 580–582.

historical category applicable to a capitalist society that would be sublated by historical development and the advent of socialism. For Hu Qiaomu alienation was neither an important tenet of Marxism nor an objectively existing, supra-historical category that could be used to analyze any society, socialist or capitalist.[9]

Hu Qiaomu and Peng Zhen's reaction to alienation theorists, critics of feudalism, and the authors of "undeveloped socialism" stemmed from the same basic assumption. To accept China's backwardness in terms of productive forces or class character as well as the thesis that alienation, in any form, existed in contemporary Chinese society was to acknowledge the limitations of "socialist transformation" or that China's socialism was not genuine.[10] Such an allegation not only undermined the achievements of the leading core but also came dangerously close to vindicating the arguments of ultraleftists and Democracy Wall theorists.[11] The moderates'

9. Hu Qiaomu, "On the Question of Humanism and Alienation," *Hongqi*, no. 2 (1984), pp. 2–28, see also *Renmin ribao*, 27 January 1984, pp. 1–5. See Ding Zhenhai and Li Zhun, "The Socialist Alientation Theory and the 'Alienation Fever' in the Realm of Literature and Art," *GMRB*, 19 November, 1983.

10. Politburo member Wang Zhen pointed out, "There are some who argue that our country is not yet socialist or that the socialism implemented in China is agrarian socialism. There are also people who consistently talk of so-called 'socialist alienation' arguing that socialism is characterized by not only ideological alienation, but also political and economic alienation, to the point of maintaining that the source of alienation is to be found in the socialist system itself. Such views run contrary to scientific socialism. See also, Wang Zhen, "Guard Against and Remove Spiritual Pollution on the Ideological Front, Raise High the Banner of Marxism and Socialism," *RMRB*, 25 October 1983, p. 1.

11. Hu Qiaomu, "Some Current Problems on the Ideological Front," *Hongqi*, no. 23 (1981), pp. 2–22. Commentator, "Take the Four Basic Principles as the Weapon to Overcome Erroneous Ideological Influences," *Jiefangjun bao*, 26 April 1981. Yu Yiding, "On Emancipating the Mind and Opposing Bourgeois Liberalization," *Hongqi*, no. 23 (1981), pp. 23–28. Feng Wenbin, "Adhere to the Ideological Line Based on Dialectical Materialism as Advocated by Comrade Mao Zedong," *Renmin ribao*, 14 September 1979, SWB/FE/6228/BII/5–8. Commentator, "Implement the Line of the Third Plenum of the Central Committee of the CCP and Uphold the Four Basic Principles," *Renmin ribao*, 24 April 1981. Deng Liqun, "Communism Is the Lofty Cause Throughout the Ages," *Gongren ribao*, 27 March 1981. Editorial Department, "Correctly Understand the Situation and the Policies and Uphold the Four Basic Principles," *Hongqi*, no. 5 (1981), pp. 2–11.

response illustrated their reluctance to countenance too rapid and fundamental a revision of doctrine, as well their concern with retaining Party prestige as a guarantee of social and political stability.[12]

Social consequences were for these individuals the most important criterion for judging ideas. According to Xing Fensi, director of the Institute of Philosophy of CASS, the neo-Marxists of the Frankfurt School, and theorists like Marcuse and Fromm replaced the concepts of class struggle with that of "man's struggle and man's revolution," but the meaning of the new terms remained "nuclear and confusing."

> It includes university students stirring up trouble, staging strikes, and their occupation of university premises and workers staging strikes and slow-downs. In May 1968, Paris University students stirred up trouble by occupying university premises. This incident was called the "May tempest." The theoretical basis for this was related to Marcuse's doctrine.[13]

In China, Xing argued, using the concept of alienation to explain bureaucratism and malpractices in the Party was not only incorrect, it was also irresponsible, for it would create pessimism, dissatisfaction, and doubts about socialism. "Preaching socialist alienation" was akin to promoting anarchy.[14]

Despite these early setbacks radical-reform theorists continued the momentum of broadening the terms of intellectual debate by analyzing and disseminating the wide array of Marxist and non-Marxist writings available outside China.[15] The critiques of Stalinism in humanist and historicist

---

12. Zhang Decheng, "Adhere to the Four Cardinal Principles and the Struggle on Two Fronts," *Hongqi*, No. 20 (1983), pp. 31–34. Ma Zhongtu, "Unfold Ideological Struggle on Two Fronts Correctly and in Good Time," *Hongqi*, no. 8 (1983), pp. 33–36.

13. Xing Fensi, "Several Questions About Alienation," *Jingji ribao*, 4 November 1983, translated in *FBIS*, 29 November 1983, pp. 13–23.

14. See "The Alienation Issue and Spiritual Pollution," *RMRB*, 5 November 1983. See also, Duan Ruofei, "Commenting on the Theory of Alienation of Socialism," *GMRB*, 29 October 1983.

15. Ru Xin, "New Tasks Facing Marxist Philosophy," *RMRB*, 20 July 1983, p. 5. Yue Ping, "Carry Forward Marxist Theory—In Preparation for the Centenary of the Death of Karl Marx," *GMRB*, 30 May, 1982. Zhou Yang, "A Probe Into Some Theoretical Problems in Marxism," *RMRB*, 16 March 1983. Yi Chen, "Louis Althusser and Structuralism," *Hongqi*, no. 9 (1983), pp. 25–32.

Marxism and the works of Althusser, Lukacs, Gramsci, Rudolf Bahro, Pavel Campeanu, the Frankfurt School, Branko Horvat, Ferenc Feher, Agnes Heller, Gyorgy Markus, and others had immense appeal. So did Kant, Locke, Montesquieu, Prigogine, Alvin Toffler, and Milton Friedman.

The presentation of this diversity followed from the need to invalidate the hitherto "standardized" and "immutable" Soviet-socialist model and to move beyond the limitations of even classical Marxism demonstrated in its flawed assumptions regarding capitalist crises and slowdown of growth, the impoverishment and expansion of the proletariat, sharpening class contradictions, and the prospect of socialist revolution in capitalist societies.[16] Following CASS president Yu Guangyuan's injunction that "even universal principles of Marxism are not ready-made formulae" and need to be "developed," dialectics, historical materialism, reflection theory, class analysis, i.e., both Marx's method and his social theory came under the critical scrutiny of theorists like Jin Guantao, Li Zehou, Wang Ruoshui, Zhang Xianyang, Su Shaozhi, and Wang Yizhou.

Some of the most significant ideological developments in this period were related to epistemology. The invocation of practice for the purposes of verification was taken forward by radical reformers to emphasize "practical materialism," and enhance the role of human subjectivity versus objective reality. Lenin's theory of reflection (as outlined in *Materialism and Empirio-Criticism*), which continued to be upheld as Party orthodoxy, came under increasing criticism from people like Wang Ruoshui and Liu Zaifu for paying attention to only material objects while ignoring the attributes of value given by men to objects and hence neglecting human feelings and will.[17] The post-Marxian view that objects are never given as

16.   Yu Guangyuan, "Perceive the Reform of the Period of Socialist Construction From the Viewpoint of World and Chinese History," *Zhongguo shehui kexue*, no. 1 (1985), pp. 53–68, also in Renda *Fuyin*, no. 1 (1985), pp.1–18. "Actively Promote Marxism as the Science of Socialist Construction," *Renmin ribao*, 5 August 1985, p. 5, also in Renda *Fuyin*, no. 8 (1985), pp. 7–8. "Develop Marxism as a Science for Socialist Construction," *Zhongguo shehui kexue*, no. 4 (1983), pp. 3–12. Liao Gailong, "Advance Along the Road of All-Round Socialist Construction: Commemorating the 100th Anniversary of Marx's Death," *Jiaoxue yu yanjiu*, no. 2 (1983), pp. 6–15, see in *Renda Fuyin*, no. 4 (1983).

17.   Wang Ruoshui, *GMRB*, 12 February 1981, also in Kelly, ed. "Wang Ruoshui," pp. 101–112. See also, "Issues on Realism and Theory of Reflection," *Wenhuibao*, (Shanghai) 12 July 1988, p. 3 also in *FBIS*, 18 August 1988, pp. 25–32.

mere "existence" but are always articulated within discursive totalities and with reference to human subjectivity found its echoes in Wang's claim that "real people and their practice have ontological significance . . . this is a historical phenomenon, which, while not denying the 'precedence of the natural world without' stresses that it is not a primitive natural world, but one that has been humanized."[18]

Developments in modern psychology and physics, the theory of relativity, and quantum mechanics had essentially rendered Engels's and Lenin's epistemological position obsolete for intellectuals like Jin Guantao:

> It is the observation of human beings that cause the irregular movements of electrons. When humans measure their positions . . . they inevitable interrupt their movement, thus causing uncertainty of their movement. . . . The fact that electrons possess certain qualities is because we observe them. We cannot talk about the quality of matter without resorting to man's sensing. The belief that matter or quality can be independent from human sense and consciousness is ridiculous . . . the moon does not exist when nobody looks at it. . . . Materialism has been falsified.[19]

The incorporation of Kant and Piaget pointed to the shortcomings of Leninist-Maoist conceptions of the birth of knowledge. In Li Zehou's exposition of the cognitive process "a priori" structures of understanding were transformed into "sedimentations"—the accumulated practical experience of mankind through history. The significance of the human subject was redefined within a materialist outlook by a creative appropriation of Kantian idealism.[20]

Wang Ruoshui affirmed his emphasis on humanism by questioning both orthodox epistemology and philosophical outlook:

> If we consider the relationship between man and the objective world as merely the relationship between the mind and the material, and consider

18.   Wang Ruoshui, "Issues on Realism," *FBIS*, p. 27.

19.   Jin Guantao, *The Philosophy of Man*, Taibei: Shangwu yinshuguan, 1988, pp. 3–17. For a rebuttal see, Hu Maoren, "Materialism Refuted?" *GMRB*, 27 November 1989, p. 3.

20.   Li Zehou, *A Critique of Critical Philosophy*, Beijing: Renmin chubanshe, 1979. For the difference between Li's humanist position and that of Wang Ruoshui and Zhou Yang, see Lin Min, "The Search for Modernity: Chinese Intellectual Discourse and Society—1978–1988, the Case of Li Zehou," *China Quarterly*, no. 132 (December 1992), pp. 969–998.

the mind as merely knowledge, then we will forget that man is an entirety. Man not only uses his mind to establish relations with the objective world, but also uses his body to establish relations with the objective world. Man's mind includes not only sense and ideology but also feelings, desire, and will. . . . Things like feelings, desire, and will cannot be described as reflection. Therefore, summarizing the relationship between mind and material as the relationship between understanding and being understood and as the relationship between reflecting and being reflected is quite one-sided. Studying man's mind merely from the viewpoint of knowledge is also inadequate. Feelings, desire, and will are the vast realm of man's mind. However, they have almost no place in our textbooks on philosophy.[21]

The political relevance of these philosophical arguments was not lost on the Party leadership. The emphasis on subjectivity and a moral-ethical interpretation of humanism undermined the centrality and significance of class, and ultimately the party's claim and authority as a representative entity. "Abstract" affirmation of humanism, therefore, repeatedly came under fire as "bourgeois individualism."[22]

The "new" Party line which emerged from the long series of debates reflected intellectual dynamism and confusion as well as opportunistic compromises between rival factions to ensure political survival and continued monopoly over the policy-making process.[23] The epistemological positions staked out by the more radically innovative practice theorists even if intellectually attractive were politically infeasible in the eyes of the leadership. The legitimacy of the moderate position on politics and economics also was consistently eroded by concrete departures from the

---

21. Wang Ruoshui, "Issues on Realism and Theory of Reflection," *Wenhuibao* (Shanghai), 12 July 1988, p. 3. Also in *FBIS*, 18 August 1988, pp. 25–32, quote on pp. 28–29.

22. He Zuoxiu, "Why Does Jin Guantao want to Negate the Objectivity of Objective Reality? Commenting on 'The Philosophy of Man,'" *Qiushi*, no. 23, 1 December 1989. Also in *FBIS*, 27 December 1989, pp. 21–25; "What Does the 'New Enlightenment' Movement Really Mean?" *GMRB*, 6 August 1990, p. 3. Also in *FBIS*, 28 August 1990, pp. 12–14

23. The conflicts and inconsistencies were most evident in documents and resolutions like Zhao Ziyang's Speech to the Thirteenth Party Congress and the "Resolution of the Central Committee of the CPC on the Guiding Principles for Building a Socialist Society With an Advanced Culture and Ideology" passed in September 1986. *FBIS*, 29 September 1986, pp. K2–12.

Soviet model in practice and radical-reformist arguments in favor of deepening reform. The acceptance of the thesis of the "primary stage of socialism" (in lieu of "undeveloped" socialism) as the main theoretical justification of the new course reflected, on the one hand, the moderate determination to preserve outmoded concepts such as the identification of nationalization with socialization. On the other hand, the assertion that China was engaged in "socialist construction" or was in any stage, primary or otherwise, of socialism was quite effectively undermined by the skepticism introduced by reformist writings with regard to basic tenets, by their contention that socialism, public ownership, 'laborers being masters,' socialist construction, etc., were terms whose meanings had never been very clear to those who professed to implement them.

The patchwork official doctrine, a product of radical-reformist innovations and the moderate ideologists' attempts to preserve basic tenets of doctrine, which had traditionally served to justify and legitimize their leading position in Chinese society, was characterized by conceptual fuzziness, inconsistency, and eclecticism.[24] One could argue that every ideology, in as much as it is a generalized interpretation of an evolving social reality, cannot but espouse both true and false principles.[25] However, all ideologies, because they are intellectual instruments and weapons, must satisfy certain intellectual requirements and rules of logic in order to be serviceable.[26] The purpose of an ideology is to provide a framework for

---

24. In *The Reassessment of Chinese Socialism, 1976–1992* (Princeton University Press, 1995), the author, Yan Sun, concludes that the radical-reformist intellectuals provided a very adept and systematic critique by first discrediting Soviet socialism in comparison with classical Marxism, and then using the Chinese experience to refute Marxism. Yan Sun also upholds the clarity of the Four Cardinal Principles. She states, "in clear and simple terms, these principles spell out who leads the country, what kind of political thought guides the country, and how the country is governed." It is doubtful whether such a claim, (particularly, the second—what kind of thought guides the country) would find support even among moderate reformers in China. Needless to say, both her conclusions are quite off the mark.

25. David Ingersoll and Richard Matthews, *The Philosophic Roots of Modern Ideology: Liberalism, Communism, Fascism*, Englewood Cliffs: Prentice Hall,1986. L.N. Moskvichov, *The End of Ideology Theory: Illusions and Reality*, Moscow: Progress Publishers, 1974, p. 67.

26. Maurice Cornforth, *Dialectical Materialism: The Theory of Knowledge*, vol. III, London: Lawrence and Wishart, 1954, p. 95.

comprehending the world in which one lives, and, at the very least, it is required to be a coherent system of ideas that square, to some extent, with the reality that one has experienced. For official Marxism, described by its practitioners as a "scientific ideology" the requirements would be even more rigorous and exacting.[27] To serve as a guide to action and a perspective for understanding objective situations and laws its basic concepts and tenets must be fairly well-defined, internally consistent, and logical. The disarray and erosion of the ruling doctrine in China, however, undermined simultaneously its utility as an analytical tool, and the legitimacy of those who sought to enforce it.

Reformist intellectuals exhibited a keen awareness of this when they repeatedly pointed out that "once a theory becomes incapable of answering the challenges of real life and dissipating the ideological doubts of the masses, it will inevitably be cold-shouldered by them and lose its prestige."[28] Hu Qili urged Chinese theorists to "have the courage to break through the few conclusions that experience has already proven to be outmoded or not entirely correct."[29] Su Shaozhi approvingly quoted the Soviet scholar G.C. Jilgansky, who wrote:

> It must be taken into consideration that the ideology of the masses, either in their knowledge or in their ability to think, is not what it was several scores of years ago. Intellectually, people want to have more independence. It will not do now to look upon the relationship between ideology and people's thought as only one of unconditionally accepting ready-made ideological formulas. . . . The masses of today have set a higher demand on ideology, requiring it to have a standard of learning and also basis.[30]

Pointing to the questions posed by historical development in directions contrary to those predicted by Marx, Engels, and Lenin, Su criticized doctrinaires for failing to understand that

27. V.I. Lenin, *Collected Works*, vol. 5, p. 342.
28. Su Shaozhi, "Prospect for Socialism as Viewed From China's Experience and Lessons," *Selected Studies*, 1985, p.5.
29. *RMRB*, 14 March 1986.
30. Su Shaozhi, "Some Questions Concerning the Writing of the History of Marxism," *Selected Studies*, 1985, p. 7. G.C. Jilgansky, "Ideological Struggle and Mass Consciousness," *Problems in Philosophy*, (USSR), no. 5 (1983), p. 165.

. . . only by creatively developing Marxism will it be possible to really persist in Marxism. . . . To analyze criticism and answer these questions presupposes studies of the reality of the contemporary world, studies which are realistic instead of apriorist, independent instead of parroting the words of others, and comprehensive instead of abstract.[31]

The ambiguity of official proclamations resulted, to some extent, from the radical reformers' need to supplement new ideas with sufficient propagandistic verbiage to thwart attacks from moderate "upholders," who interpreted signs of ideological laxity as a dangerous diminution of the Party's prestige and an indication of a "peaceful evolution to capitalism."[32] However, even bearing in mind that radical-reformist intellectuals wrote in a political atmosphere that was not always conducive to frank and forthright expression,[33] it is clear that inconsistency and eclecticism were traits that they shared with their rivals. Individuals like Liao Gailong and Yu Guangyuan exhibited ambiguity when they complained of "laborers not being masters" in Chinese society on the one hand, and on the other, sanguinely asserted that "capitalist factors" posed no danger in a workers' state implementing the Dictatorship of the Proletariat. The moderate myth

31.   Su Shaozhi, "Develop Marxism Under Contemporary Conditions—In Commemoration of the Centenary of the Death of Karl Marx," *Selected Studies*, 1983, pp. 10–11.
32.   Commentator, "A Serious Struggle Against Enemies in the Political Realm," *Hongqi*, no. 18 (1983), pp. 2–8. Commentator, "Four Great Pillars that Hold Up the Sky—On the Importance of Upholding the Four Basic Principles," *RMRB*, 23 October 1983. "Theoretical Work Must Serve Socialist Modernization," *Hongqi*, no. 13 (1983), pp. 28–31.
33.   Decades of policy vacillation had finally convinced Chinese intellectuals of the need to devise a strategy of survival. As Su Shaozhi put it, "in China . . . some people posing as 'theoretical authorities' and 'defenders of the purity of Marxism' rely on the power and influence of leaders to make conclusions and to criticize, to put labels on, and to attack those who disagree with them. Yet, China's intellectuals today are no longer the obedient slaves of the Cultural Revolution period, who 'acted according to Chairman Mao's instructions even if they did not understand'. And, even if they are forced into temporary silence when they are under attack, they will offer new arguments and become active again when they get the opportunity. 'Criticism, silence, activity, again criticism, again silence, and again activity.' This is the cycle through which China's ideological circles have moved repeatedly since the Third Plenum." See "The Historical Destiny of Marxism in China From 1949–1989," *Pai hsing*, no. 201 1 October 1989, pp. 31–33.

about workers being "masters of the socialist state" found its counterpart in the radical-reformist myth of hired laborers being "masters" of enterprises after the comprehensive adoption of the labor contract system to counter the iron-rice bowl had accentuated an already evident shift of power within the enterprise in favor of managers.[34] The freedom and equality of opportunity accompanying the commodification of labor was more obvious to CASS economists and Zhao Ziyang's advisors than to workers where greater discretionary power was devolved to personnel managers to dismiss employees in response to changing market conditions, and managers who focused more on workers' rights and benefits were assailed for not living up to the ideal of cost-cutting efficient entrepreneurs. Radical-reformist admiration for Yugoslavia did not translate into an endorsement for a worker-management system for China.

Similarly, criticism of Mao and other leftists for arbitrary definitions of class status could scarcely be sustained by theorists who themselves identified class positions on the basis of commitment to the "socialist system and reform," rather than relationship to the means of production or sources of income. Yu Guangyuan's new social contradiction between "advancing and holding on" could not but end up with an identification of "progressive" rural capitalists and business entrepreneurs who, for obvious reasons, would be favorably disposed toward reform, and a "conservative" working class and poor peasantry, which would resist further encroachments upon jobs and social security. Neo-authoritarians simply drew the logical conclusions from such formulations and were far more candid than their liberal democratic colleagues in pointing out the need for autocratic authority to override "vested interests" such as "consumers" and "imperial workers" who sought to resist the march toward a market economy.[35]

Indeed, discussions of "equality of opportunity," "fair exchange of value," and "social individual ownership" by radical reformers and liberal intellectuals were as one-sided and simplistic in their denial of differences

34. Gordon White, "Restructuring the Working Class: Labor Reform in Post-Mao China," in *Marxism and the Chinese Experience*, pp. 152–171. Jiang Yiwei, "If All Workers Are on the Contract System It Will Not Be Conducive to the Socialist Character of the Enterprise," *Jingji tizhi gaige*, no. 1 (1985), pp. 11–13.

35. Wu Jiaxiang, "The New Authoritarianism: An Express Train Toward Democracy by Building Markets," p. 40.

as the ultraleftist egalitarianism that they contemptuously denounced. Arguments touting the equality of opportunity inherent in a liberal democratic market-economy reflected the same blindness to socially constructed realities of class and gender as the Party leadership that denied the existence of privilege and inequality in "socialist" society. Yan Jiaqi's oft-quoted assumption that people will tolerate disparities based on differences in human abilities was naive and cavalier, at best, as was the dismissal of popular discontent with inequality as the "green-eyed disease."[36] Radical-reformist and liberal writings suffered from a serious shortcoming in their failure to assess the long-term political and socioeconomic consequences of economic liberalization.

The tension between economic determinism and the concept of revolutionary praxis or anthropocentrism remained unresolved in radical-reformist critiques of the past, and their prescriptions for reform. Articles by Sun Changjiang, Wu Jiang, Yu Guangyuan, et al., on the tenth anniversary of the practice-criterion discussions unequivocally equated the criterion of productive forces with the criterion of practice.[37] Zhang Xianyang, curiously enough, criticized Marx for "mechanistic determinism" and rationalism, yet joined his colleagues in emphasizing objective laws of development, especially the determination of production relations and the superstructure by productive forces, and in the evaluation of theories and policies in terms of their contribution to economic growth.[38]

Su Shaozhi invoked Marx's injunction that "no social order ever perishes before all the productive forces for which there is room in it have developed; and new higher relations of production never appear before the material conditions of their existence have matured in the womb of the old society itself," to explain the continued vitality of capitalism, and

36. Yan Jiaqi, "Democracy and Social Equity: A Comparative Analysis of the Role of the Government," *GMRB*, 7 July 1988.
37. Wu Jiang, "On the Historical Stage of Socialist Construction," *RMRB*, 5 May 1988. Yu Guangyuan, "Commemorating the Tenth Anniversary of the Debate on the Criterion of Truth," *RMRB*, 8 May 1988. Sun Changjiang, "From the Practice Criterion to the Production Criterion," *RMRB*, 9 May 1988.
38. Zhang Xianyang, "Marxism: Reflection and Transcendence," *Wenhuibao*, (Hong Kong), 29 January 1989, p. 2. Also in, *FBIS*, 30 January 1989, pp. 37–38.

to chastise Communist parties for violating this theory.[39] But the logic of this argument also pointed to the futility of conscious tampering or popular mobilization to undermine the authority of the contemporary "feudal despotic" Chinese state based on what Su, Zhang, Wang Yizhou, and others still considered a predominantly small-producer economy. Yu Guangyuan justified the adoption of capitalist policies on the grounds of China's immaturity for socialism. However, his arguments for dismantling the dictatorship of the proletariat harked back to Marx's notion of the withering away of the state under conditions of economic abundance in a mature, classless Communist society.

The attraction of economic determinism (although the unilinear development of history was substituted by many for multilinear view)[40] was reflected in both neo-authoritarian and liberal democratic arguments for transition to a market economy. Although many of the economic and technological determinists maintained more than a residual commitment to Marxism-socialist goals and values as commonly understood had ceased to be meaningful guides to social and political action. For the liberal democrats to raise the issue of means and ends and ask the neo-authoritarians how despotism would lead to democracy was ironic indeed, for they themselves had chosen to pass over the question of how widening socioeconomic inequality and the reinstitution of private property in the "primary stage" would lead to socialism.[41]

"Critical and humanist" Marxists like Wang Ruoshui, who emphasize the subject-centered view of history, have, to some extent, resisted the overwhelming of teleological goals by the imperatives of modernization and industrialism. Against the equation of the criterion of practice with productive forces Wang, early on, had identified "people's needs and interests" as the criterion for evaluating aims and the results of practice.

39. "All Roads Lead to Democracy," *Bulletin of Concerned Asian Scholars*, vol. 24, no. 1 (January–March 1992, p. 56.

40. See for example, Su Shaozhi, "Rethinking Socialism in the Light of Chinese Reforms," *China Information*, vol. 5, no. 4 (Spring 1991).

41. Yu Haocheng, "Does China Need New Authoritarianism?" *CSA*, vol. 23, no. 4 (Summer 1991), pp. 44–45; Wang Yizhou, "Why We Cannot Agree With the New Authoritarianism" in same issue, pp. 56–66; Qin Xiaoying, "Escaping From a Historical Cycle" also in same issue, pp. 7–30; Rong Jian, "Does China Need an Authoritarian Political System in the Course of Modernization?" *CSA*, vol. 23, no. 2 (Winter 1990–91), pp. 113–31.

Despite his critique of Maoist voluntarism Wang continued to uphold the role of practice and the human subject in constituting objective reality and the knowledge of that reality. Nevertheless, the commitment of alienation theorists to Marx's notion of "recovery of human species essence" remains both partial and selective. For Wang and his colleagues bureaucratism and loss of freedom leading to intellectual and political alienation are unacceptable "obstacles to progress." However, the alienation fostered by commodification and capitalist-market relations along with a perpetuating division of labor based on enhanced mental/manual, worker/intellectual, rural/urban distinctions—"a special form of alienation" is "the price of progress."[42] For these Chinese intellectuals as for other post-Marxists like Laclau and Mouffe the "classism" of Marx, Engels, and their followers is untenable.[43] The proletariat is longer the privileged class in history, and there is no "inherent antagonism" between the interests of capital and labor.

Overall, radical reformers proved more able at undermining the existing doctrine than at furnishing a new persuasively and coherently articulated ideological framework. The most striking aspect of the intellectual reassessment that occurred in the two decades since Mao's death is that, for all the critiques of ultraleftism, Mao's successors never really succeeded in marginalizing his concerns regarding the emergence of oppressive, exploitative groups in socialist society. Mao's fears of capitalist restoration were echoed by Chen Yun, Peng Zhen, Hu Qiaomu, and Deng Liqun in the years leading up to and after the Tiananmen movement. The radical reformers' and liberal intellectuals' indictment of the Stalinist "socialist system" reflected strains of the 1960s Maoist analysis of bureaucratic degeneration. Their panacea, of course, was democratization and representative institutions, not political mobilization and cultural revolutions. Such a resolution was in line with the interests of the group that articulated it, and it was all the more attractive and justifiable because it coincided with a rational public interest. Its omissions were equally significant for it marginalized the issues of socioeconomic equality, class, and hierarchy that have, for so long, sustained the power and attraction of the Communist idea.

---

42. "All Roads Lead to Democracy," *Bulletin of Concerned Asian Scholars*, vol. 24, no. 1 (January–March 1992), p. 57.

43. E. Laclau and C. Mouffe, *Hegemony and Socialist Strategy*, London: 1985. See also, "Post-Marxism Without Apologies," *New Left Review*, vol. 166 (1987), pp. 79–106.

Despite their harsh denunciations of Party work style and policies in 1979 and 1988–89, and their radical reassessment of Marxism and the viability of socialism as a system or model of development Chinese establishment intellectuals remained essentially reformers rather than revolutionaries in their outlook. In 1979, the Party leadership's explanation of the Great Leap Forward and the Cultural Revolution in terms of "individual opportunism and adventurism" was decried by Li Honglin, Guo Luoji, and Liu Binyan as neither convincing nor Marxist.[44] However, in marking a retreat on the questions of feudalism and bureaucratic class, their own critiques at the time focused on political and personal shortcomings. Wang Ruoshui attempted to maintain his ideological consistency by continuing to identify Mao's personal character and his flawed understanding of dialectics (overemphasis on struggle, i.e., "one divides into two" and neglect of the law of identity of opposites) as the major source of ultraleftist mistakes and tyranny.[45] Others like Yan Jiaqi, Liao Gailong, Su Shaozhi, and Yu Guangyuan emphasized procedural politics and democratic mechanisms to prevent a recurrence of previous policies and work style.[46] As Janos Kadar had remarked on the Soviet treatment of the Stalin question the position that violation of democratic rights and legality occurred in "socialist societies" stopped short of a systemic criticism. "Grave mistakes . . . did not occur because of the nature of the regime but on the contrary because of *political and personal errors* which conflict with the essence of socialism and are alien to it."[47]

44. Li Honglin, "Exposing and Criticizing the 'Gang of Four' Constitutes a Decisive Battle of a Historical Nature," *Lishi yanjiu*, no. 3 (1978), pp. 3–15. Liu Binyan, "Listen Carefully to the Voice of the People," *RMRB*, 26 November 1979. Shi Zhu, "The 'Leftist' line of Lin Biao and the Gang of Four and Its Social and Historical Root Causes," *Hongqi*, no. 4 (1979), pp. 21–26.

45. Wang Ruoshui, "The Maid of Chinese Politics," *The Journal of Contemporary China*, no. 10 (Fall 1995), pp. 66–80.

46. Yan Jiaqi, "From Non-Procedural Politics to Procedural Politics," *Shehui Kexue*, 15 August 1988, pp. 3–7. Liao Gailong, "Zhou Enlai's Thought on Socialist Construction," *Mao Zedong sixiang yanjiu*, no. 3 (1985), p. 1–6. Su Shaozhi, "In the Midst of All-Round Reform Develop Marxism and Construct Socialism With Chinese Characteristics," *RMRB*, 11 March 1983, p. 5. "The Most Important Development of Marxism," *RMRB*, 21 July 1981. "The Goal of Socialist Production and Socialist Democracy," *FBIS*, 23 June 1981, pp. 1–7.

47. Janos Kadar, "Answers to the Questions of the Correspondent of 'New Age,' Newspaper of the Indian Communist Party," November 1970, in *For a Socialist Hungary*, Budapest: Corvina Press, 1974, p. 229.

Affirmation of the democratic component in the definition of socialism, which began soon after the 1978 Third Plenum, was consistent with the policy initiatives of leaders like Hu Yaobang and Zhao Ziyang. Their intellectual followers argued that the continued monopolization of power by the Communist Party was eroding its legitimacy and deepening the "crisis of faith" in the population. Yan Jiaqi warned ominously, "once the sound of the anguish of the people is silenced by the emperor, the people can express their demands through violence only."[48] In his speech at the February 1979 Conference, Wang Ruoshui argued, "the fact that the masses dare not criticize the Party is very harmful to the Party and very dangerous."[49] Presenting his case in terms that would appeal to a modernizing oligarchy Su Shaozhi pointed out that "democratization is a good remedy for removing the bottlenecks impeding economic development."[50] Li Shu focused on the disastrous effect of "political despotism" on intellectual creativity and the development of science and culture. Denying the validity of a "demarcation between academia and politics" he argued that there could be no freedom of speech on academic issues without freedom of speech on political issues.[51] The Hundred Flowers failed because "it remained an idea carrying neither legal protection of the citizens' inalienable democratic rights under the socialist system nor the legal functions punishing those who violated them."[52] Equating democratization with modernization Yu Guangyuan joined in the general resurrection of the May Fourth spirit by emphasizing that what China needed most was science and democracy.[53]

By the mid-1980s, with the renewed support of Hu Yaobang, Hu Qili, and Wang Zhaoguo in the higher levels of the party apparatus, Yan Jiaqi, Wang Ruoshui, Yu Haocheng, and others were integrating the instrumental

48. Reprinted in *Xinhua Wenzhai*, February 1989, pp. 130–134.

49. "The Greatest Lesson of the Cultural Revolution Is That the Personality Cult Should be Opposed," Speech at the Theory Conference, 13 February 1979, *Mingbao* (Hong Kong), no. 2 (1980), pp. 2–15. Also in *JPRS*, 12 March 1980, pp 78–99.

50. Su Shaozhi, "Economic Development and Democratization," *Selected Studies*, 1981, pp. 5–6.

51. Xinhua, 17 October 1979. *JPRS*, no. 74564, pp. 1–3.

52. Li Shu, "Identify the Essence and Absorb It," *Lishi yanjiu*, November 1979, translated in *JPRS*, no. 75064, p. 36.

53. Yu Guangyuan, "On the Liberation of Thought," *Ziran bianzhengfa tongxun*, no. 1 (1981), pp. 1–2, also in, Renda *Fuyin*, no. 4 (1981), pp. 43–44.

view of democracy with a more teleological one.[54] Unlike Hu Qiaomu and Wu Jianguo, who continued to discuss freedom from necessity/constraints of nature (or as working within objective laws), radical-reformist intellectuals proceeded from Kant's categorical imperative and defined freedom in terms of spontaneity, creativity, enterprise, self-development, and self-realization.[55] Their defense of human rights and demands that "people really be seen as people," although couched in what Li Zehou perceived as ethical-purist terms were linked concretely to constitutional protection of the "sanctity of personal freedom and dignity," and the revival of the double-hundred policy. This was also true for arch critics like Liu Xiaobo, who despite his attraction for Nietzsche and Sartre defended freedom in a liberal Lockean sense and argued for institutional arrangements based on human rights.[56] Yu Haocheng summed up the views of his colleagues by pointing out:

> If socialist society cannot offer the individual more and greater freedom, how can it display its superiority? . . . Even in capitalist society there is law and discipline in order to maintain social stability. . . . We, on the one hand, set a high level of democracy as one of the objectives of our struggle, while on the other we proclaim that socialist society cannot offer the individual more and greater freedom. Is there not a contradiction here?[57]

54. Hu Qili's speech on May Day in *RMRB*, 14 March 1986. Translated in *FBIS*, 25 March 1986, pp. 27–29. Also in, *FBIS*, 22 September 1986, pp. K8–21. Yan Jiaqi in *Guangming ribao*, 30 June 1986. Speeches by Su Shaozhi, Lu Dingyi, and Yu Guangyuan on the "Thirty Years of the Double Hundred Policy," *Selected Studies*, 1988, pp. 5–6. Feng Lanrui, "Thriving of Academic Research Presupposes Freedom and Democracy," *World Economic Herald*, (Shanghai) 5 May 1986, also in *Selected Studies*, 1988, pp. 43–50. Yu Guangyuan, *RMRB* 16 May 1986. Wang Ruoshui, "The Double Hundred Policy and Civil Rights," *Survey of World Broadcasts/Far East* 8360, 10 September 1986, pp. BII, 8–9. Also Kelly, ed. "Wang Ruoshui," pp. 71–88.

55. Wu Jianguo, "Reflections on the Question of Freedom," *Hongqi*, 1 September 1986, pp. 32–38. *Zhengming*, 1 December 1986, pp. 9–12. See also Brugger and Kelly, *Chinese Marxism*, p. 167–68. David Kelly, "The Chinese Search for Freedom as a Universal Value," in David Kelly and Tony Reid, ed., *Ideas of Freedom in Asia*, (forthcoming).

56. Woei Lien Chong, "The Tragic Duality of Man: Liu Xiaobo on Western Philosophy," in Kurt Werner Radtke and Tony Saich, eds. *China's Modernization: Westernization and Acculturation*, Stuttgart: Franz Steiner Verlag 1993, pp. 139.

57. *Wenhuibao*, 7 November 1986, p. 2.

Drawing upon the conceptual distinction made between system legitimacy and the legitimation of a particular regime by scholars of East European societies one can argue that the critiques offered by radical-refomist intellectuals demonstrated that, in China, the system as such enjoyed varying degrees of legitimacy, but not so the regime.[58] The latter, with some notable exceptions, was still identified to a significant extent with the previous discredited Maoist era, and the convoluted efforts at selective rejection and affirmation of various aspects of Maoism contributed further to the belief that little had changed. Since the crisis was one of regime rather than system legitimacy, it was, for many, "derivative" rather than fundamental.[59] For addressing such a "derivative" crisis, Chinese radical reformers and theorists as well as leaders like Hu Yaobang preferred to emulate the Hungarian two-pronged strategy of increasing political participation and improved economic performance with a "calculated depoliticization of public affairs and a lower profile for the party."[60] Limited political and ideological pluralism would obviate the need for an officially sanctioned and rigidly enforced doctrine and allow the leadership to draw its legitimacy from popular perception of its willingness to respect individual rights and pursue the satisfaction of broadly accepted social needs.

For moderate political leaders, such an ideological reorientation came at too high a price. The ideal for such leaders continued to be "crypto-politics" whereby the legitimation of the elite was still derived from teleological formulae and the constraints to its rule were normative rather than electoral.[61] Insofar as Deng Xiaoping, Chen Yun, Peng Zhen, and others rejected the revolutionary mobilizational politics of the Maoist period, they could not but countenance some transformation of "crypto-politics"

58.   Bennett Kovrig, "Hungarian Socialism: The Deceptive Hybrid," *Eastern European Politics and Societies*, vol. 1, no. 1 (1987), pp. 113–134. Bill Lomax, "Hungary: The Quest for Legitimacy," in *Eastern Europe: Political Crisis and Legitimation*, Paul Lewis, ed. London: Croom Helm, 1984, p. 102.

59.   Lucian Pye, "The Legitimacy Crisis," in *Crisis and Sequences in Political Development*, Leonard Binder, ed., et al., Princeton: Princeton University Press, 1971, pp. 136–138.

60.   Kovrig, *Hungarian Socialism*, p. 123.

61.   Andrew C. Janos, "Systemic Models and the Theory of Change in the Comparative Study of Communist Politics," *Authoritarian Politics in Communist Europe*, Andrew Janos, ed., Berkeley: University of California Institute of International Studies, 1976, pp. 3–4.

into "parapolitics," which according to Andrew Janos is typical of a managerial-bureaucratic model. In the latter, characterized as it is by the values of stability and technological rationality, there emerges a "more pragmatic and limited view of social engineering."[62] Consequently, while the "rationalization of controls" does not give "politics a 'public' character, the restoration of fixed responsibilities" provides "sufficient leverage to subordinates in the complex and multifaceted network of social organization."[63] For Chinese moderate reformers, as for their East European and Soviet counterparts in an earlier era, the democratization demanded by reformist or dissident intellectuals was, at once, too destabilizing and too diminutive of the Party's role.

The moderate response reflected also their sensitivity to the broader context in which the demands for intellectual pluralism and political democratization took shape. From the mid-1980s onward the introspection on the Cultural Revolution and the source of past and present failings in the Chinese sociopolitical order manifested in a widespread "culture fever" (*wenhuare*) or cultural reflection (*wenhua fansi*).[64] A surge of artistic and literary creativity marked by a spirit of iconoclasm and defiance strongly reminiscent of the May Fourth movement turned to an exploration of Chinese tradition and culture for the roots of the repressive ideological and bureaucratic apparatus of the Party-state.

The most simplistic, hard-hitting, and controversial representation of such cultural critiques was the television series *River Elegy* (*He shang*), which aired in the summer of 1988 and focused on the backwardness and decline of Chinese civilization (symbolized by the destructive force of the Yellow River and its mass of sedimentation that blocked its flow toward the clear azure Pacific Ocean representing the liberated progressive Western civilization), and underscored the need for its total rejection and replacement with the values and institutions of the modern West. The central argument of *River Elegy* was reflected in the works of younger artists and writers and had also been put forward in a more nuanced and subtle way by critics like Liu Zaifu, Liu Xiaobo, Gan Yang, and Li Zehou.

62. Ibid., pp. 6, 20–21, 25–27.
63. Ibid.
64. Lee Ou-fan Lee, "The Crisis of Culture," in Anthony Kane, ed., *China Briefing 1990*, Boulder: Westview Press, 1990, pp. 83–106.

Liu Zaifu's literary themes of subjectivity and multiple composition of character (*xinge zuhe lun*) challenged both Party-sponsored socialist realism and the demand that literature (and art) serve politics in favor of transcending the limits on cultural expression set by Confucianism and its latter-day Marxist-Leninist variant. Liu Xiaobo, Bao Zunxin, and Gan Yang more openly identified Chinese Communism as a continuation of traditional Confucian despotism with its unity of ethics and politics, its preoccupation with social order, harmony, and uniformity, and its repression of the individual for the sake of the collective. For all of these critics the destruction and brutality of the Cultural Revolution as also the tyranny and corruption of the Party-state bureaucracy was not a matter of work style or political institutions, but had pervasive and deeper roots in feudal, traditional, peasant-based authoritarian culture.[65]

Jin Guantao analyzed the "sinification of Marxism-Leninism" by referring to the failure of Confucian ideology to accomplish both social integration and modernization to resist being overrun by the West.[66] The May Fourth movement brought about the adoption of "reactive values" such as science, democracy, knowledge, and equality in place of Confucian ethical centrism and hierarchy. The deep structure of traditional Chinese culture, which consisted of rationality from direct observation, monism of moral ethics, utopianism and Sino-centrism, however, remained intact. The new ideologies of Marxism-Leninism and the Three People's Principles were chosen for their combination of "reactive values," organizational capacity of mobilizing for modernization, and compatibility with tradition. Over a period of time the deep structure of traditional culture asserted itself in the politics of the KMT and the CCP. Under Chiang Kaishek's leadership the Three People's Principles acquired fascist tendencies and became Confucianized. With the eclipse of May Fourth leaders in the CCP and the rise of Mao, the "peasantization" and Sinification of Marxism-Leninism was accomplished. In continuing the application of systems theory to the study

---

65.   Lin Yu-sheng, et al., *May Fourth: Pluralistic Reflections,*" Hong Kong: Joint Publishing Company, 1989.

66.   Jin Guantao, "The Effect of the Deep Structure of Confucian Culture on the Sinification of Marxism," *Xinqimeng,* no. 2, Hunan: Jiaoyu Chubanshe, 1988. "Socialism and Tradition: The Formation and Development of Modern Chinese Political Culture," *The Journal of Contemporary China,* no. 3 (Summer 1993), pp. 3–17.

of traditional Chinese society Jin concluded that the conservativism and ultra-stability of that system was reproduced in the new order as well.[67]

Li Zehou's contribution to this debate characteristically avoided extremes and emphasized the need for a conscious creative transformation of traditional philosophy and the cultural-psychological structure that has sedimented in the individual and collective Chinese consciousness according to the formula, "Western learning for substance and Chinese learning for application (*Xiti-Zhongyong*)."[68] This reversal (suggested originally by the historian Li Shu) of the 19th-century reformer Zhang Zhidong's more famous "*Zhongti-Xiyong*" formulation advocated a selective appropriation of Western philosophy, the concept of personal autonomy, and science for modern Chinese society, culture, and institutions. For Li there were elements of traditional culture worth retaining that would be invigorated and balanced by the importation of modern rational Western values.

The implication of Li's exposition that the Communist Party had not yet accomplished the modernization of China was spelled out more clearly in his article, "Dual Variations on Enlightenment and National Salvation." According to Li, the twin tasks of the May Fourth movement comprised of national salvation and intellectual enlightenment. However, in the decades that followed, the anti-imperialist political imperative overwhelmed the cultural-intellectual dimension, hence both the Marxist-Leninist Revolution and the intellectuals who supported it failed to accomplish the complete agenda of May Fourth.[69]

For the Chinese Communist leadership, which considered itself the true heir of the modernizing transformative spirit of May Fourth, these were serious indictments indeed. The critiques of tradition, emphasis on subjectivity, and the attempt by newly emerging avant garde artists and writers to give the cultural realm a true measure of autonomy were fraught with political implications for they challenged the Party's competence, achievements, and representative role. Radical-reformist demands for democratization were received by the political leadership within this

---

67. Jin Guantao and Liu Qinfeng, *The Cycle of Growth and Decline—On the Ultrastable Structure of Chinese Society*, Hong Kong: Chinese University Press, 1992.
68. Lin Min, "The Search for Modernity."
69. Lin Yu-sheng, *May Fourth: Pluralistic Reflections*. See also, Lin Min, "The Search for Modernity."

broader context of a more fundamental denial of its legitimacy. Against such an onslaught the radical-reformist prescription of political democratization could only have been perceived as a step that would hasten the disintegration of the CCP rather than ensuring its continued predominance with a socialist human face.

On the eve of the Tiananmen movement reformist discourse had been radicalized to the point where Su Shaozhi could ask:

> Is Marxism science or ideology? This has been a controversial issue among Marxists in modern times. In countries where Communist Parties are in power, we cannot deny that Marxism takes an ideological form because Marxism is recognized there as a guiding ideology. In China, Marxism is one of the Four Cardinal Principles. . . . If Marxism is not a science and if it can be backed only by state power, then it loses its vitality. If Marxism is a science, we must utilize a scientific attitude toward it . . . science is not afraid of criticism and may be proved wrong.[70]

This usage of the term *ideology* was clearly closer to the Marxian notion of "false consciousness," or the Althusserian conception of "non knowledge" as opposed to knowledge, i.e., science. Either way, it implied that the ruling doctrine was a distortion of Chinese reality, maintained and preserved by a social group that could no longer claim to be representative of the working class. Su's contention was a reaffirmation, with renewed urgency, of Wang Ruoshui's in 1980:

> Marxism must constantly be supplemented, revised, developed through testing practice; as soon as it comes to a stop, its life is over; it will be Marxism no longer but dogmatism. Not only is dogma not Marxism, it is the antithesis of Marxism. Originally, Marxism was intellectually emancipated, but in its developmental process it was susceptible to dogmatization at the hands of some people. In this way, the instrument of intellectual emancipation became a fetter constricting the mind. If I may use a somewhat unfamiliar philosophical term, this is the "alienation" of Marxism.[71]

70. Response by Su Shaozhi, *Bulletin of Concerned Asian Scholars*, no. 1 (1988), pp. 30. See also, "Some Questions Concerning the Writing of the History of the Development of Marxism," *Selected Studies* (1988).

71. Wang Ruoshui, "Marxism and Intellectual Emancipation," *Xin shiqi*, no. 4 (1980), pp. 2–3.

The radical-reformist challenge to the Party leadership could scarcely go unanswered. The "victory" achieved by Party elders over their reformist rivals was a reflection not of the validity of one reconstruction of Marxism over another, but an unfortunate reminder that quite often in the history of official Marxism the "seal of authority" in many disputes was provided by the coercive organs of state power.

After Tiananmen

The Democracy Movement of 1989 and its suppression have been described, not at all inaccurately, as a watershed. The post-Tiananmen era is more commonly referred to as the post-Deng era. The use of such terminology reflects both a recognition of Deng's relative dominance within China from the late 1970s to the late 1980s and his declining participation since 1992, and also the centrality of the ideological and political conflict between moderates and radicals in the previous period and its replacement by a more complex and uncertain phase of transition beginning in the early 1990s.

There are, however, continuities and fundamental similarities between the pre- and post-Tiananmen periods. China's rapid economic growth, the erosion of the planned and state sector, the marketization of economic life and the pluralization of society continue as before. Equally significant and cogent as in the earlier period are the attendant problems and concerns over the adverse consequences of reform. Chen Yizi summarizes the situation succinctly and paradoxically:

> No Chinese leader in power can achieve an overall success in putting China back after ten years of reform especially the economic reforms, and therefore, there is no reason for unwarranted pessimism; no Chinese leader in power can achieve a substantial step forward in solving problems unsolved in the ten years of reform especially those of a political nature, and therefore, there is no reason for unwarranted optimism.[72]

The ideological debate in the post-Tiananmen phase has been muted somewhat by the partial silencing within China and the exile of the most

72. Chen Yizi, "Problems of Communism and Changes in China," *Journal of Contemporary China*, vol. 2, no. 1–2 (Winter 1993), pp. 82–86.

strident intellectual voices for radical reform. However, apprehensions regarding an ideological vacuum and the search for a "new ideology," some sort of coherent framework of beliefs and values to unify and guide the society and state through a crucial phase of transition continues with the same sense of urgency.[73]

Within the Party the passing of the old guard and rising prominence of second-generation leaders like Chen Yuan points to a transformation of the moderate-reformist stance into a more genuine conservative or neo-conservative orientation. Since late 1990, and despite the endorsement of fast-paced reform policy by Deng Xiaoping and the Fourteenth Party Congress in 1992, neoconservatives have inherited the mantle of moderate reform by emphasizing the reassertion of planning and economic and administrative controls. They have also, however, gone far beyond moderate reformism in their acceptance of market forces and contemporary Western economic theories and concepts.[74]

Intellectual support for neoconservatism comes, not surprisingly, from previous advocates of neo-authoritarianism like Xiao Gongqin who share the gradual and incremental approach to the changing of leaders like Chen Yuan, and place a high premium on a guiding or "visible hand" of an elite in the process of modernization.[75] Inspired by the evolutionary approach of the late 19th-century and early 20th-century reformer Yan Fu, Xiao's strategy for China's transition from tradition to modernity consists of a blend of selective Western ideas and institutions (to promote economic rationality, market forces, the emergence of autonomous interests, and eventually a middle class), with

73. Media articles stressed the significance of socialist culture and ideology and intensified education in "patriotism, collectivism and socialism." See *RMRB* 13 July and 22 August 1996. Jiang Zemin's speech at the Fifth Plenary session of the CCP Central Committee's Central Discipline Inspection Commission emphasized the need for ideological and political work and pointed out that unless the Party concentrated its effort on maintaining its "progressiveness and purity" it would "collapse." *RMRB* 25 January 1995.

74. Joseph Fewsmith, "Neoconservatism and the End of the Dengist Era," *Asian Survey*, vol. XXXV, no. 7 (July 1995), pp. 635–651.

75. Chen Yuan, "Profound Questions and Choices in China's Economy," *Jingji yanjiu*, April 1991, pp. 18–19.

traditional Chinese values propagated and maintained by a modernizing elite.[76]

Xiao's concern for political order and stability is shared by others like He Xin and Wang Huning, who deplore loss of central authority and the consequent ideological and political disintegration and fragmentation that threaten to undermine the Chinese social fabric.[77] Harshly critical of radical reformers as utopians and romantics and thus unable to comprehend the destabilizing effects of the policies they espoused, the neoconservatives also revive the appeal of a new coherent, officially sanctioned ideology which can be used to unite and mobilize the pursuit of elite-defined national, modernizational goals.

The simplistic polemical counterpart to *River Elegy* in the 1990s is a document entitled, "Realistic Responses and Strategic Choices for China After the Soviet Upheaval," meant for internal circulation but printed by *Zhong-guo Qingnian bao* in 1991. This piece, which exhibited a spirit of "extraordinary Machiavellianism," according to Gu Xin and David Kelly, cynically renounced the Marxist-Leninist legacy as a liability for the Party after the collapse of Communism in Eastern Europe and the Soviet Union, and pointed to nationalism as a renewed-rallying and cohesive force within an ideological framework combining Western rationalism and the "lofty and noble traditional culture of the Chinese people."[78]

Both the "Realistic Responses" article and the discussions of the neoconservatives display an economic determinism and a distrust of the spontaneity of the masses as legacies from the past but this is where the resemblance ends. The nexus between the ideologists of neoconservatism and their princeling political allies reflects the significant shift in issues and perceptions from the 1980s to the 1990s. In the mid-1980s, the Party leadership was on the defensive concerning newly emerging socioeconomic configurations, and felt vulnerable to indictments such as those of

76. Xiao Gongqin and Zhuwei, "A Painful Dilemma: A Dialogue on the Theory of 'New Authoritarianism,'" in Rosen and Zou, eds. "The Chinese Debate on New Authoritarianism." See also, Gu Xin and David Kelly, "New Conservativism: Intermediate Ideology of a 'New Elite,'" in *China's Quiet Revolution*, pp. 219–233.

77. Wang Huning, "Political Aesthetics and Political Development," *Shehui Kexue zhanxian*, no. 1, pp. 134–41.

78. Gu Xin and David Kelly, p. 225. Fewsmith, p. 643.

Li Zehou regarding its commitment to national salvation over enlightenment values. In the 1990s the backlash against cultural and national nihilism and wholesale Westernization of the previous decade has allowed the Party to recoup a measure of legitimacy on the basis of past achievements in repulsing imperialism, and in the present context to promote itself as the defender of Chinese sovereignty and national interest in a post–Cold War global environment marked by the resurgence of a U.S. now poised to contain China.[79] Western mercantilism rather than enlightenment values have encited popular imagination in more recent years.

Whereas a displacement of class by emphasis on individual subjectivity threatened the self-identity and legitimacy of the Marxist party in the 1980s, a decade later a core of leading figures seem to have adjusted fairly comfortably to the image of a modernizing neo-authoritarian elite promoting the emergence of diverse autonomous interests that may one day provide the basis for a more democratic system. However, neoconservatism, as Joseph Fewsmith points out, is not yet a coherent socioeconomic political program for it has provided few specific prescriptions for the problems that it has identified in the realm of politics and economics.[80]

The general disaffection with rising levels of inequality, declining social mores, dislocation, and accompanying socioeconomic tensions evident in the late 1980s has been magnified in recent years by the scale and intensity of corruption and speculation rife within the system. This gives neoconservatism its appeal, but it also supports a revival of other streams and currents that had been marginalized in the past decade. A notable example is the attention received by the book *Looking at China Through a Third Eye*. Published in 1994, it also focuses on the adverse destabilizing consequences of unbridled reform, the loss of central ideological and political control, and the alarming decline of public morality. It differs from "Realistic Responses and Strategic Choices" and the general neoconservatism position in its attention to the reemergence of class conflict and polarization in Chinese society and its advocacy of a return to revolutionary ideals and Mao Zedong Thought as the way out of the current dilemma.[81]

79.   I am indebted to Professor Tu Wei-ming for his suggestion that I point out more explicitly the shift in perceptions of the West, and particularly the U.S. from the 1980s to 1990s.
80.   Fewsmith, p. 649.
81.   Fewsmith, p. 649.

The apprehensions voiced by the *Third Eye* find an echo in more academic analyses as well. In an article entitled, "The First Anniversary of the Market Economy," the economist Yang Fan points out:

> Utilitarian standards replace rational standards as the basis for judging things, the ideological standard of surnamed socialism or surnamed capitalism is replaced by the standard of productive forces, and the standard of morality and conscience is replaced by the standard of money. . . . Stimulated by a small minority getting rich quickly, people's desire to pursue wealth has become unprecedentedly strong, and the principles of the commodity economy have corroded everything. . . . The activity of the whole society revolves around the word "money". . . . It can be said that the secularization of China's society is complete and that it is developing in an unhealthy direction.[82]

The similarity with Yao Wenyuan's predictions about the consequence of consolidating bourgeois right is striking.[83] The Mao fever of the 1990s may have its eccentric, commercial manifestations,[84] but, at a deeper more serious level, it underscores the shortcomings of the radical-reformist and moderate ideological reorientation referred to earlier in this chapter.

The new intellectual currents also demonstrate that the May Fourth-type "totalistic antitraditionalism" seems to be a necessary but ultimately short-lived phenomenon in the Chinese discourse on tradition and modernity. On the heels of the Culture Fever followed a new receptivity to the ideas of New Confucianism introduced by overseas scholars like Tu Wei-ming, but sustained and supported by the engagement and support of individuals like Zhang Dainian and Tang Yijie.

82. Yang Fan, "First Anniversary of the Market Economy," *Fazhan yu guanli*, no. 1 (November 1993), p. 26. Originally quoted in Fewsmith, p. 646.

83. A "10,000 characters statement" attributed to Deng Liqun by the Hong Kong press addressed the implications of the shrinking public sector and argued that a "non-governmental bourgeois class" and petty bourgeoisie" had already emerged in China. The subsidizing of "bourgeois liberal" intellectual activity by private entrepreneurs had facilitated an ideological alliance which "without doubt" would "accelerate the change of the bourgeois class from a class-in-itself to a class-for-itself. " Full text in *The China Quarterly* no. 148, December 1996, pp. 1426–41.

84. Edward Friedman, "Democracy and Mao Fever," *The Journal of Contemporary China*, no. 6, Summer 1994, pp. 84–95.

Interest in the concept of a "third epoch of Confucianism" is a continuation of the search for "self" and cultural identity that has absorbed Chinese intellectuals since the closing of the Maoist era. The New Confucian emphasis on the inherent value of humanity and the moral autonomy of the individual made it consistent with the humanist and subjectivist orientation of the new discourse prompting a reevaluation of the Confucian heritage that diverged significantly from that of Jin Guantao, Bao Zunxin, and others.[85] The new more-balanced assessments looked to the concepts of "self-cultivation" and "inner sageliness" as examples of the Confucian regard for subjectivity as well as acceptance of a basic equality among human beings.[86] In the concept of "ren," pointed out Li Zehou, "there is not only democratic character but also humanistic character."[87]

For other scholars like Li Jinquan, the Confucian reciprocal juxtaposition of the sovereign and the subjects (the idea that benevolent government serves and cares for the people also includes the notion of people or subjects being selective in serving the sovereign) along with the basic humanism of Confucian philosophy make it compatible with the development of science and democracy.[88] Li and others do not deny the "hierarchy and despotic elements" in Confucianism but point out their historical and time-specific nature. The ideas of freedom, equality, and human rights, they argue, could only be produced in modern capitalist society. Had Confucian humanism included the modern concepts of democracy and popular rights it would have been an ideology too far ahead of its time to be credible.[89]

In referring to the 1980s cultural self-criticism, He Baogang and David Kelly commented that, "while defining democracy, legality, and human rights as cultural universals, Chinese intellectuals know that access to them

85. Media articles urged cadres to integrate Confucian ethics with Marxism with particular emphasis on the notion of "self-accomplishment" as a key to improved ethical standards. They cautioned, however, that far from holding the key to all problems the current "Confucian craze" had become "excessive. " *RMRB* 25 June 1996.

86. Li Jinquan, "On the Historical Status of Confucianist Humanistic Thought, *Zhexue yanjiu*, no. 11 (1989), pp. 47–52. Also in, *Chinese Studies in Philosophy*, nos. 3–4 (Fall 1991), pp. 34–56.

87. Li Zehou, *Ancient Chinese Intellectual History*, Beijing: Renmin chubanshe, 1985, p. 15.

88. Li Jinquan, p.41.

89. p. 48.

can be gained only in the context of a politically loaded act of cultural critique. They cannot appeal to the symbolic order of European civilization as their lost spiritual home."[90] Tu Wei-ming, on the other hand, argues:

> The Chinese intellectual must resolve to face up to the essential intellectual significance of the challenge of the West; this is not merely an economic or military conflict, but a confrontation of fundamental human values. Therefore, to rescue China as a social and political entity, the path would not be simply to kneel in deference to obvious Western advantages, or to subserviently emulate them; if the intellectual is to save China from the pitiful state in which it has no strength even to be summoned, he must first attempt to overcome the obstinate illusion that internally (China's) cultural fountain has already dried up completely and that saving grace can only come from some external largesse.[91]

The dilemma between learning from abroad and shaping a consensus on the basis of a shared cultural identity may be resolved by a reaffirmation of the living spirit of Chinese tradition urged by New Confucianism.[92] The idea that Confucianism in its third epoch provides a happier balance between self and community than Western liberalism has begun to strike a chord among Chinese intellectuals who look beyond the development of productive forces and face the challenges posed by modernism and postmodernism. The appeal of the Confucian adage, "inner sage, outward king," translated as perfecting the inner subjective world and making use of the spiritual strength of the self to transform and perfect the external world to philosophers like Li Zehou is obvious.[93]

90. He Baogang and David Kelly, "Emergent Civil Society and the Intellectuals in China," in Robert Miller, ed. *The Development of Civil Society in Communist Systems*, North Sydney: Allen & Unwin, 1992, p. 37.

91. Quoted in Shi Zhonglian, "Neo-Confucianism and the Living Spirit of China's Civilization," *Zhexue yanjiu*, no. 9 (1989), pp. 31–36. Also in, *Chinese Studies Philosophy*, nos. 3–4 (Fall 1991), pp. 74–95. Quote on p. 78.

92. Tu Wei-ming, "The Modern Chinese Intellectual Quest," p. 173.

93. There are, of course, limits to this for Li Zehou also believes that an excessive emphasis on the power of the human subject to transform external reality was the source of Maoist voluntarism. See Woei Lien Chong, "Mankind and Nature in Chinese Thought: Li Zehou on the Traditional Roots of Maoist Voluntarism," *China Information*, vol. XI, nos. 2–3 (Autumn–Winter 1996), pp. 138–175.

The emergence of neoconservatism, the nostalgia for the Mao era, and the new receptivity to and reassessment of New Confucianism are a part of the ongoing attempt to address what Chang Hao calls an "orientational crisis."[94] Neoconservatism's (as formulated by Xiao Gongqin and others) attempt to provide a new simple cognitive scheme that can reimpose order and provide a sense of direction are understandable, but most likely a futile exercise. The failure of the gigantic intellectual effort aimed at providing a new ideological framework for the post-Mao change of course illustrates that the complexity of the Chinese socioeconomic cultural order at this time can scarcely be contained by an official orthodoxy. It is also unlikely that the "communal critical self-consciousness" that the Chinese intelligentsia has begun to acquire in the past two decades of soul searching will be exchanged for a new "self-inflicted immaturity" provided by another state-sponsored ideology.[95]

The lessons of May Fourth were brought home once again in the intellectual reawakening of the post-Mao period. Regeneration and revitalization requires acceptance and incorporation of new ideas, concepts, and language. But, the new discourse cannot and need not sever itself completely from the old one. Nick Knight emphasizes that the study of Mao Zedong Thought still constitutes a "realm of discourse intimately integrated with the structure of power within Chinese society."[96] "Orthodox Marxism," points out Kelly, "continues to provide and propagate a discursive field, setting up the ways in which social and political reality is categorized, and thus the ways in which political problems are resolved."[97] This is true, also of those who have more consciously renounced Marxism like Jin Guantao, Chen Yize, and others. Advocates of neo-authoritarianism

94.   Chang Hao, "Intellectual Crisis of Modern China in Historical Perspective," in Tu Wei-ming, ed., *The Triadic Chord: Confucian Ethics, Industrial East Asia and Max Weber*, Singapore: Institute of East Asian Philosophy, 1991.

95.   Tu Wei-ming, "Intellectual Effervescence."

96.   Nick Knight, "Introduction: The Study of Mao Zedong's Philosophical Thought in Contemporary China," *Chinese Studies in Philosophy*, vol. 23, nos. 3–4 (Spring–Summer 1991), p. 3–56.

97.   David Kelly, "Chinese Marxism Since Tiananmen: Between Evaporation and Dismemberment," in David Goodman and Gerald Segal, eds., *China in the Nineties*, Oxford: Oxford University Press, 1991, p 21.

and neoconservatism have substituted the capitalist telos for the socialist one but continue to be inspired by economic determinism and a belief in linear progress.

Socialism was adopted by May Fourth intellectuals in the 1920s as a model for state building and economic development while avoiding the social conflict, class oppression, and exploitation associated with early capitalism.[98] The critical questioning of this choice in the 1980s prompted much rejection and even total denial. Yet, leading intellectuals like Su Shaozhi, Wang Ruoshui, Li Honglin, and Li Zehou still identify themselves as Marxists and profess their commitment to socialist goals. What they reject totally and unconditionally are its distorted and degenerate social and political forms—Stalinist or Chinese ultra-leftist. (Even an arch critic like Fang Lizhi demonstrates primarily an ambivalence when he maintains that socialism is a complete failure and also claims that what one has in China is "feudalism painted with a socialist face.")

One can appreciate the dilemma of these intellectuals by referring to Alex Callinicos's point that, "as both an intellectual tradition and a political movement, Marxism has operated in two registers, and submits itself to two standards of judgment." It is the defeat of Marxism as a political project not its complete theoretical refutation as a critical theory that accounts for its current recession.[99] While stressing the plurality of Marxism and delegitimizing the Soviet-Chinese variants, most Chinese-Marxist intellectuals refrained from taking the easy way out by separating the critical theory from the political project, i.e., abandoning the latter to save the former. Establishment intellectuals took tremendous risks to retain the theory and save the project. To question the success of their endeavors is not to undermine the valor of their effort. As Chinese Marxists continue in their attempts to overcome the "crisis" of Marxism by creatively and imaginatively exploring the possibility of its synthesis with democratic liberalism and Confucian humanism their intellectual discourse may move beyond post-Maoism to post-Marxism. It will, however, continue to be post-"Maoist" and post-"Marxist" as well.

98. Arif Dirlik, "Socialism and Capitalism in Chinese Socialist Thinking," *Studies in Comparative Communism*, vol. XXI, no. 2 (Summer 1988), pp. 131–352.

99. Alex Callinicos, "Whither Marxism?" *Economic and Political Weekly*, vol. XXXI no. 4 (27 January 1996), pp. PE9–PE17.

Glossary of Names

CHEN YUN   Economic planner who commanded considerable influence and prestige in the 1950s. Chen suffered an eclipse in authority during the Great Leap Forward and Cultural Revolution but reemerged in the late 1970s as a major figure within the post-Mao coalition. As first secretary, Central Discipline Inspection Commission (1978–87), and chairman, Central Advisory Commission (1987–92), Chen spearheaded the call for "seeking truth from facts," providing an accurate appraisal of Mao Zedong's errors and failures and initiating necessary political- and economic-reform measures. Most famous for his "bird and cage" analogy in the economic realm, Chen favored limited economic decentralization and continued reliance on central planning, and was wary of unleashing destabilizing growth.

DENG LIQUN   Formerly Liu Shaoqi's political secretary, Deng served as director of the Central Propaganda Department from 1982–85. Deng was aligned with Chen Yun and Peng Zhen and, along with the Chinese Academy of Social Sciences (CASS) president Hu Qiaomu, was a formidable opponent of "spiritual pollution" or ideological revision and liberalization. Zhao Ziyang's strengthened position in 1986 led to the weakening of Deng's influence over the propaganda apparatus and the Policy Research Office. At the Thirteenth Party Congress, Deng failed to get elected to the Central Committee, but regained his authority in the period immediately following the Tiananmen crackdown when his followers were appointed to key positions in the editorial boards of major newspapers like the *Renmin ribao* (*People's Daily*).

FANG LIZHI   Dubbed "China's Sakharov," astrophysicist and former vice-president of the Chinese University of Science and Technology, Hefei (1985–87) Fang Lizhi attracted a great deal of Western media attention and a following among Chinese students for his attacks on socialism and traditional culture. Through the 1980s Fang's speeches on university campuses across China stressed "all-around Westernization" as the solution to the country's problems. In June 1989, Fang sought refuge in the U.S. embassy in Beijing and remained there until granted permission to leave China the following year.

GANG OF FOUR   Jiang Qing, Yao Wenyuan, Zhang Chunqiao, and Wang Hongwen were followers of Mao Zedong who upheld the politics and ideals of the Cultural Revolution and resisted the social and economic policies of Zhou Enlai and Deng Xiaoping. Their removal by a coup within eight weeks of Mao's death facilitated the institution of pre-Cultural Revolution policies in the spheres of education and culture as well as a new emphasis on stability and unity for the sake of economic growth and development. The Gang's emphasis on class struggle and continuous revolution and its opposition to material incentives and income differences cme to be castigated as "ultraleftist" petty-bourgeois fanaticism by the radical reformers.

GUO LUOJI   A philosopher at Beijing University, Guo distinguished himself by being one of the few radical-reformist intellectuals who in 1979 publicly defended the right of Democracy Wall activists to express themselves. A vocal critic of bureaucratism and ideological dogmatism, Guo Luoji derided the policy of allowing academic liberalization but not political liberalization as impractical, and supported the people's right to express all kinds of opinions, including "counterrevolutionary" ones.

HU JIWEI   Editor-in-chief of the leading newspaper *Renmin ribao* (*People's Daily*). Hu was closely allied with Hu Yaobang and played a crucial role in the media campaign on "practice is the sole criterion of truth." Under Hu's editorship, the *Renmin ribao* resisted Hu Qiaomu and Deng Liqun's efforts to use the media for attacks against radical-reformist intellectuals. As a member of the National People's Congress (NPC) Hu called for freedom of the press and political structural reform along with economic change. Hu played a prominent role in the Tiananmen events of 1989 when he attempted to invoke the NPC's right to review Li Peng's declaration of martial law.

HU QIAOMU   President of the Chinese Academy of Social Sciences (CASS) from 1978–82. Hu, the principal theorist for the moderate reformers, took a leading part in discrediting the economic policies associated with ultraleftism and launching a media barrage in favor of the policy of "distribution according to work" in the late 1970s. Although he aligned himself with the radical reformers against residual Maoists in the successor leadership, Hu had reservations about the discussions on practice and the attacks on Mao by intellectuals like Wang Ruoshui. As the reforms unfolded, Hu joined forces with Deng Liqun to oppose ideological and political liberalization.

HU YAOBANG   Criticized during the Cultural Revolution for his resistance to the Anti-Rightist Campaign of 1957–59, Hu was rehabilitated in 1973 and served as vice-president of the Chinese Academy of Sciences (CAS) until 1975 when he was purged again for his policy proposals regarding intellectuals, education, science, and technology. After his return to power in 1977 as vice-president of the Central Party School, Hu played a major role in directing an ideological offensive against Cultural Revolutionary radicalism and remnant leftists within the Party and the administration. As general secretary of the CCP from 1980–87 Hu came to be identified as the highest-level patron of Chinese intellectuals and their most influential voice for professionalism, intellectual freedom, and security from arbitrary persecution. Hu's death in April 1989, a little over two years after dismissal from his Party posts for failure to curb student demonstrations and protests in December 1986, sparked off the democracy movement that culminated in the Tiananmen tragedy of June 1989.

HUA GUOFENG   The former head of the Public Security apparatus who had supervised the quelling of the Tiananmen demonstrations in the wake of Zhou Enlai's death in 1976, Hua Guofeng was the immediate successor of both Mao Zedong and Zhou Enlai. Discredited for his reluctance to countenance too rapid a shift away from Maoist policies, and outmaneuvered by Deng Xiaoping, Hau lost his premiership of the State Council to Zhao Ziyang in 1980, and his leadership of the CCP to Hu Yaobang in 1981.

JIN GUANTAO As chief editor of the series *Toward the Future* and the author of books like *Philosophy of Man* and *Philosophy of the Whole*, Jin Guantao's main contribution was to introduce "new" Western theories and methodologies such as cybernetics, systems theory, econometrics, and comparative sociology to a Chinese audience. By the late 1980s, Jin had abandoned Marxian dialectics altogether and began to focus on the sinification of Marxism-Leninism as an explanation for the continued conservatism and ultra-stability of the contemporary Chinese social and political order.

LI HONGLIN Currently a historian at the Fujian Academy of Social Sciences, Li Honglin has been one of the most ardent advocates of democracy in the ranks of radical-reformist intellectuals. Unlike most of his colleagues who favor elite democracy, Li has pressed for political rights for workers and peasants as well. In the mid-1980s, he came under attack from Deng Liqun and voluntarily transferred from Beijing to Fujian. In the aftermath of the 1989 Tiananmen student demonstrations, Li was subjected to a year's imprisonment as punishment for his active participation in the democracy movement and support for the demands of students.

LI ZEHOU One of the most original philosophers to gain recognition in the post-Mao era, Li Zehou of the Insititute of Philosophy (CASS) contributed to the debates on epistemology and critical-humanist Marxism by a creative appropriation of Kantian idealism. In Li's writings, the significance of the human subject was redefined within a materialist outlook and aesthetics was determined by the ethical category of freedom. Li's contention that the CCP had failed to promote May Fourth goals of intellectual enlightenment made him the subject of intense criticism in the late 1980s and early 1990s.

LIAO GAILONG As deputy director of the Party History Research Center, Liao Gailong was an influential critic of the Leninist Party organization and its work style. Liao pushed not only for separation of party and Government but also a streamlined NPC which would serve as a check on the arbitrary exercise of political power. Liao envisaged a reduced role for the Party in the social and cultural arenas along with autonomy for the press, judiciary, and mass organizations.

SU SHAOZHI   Su Shaozhi has been one of the most prominent and vocal theorists in the radical-reformist camp. Su was the coauthor of the theory of "undeveloped socialism," which brought upon him the ire of moderate leaders and ideologists like Hu Qiaomu. As director of the Institute of Marxism-Leninism and Mao Zedong Thought from 1982 to 1987, Su encouraged ideological pluralism and the "development" of Marxism through critical questioning of orthodoxy and an openness to new ideas and perspectives from diverse intellectual traditions. In 1987, even as his theory of "undeveloped socialism" was officially espoused under the modified nomenclature of the "primary stage of socialism" by the Thirteenth party Congress, Su himself came under harsh criticism once again for his association with Hu Yaobang and his outspoken advocacy of political democratization and pluralism.

WANG RUOSHUI   Deputy editor of the *Renmin ribao* (*People's Daily,*) 1977–83. Wang's speech at the 1979 Theory Conferences and his subsequent writings made him a central figure in the Chinese debate on alienation and humanism. Despite denunciation during the Anti-Spiritual Pollution Campaign of 1983 and Hu Yaobang's dismissal in 1987, Wang continued to maintain that phenomena such as the Cultural Revolution, Mao's cult of personality, and lack of democracy were manifestations of alienation in Chinese society, as well as consequences of the subordination of the rights of the individual to other goals.

"WHATEVER FACTION"   Led by Hua Guofeng, this group included Wang Dongxing, Ji Dengkui, Chen Yonggui, Chen Xilian, Zhang Binghua, and Li Xing. These surviving leftists, who had conspired with moderate elements within the post-Mao coalition to overthrow the Gang of Four came to be labeled the "whatever faction" because of their pledge to "support whatever policy decisions were made by Chairman Mao and to unswervingly follow whatever instructions were given by him." The "whateverism" of this group implied opposition to the rehabilitation of Deng Xiaoping, the reversal of verdict on the Tiananmen incident of 1976, criticism of Mao and the Cultural Revolution, (or leftism in general) as a deviant phenomenon. The success of Deng Xiaoping and his allies in promoting "practice" as "the sole criterion of truth" as a more authentic Maoist legacy undercut the position of the "whateverists" and led to their virtual elimination as a political force by 1980–81.

XIAO GONGQIN   An associate professor of history at Shanghai Normal University, Xiao Gongqin continued to be one of the foremost proponents of "neo-authoritarianism." In 1988–89, Xiao joined intellectuals like Chen Yizi and Wu Jiaxiang (based in official think tanks like the Institute for Research on the Economic System Reform under the State Council and the Investigation and Research Division of the General Office of the Party Central Committee) to propose an "enlightened despotism" to guide China's transition to a full-fledged market economy and political democracy. In the post-Tiananmen phase Xiao has been identified with the trend of "new conservatism," which opposes the "radicalism" and "political romanticism" of advocates for immediate democratization like Yan Jiaqi, Hu Jiwei, and Su Shaozhi. Xiao's writings support the accommodation of traditional values and a strategy of gradual change effected by a "transitional authority with a modernizing orientation."

YAN JIAQI   Yan was the first director of the Institute of Political Science of CASS (1985–89). During the Theory Conference of February–March 1979, Yan voiced the need for limited terms of office for political leaders. Through the 1980s he recommended strengthening the system of people's congresses including the NPC and implementing a "division of power" and "procedural politics." For Yan Jiaqi, new institutions and the rule of law, not virtuous officials, were the only guarantee against abuse of power.

YU GUANGYAUN   Advisor to the Party Central Propaganda Department and vice-president of CASS, Yu Guangyuan helped establish the Institute of Marxism-Leninism and Mao Zedong Thought and was its first director from 1979 to 1982. Under his leadership the Institute became a focal point for reformists intellectuals committed to ideological pluralism, academic freedom, and a nondogmatic approach to Marxism.

ZHAO ZIYANG   The success of Zhao Ziyang's experiment in economic reform in Sichuan province led to his replacement of Hua Guofeng as premier of the State Council in 1980. As head of the Chinese government from 1980–87 Zhao oversaw far-reaching changes in China's rural and urban economy. Zhao's radical-reformist economic vision brought him into conflict with moderates like Chen Yun and Peng Zhen who deplored the undermining of central control and opposed the emergence of a full-scale market economy system. The perception of an impending economic crisis in late 1988 and early 1989 coupled with his reluctance to come down heavily against the student demonstrators eroded Zhao's position within the official hierarchy and led to his dismissal in late June 1989. Although permitted to retain his party membership, Zhao has since then been marginalized in public life.

ZHOU YANG   As deputy director of the Propaganda Department, 1978–83, and Chairman, All-China Federation of Literary and Art Circles, 1978–83, Zhou Yang reversed his pre-Cultural Revolutionary stance to support intellectual autonomy and diversity. His speech commemorating Marx's death centennial raised a storm in moderate circles by contending that all kinds of alienation—political, economic, and ideological—still existed in China and could only be rooted out by democratization. In the Anti-Spiritual Pollution Campaign that followed, Zhou was criticized for ideological disruption. However, as in the case of colleagues like Su Shaozhi and Wang Ruoshui, such criticism only served to heighten Zhou's prestige and popularity among fellow intellectuals.

Bibliography

Ai Siqi. "Philosophy for the Masses." *Ai Siqi Wenji*, vol. 1. Beijing: People's Publishing House, 1981, pp. 129–282.

———. "A Rebuttal of Comrade Yang Hsien-chen's 'Composite Economic Foundation Theory.'" *Renmin ribao*, 1 November 1964, p. 6. In *JPRS*, 27414, 17 November 1964, pp. 52–67.

———. "Engels Had Affirmed the Identity of Thought and Existence." *Renmin ribao*, 21 July 1960.

Ali, Tariq, ed. *The Stalinist Legacy*. Harmondsworth, Middlesex, England: Penguin Books, 1984.

Althusser, Louis. *For Marx*. Harmondsworth, Middlesex, England: Penguin Books, 1966.

Avineri, Schlomo. *The Social and Political Thought of Karl Marx*. Cambridge: Cambridge University Press, 1968.

Bachman, David. *Chen Yun and the Chinese Political System*. Berkeley: University of California Press, 1985.

Bachman, David and Dali Yang, ed. and trans. *Yan Jiaqi and China's Struggle for Democracy*, Armonk, N.Y.: M.E. Sharpe, 1991.

Bellis, Paul. *Marxism and the USSR*, Atlantic Highlands, N.J.: Humanities Press, 1979.

Benton, Ted. *The Rise and Fall of Structural Marxism: Althusser and His Influence*. New York: St. Martin's Press, 1984.

Bettelheim, Charles. *Class Struggle in the USSR, First Period: 1917–1923*. New York: Monthly Review Press, 1976.

Binder, Leonard, et al., ed. *Crises and Sequences in Political Development*. Princeton: Princeton University Press, 1971.

Brugger, Bill, ed. *Chinese Marxism in Flux 1978–84*. New York: M.E. Sharpe, 1985.

Brugger, Bill and David Kelly. *Chinese Marxism in the Post–Mao Era, 1978–84*. Stanford: Stanford University Press, 1990.

Brus, Wlodzimiercz. *Socialist Ownership and Political Systems*. London: Routledge and Kegan Paul, 1975.

Buchanan, Ray. "Lenin and Bukharin on the Transition From Capitalism to Socialism: The Meshchersky Controversy, 1918." *Soviet Studies*, vol. XXVIII, no. 1 (1976), pp. 66–82.

Callinicos, Alex. "Whither Marxism," *Economic and Political Weekly*, vol. XXXI, no. 4, pp. PE9–PE17.

Cao Siyuan. "Thoughts on the Reform of the NPC." *FBIS*, 23 November 1984.

Cao Tianyu. "A Brief Discussion of Marx's Theory of Alienation." *Zhexue yanjiu*, no. 8 (1983), pp. 18–22.

Cao Yuanzheng. "The Model of the Market Under a 'Soft' Government." *Chinese Sociology and Anthropology*, vol. 23, no. 3 (Spring 1991), pp. 24–31.

———. "The Model of the Market Under a 'Hard' Government." *Chinese Sociology and Anthropology*, vol. 23, no. 3 (Spring 1991), pp. 32–38.

Carchedi, Guglielmo. "On the Economic Identification of the New Middle Class." *Economy and Society*, vol. 4, no. 1 (1975), pp. 1–86.

Casals, Felipe Garcia. *The Syncretic Society*. White Plains, N.Y.: M.E. Sharpe, 1980.

CCP Central Party School Research and Writing Group on Scientific Socialism. "The Class Content and Historical Task of the Dictatorship of the Proletariat." *Guangming ribao*, 11 July 1983, p. 3.

———. "The Basic Characteristics of Socialist Society." *Guangming ribao*, 3 October 1983, p. 3.

———. "Contradictions in Socialist Society." *Guangming ribao*, 31 October 1983, p. 3.

———. "The Basic Characteristics of Socialist Society." *Guangming ribao*, 3 October 1983, p. 3.

Chan Peng. "The Situation on the Discussions of the Question of the Criterion of Practice." *JPRS*, 25624, 29 July 1964, pp. 76–80.

Chang Chen-pang. "The Sixth Plenary Session of the Eleventh CCP Central Committee—An Analysis." *Issues and Studies*, no. 9 (1981), pp. 13–26.

Chang, Gordon. "Interview With Su Shaozhi." *Bulletin of Concerned Asian Scholars*, no. 1 (1988).

Chang Hao. "Intellectual Crisis of Contemporary China in Historical Perspective." In *The Triadic Chord: Confucian Ethics, Industrial East Asia and Max Weber*.

Cheek, Timothy. "Habits of the Heart: Intellectual Assumptions Reflected by Mainland Chinese Reformers From Teng T'o to Fang Li-chih." *Issues and Studies*, vol. 24, no. 3 (1988), pp. 31–52.

Chen Daisun. "Study Modern Economies of the West and Socialist Economic Modernization of Our Country." *Renmin ribao*, 16 November 1983.

Chen Duxiu. "On the Discussion of Socialism." *Shehui zhuyi taolunji*, Guangzhou: New Youth Press, 1922, pp. 32–73.

Chen Erjin. *China: Crossroads Socialism*, translated by Robin Munro. Verso, 1984.

Chen Xiuzhai. "Clearly Demarcate Between the Marxist Criterion of Practice and That of Pragmatism." *Zhexue yanjiu*, no. 3 (1979), pp. 21–24.

Chen Yizi. "Problems of Communism and Changes in China." *The Journal of Contemporary China*, vol. 2, nos. 1–2 (Winter 1993), pp. 82–86.

Chen Yizi, Wang Xiaoqiang, and Li Jun. "The Deep-Seated Questions and the Strategic Choice China's Reform Faces." *Zhongguo: fazhan yu gaige*, no. 4 (1989), pp. 3–9.

Chen Yuan. "Profound Questions and Choices in China's Economy." *Jingji yanjiu*, April 1991, pp. 18–19.

Chen Yun. "Uphold Seeking Truth From Facts—Commemorating the First Anniversary of the Death of the Great Leader and Teacher Chairman Mao." *Renmin ribao*, 28 September 1977.

———. "Report of the Discipline Inspection Commission." *FBIS*, 3 September 1982.

———. "Speech Delivered at the National Conference." *FBIS*, 23 September 1985, pp. 13–16.

Chen Zhongli. "When Were the Exploiting Classes in China Eliminated?" *Beijing Review*, no. 22 (1980).

Chester, Eric. "Revolutionary Socialism and the Dictatorship of the Proletariat." *Critique*, no. 17 (1986), pp. 83–89.

Chinese Academy of Social Sciences, Philosophy Research Branch, *Zhexue Zhenglun* Editorial Group, ed. *Zhexue zhenglun, 1977–1980 nianchu* (Philosophical debates, 1977–early 1980). Xian: Shanxi People's Publishing House, 1980.

Chu Jingning. "Practice Is the Medium of Rational Knowledge—More on the Objective World Is the Source of Knowledge." *Shehui kexue*, no. 6 (1981), pp. 88–91.

Cohen, Stephen *Bukharin and the Bolshevik Revolution*. New York: Alfred Knopf, 1973.

Collier, Andrew. "In Defense of Epistemology." In *Issues in Marxist Philosophy*, edited by John Mepham and David-Hillel Ruben. Brighton, England: Harvester Press, 1979.

Commentator. "Implement the Line of the Third Plenum of the Central Committee of the CCP and Uphold the Four Basic Principles." *Renmin ribao*, 24 April 1981.

———. "Take the Four Basic Principles as the Weapon to Overcome Erroneous Ideological Influences." *Jiefangjun bao*, 26 April 1981.

———. "Correctly Understand the Fundamental Changes in China's Class Situation." *Jiefang ribao*, 19 July 1979.

———. "A Scientific Understanding and Handling of Questions Concerning Class Struggle." *Jiefangjun bao*, 9 October 1982. Also in *Renmin ribao*, p. 2.

———. "Correctly Appraise and Handle the Class Struggle in the Current Stage." *Renmin ribao*, 6 November 1982.

———. "A Serious Struggle Against Enemies in the Political Realm." *Hongqi*, no. 18 (1983), pp. 2–8.

———. "Four Great Pillars That Hold Up the Sky—On the Importance of Upholding the Four Basic Principles." *Renmin ribao*, 23 October 1983.

———. "Common Prosperity not 'Concurrent' Prosperity." *Guangming ribao*, 22 July 1984.

———. "Communique of the Third Plenum of the Eleventh Central Committee of the Communist Party of China." *Peking Review*, no. 52 (1978), pp. 6–16.

Contributing Commentator. "One of the Fundamental Principles of Marxism". *Renmin ribao*, 24 June 1978. In SWB/FE/5851/BII/1–4.

———. "Talk on the Question of Abstract Affirmation and Specific Negation." *Renmin ribao*, 22 September 1978.

———. "Open Up the Broad Prospect of Theoretical Work." *Renmin ribao*, 22 December 1978. In Survey of World Broadcasts/Far SWB/FE/6004/BII/8-11.

———. "All Things in the Subjective World Must Be Verified by Practice." *Renmin ribao*, 25 September 1978.

———. "Uphold the Marxist Scientific Approach." *Renmin ribao*, 19 September 1978. In Survey of World Broadcasts/Far East SWB/FE/5923/BII/1-7.

———. "Implement the Socialist Principle of 'to Each According to His Work.'" *Renmin ribao*, 5 May 1978.

———. "To Uphold the People's Democratic Dictatorship Is an Unshakeable Principle." *Guangming ribao*, 23 April 1981.

———. "On Rethinking." *Hongqi*, no. 12 (1984), pp. 2–8.

———. "Deepen Theoretical Understanding of Reform." *Hongqi*, no. 12 (1984), pp. 38–40.

Cornforth, Maurice. *Dialectical Materialism: The Theory of Knowledge*, vol. III. Calcutta: National Book Agency, 1955.

———. *Communism and Philosophy*. London: Lawrence and Wishart, 1980.

Cui Wenyu. "Discussion on the Question of the Source of Knowledge." *Renmin ribao*, 17 September 1981, p. 5.

Dai Qing. "From Lin Zexu to Jiang Jingguo. "In *Chinese Sociology and Anthropology*, vol. 23, no.3 (Spring 1991), pp. 61–66.

"Decision of the Central Committee of the Communist Party of China on Reform of the Economic Structure." In *FBIS*, 22 October 1984, pp. K1–K19.

Deng Liqun. "Communism Is the Lofty Cause Throughout the Ages." *Gongren ribao*, 27 March 1981.

———. "It Is an Excellent Thing to Discuss Humanism and the Theory of Human Nature." *Renmin ribao*, 12 April 1983, p. 1.

Deng Xiaoping. "Speech at the Opening Ceremony of the National Conference on Science," 18 March 1978. *Selected Works of Deng Xiaoping, 1975–82*, Beijing: Foreign Languages Press, 1984, pp. 101–116.

———. "Vice Chairman Deng Xiaoping's Speech at the All-Army Political Work Conference." *Renmin ribao*, 6 June 1978, pp. 1–2.

———. "Emancipate the Mind, Seek Truth From Facts and Unite as One in Looking to the Future." *Selected Works*, 13 December 1978 pp. 151–165.

———. "Uphold the Four Cardinal Principles." *Selected Works* 30 March 1979. pp. 166–191.

———. "Remarks on Successive Drafts of the 'Resolution on Certain Questions in the History of Our Party Since the Founding of the People's Republic of China.'" *Selected Works* March 1980–June 1981. pp. 276–296.

———. "Implement the Policy of Readjustment, Ensure Stability and Unity." *Selected Works* 25 December 1980. pp. 335–355.

———. "Adhere to the Principle of 'to Each According to His Work.'" Ibid., pp. 117–118.

———. "Carrying Through the Principle of Adjustment, Improving the Working of the Party and Guaranteeing Stability and Solidarity." *Issues and Studies*, no. 7 (1981), pp. 101–119.

Ding Xueliang. *The Decline of Communism in China: Legitimacy Crisis, 1978–1989*. Cambridge: Cambridge University Press, 1994.

———. "The Disparity Between the Idealistic and Instrumental Chinese Reformers," *Asian Survey*, vol. XXXVIII, pp. 1117–1139.

Ding Zhenhai, and Li Zhun. "The Socialist Alienation Theory and the 'Alienation Fever' in the Realm of Literature and Art." *Guangming ribao*, 19 November 1983, p. 3. In SWB/FE/7518/BII/5-12.

Dirlik, Arif. *The Origins of Chinese Communism*. New York: Oxford University Press, 1989.

———. "Socialism and Capitalism in Chinese Socialist Thinking: The Origins." *Studies in Comparative Communism*, vol. XXI, no. 2 (Summer 1988), pp. 131–152.

Dirlik, Arif and Maurice Meisner, eds. *Marxism and the Chinese Experience.* Armonke, N.Y.: M.E. Sharpe, 1989.

Dittmer, Lowell. *Liu Shao-ch'i and the Chinese Cultural Revolution.* Berkeley: University of California Press, 1974.

Dong Fureng, "Develop a Socialist Economy of Benefit to the People," *Renmin ribao,* 29 January 1981.

———. "On the Form of Socialist Ownership in Our Country." *Jingji yanjiu,* no. 1 (1979).

Du Runsheng. "The Agricultural Responsibility System and the Reform of the Rural Economic System." *Hongqi,* no. 19 (1981), pp. 17–25.

Duan Ruofei. "Commenting on the Theory of Alienation of Socialism." *Guangming ribao,* 29 October 1983. In SWB/FE/7485/BII/4-7.

Editorial Department. "Correctly Understand the Situation and the Policies and Uphold the Four Cardinal Principles." *Hongqi,* no. 5 (1981), pp. 2–11.

———. "Communist Ideology and Our Practice." *Hongqi,* no. 17 (1982), pp. 2–8.

———. "Our Banner Is Communism." *Hongqi,* no. 10 (1982), pp. 2–6.

———. "Some Questions That Merit Our Attention." *Hongqi,* no. 24 (1981), pp. 2–7.

———. "Accurately Appraise and Handle Class Struggle in the Current Phase." *Renmin ribao,* 6 November 1982.

———. "Theoretical Work Must Serve Socialist Modernization." *Hongqi,* no. 13 (1983), pp. 28–31.

Engels, Frederick. "Ludwig Feuerbach and the End of Classical German Philosophy." *Marx–Engels Selected Works,* vol. II. Moscow: Foreign Language Publishing House, 1958.

Esherick, Joseph. "On the 'Restoration of Capitalism'—Mao and Marxist Theory." *Modern China,* vol. 5, no. 1 (1979), pp. 41–77.

Evans, Alfred Jr. "Developed Socialism in Soviet Ideology." *Soviet Studies,* no. 29 (1977), pp. 409–428.

Fan Ruoyu. "On the Comprehensive and Accurate Understanding and Mastery of the Fundamental Principles of Marxism." *Zhexue yanjiu,* no. 4 (1978), pp. 2–8, 22.

———. "The Origin of the Polemic Against 'Two Combining Into One.'" *Hongqi,* no. 10 (1979), pp. 64–69. In *JPRS–RF,* 74680, 30 November 1979, pp. 109–118.

Fang Qiao. "On Leftist Mistakes and Their Origin." *Hongqi,* no. 5 (1981), pp. 29–30.

Feng Lanrui. "Thriving of Academic Research Presupposes Freedom and Democracy." *World Economic Herald,* 5 May 1986.

Feng Wenbin. "Consciously Implement the Line of the Third Plenary Session of the Eleventh CCP Central Committee and Firmly Advance Along the Track of Scientific Socialism." *Hongqi,* no. 10 (1981), pp. 2–12.

――――. "Adhere to the Ideological Line Based on Dialectical Materialism as Advocated by Comrade Mao Zedong." *Renmin ribao*, 14 September 1979. In SWB/FE/6228/BII/5-8.

Fewsmith, Joseph. "Neoconservatism and the End of the Dengist Era." *Asian Survey*, vol. XXXV, no. 7 (July 1995), pp. 635–651.

Fogel, Joshua. *Ai Ssu–ch'is Contribution to the Development of Chinese Marxism.* Harvard Contemporary China Series, no. 4. Cambridge: Harvard University Press, 1987.

Friedman, Edward. "Democracy and 'Mao Fever.'" *The Journal of Contemporary China*, no. 6 (Summer 1994), pp. 84–95.

Gao Ertai. "On the Essence of Man," *Chinese Studies in Philosophy*, Fall 1993, pp. 27–53.

――――. "An In-Depth Examination of Alienation," in *"Man is the Starting Point of Marxism"—A collection of Articles Discussing Human Nature and Humanism.* Beijing: Renmin chubanshe, 1981, pp. 72–98.

Gao Hongfan. "Theoretical Abstraction of the Profound Changes in the Countryside—Reading *Economic Reform in Rural China.*" *Renmin ribao*, 30 January 1986.

Goldman, Merle. *China's Intellectuals.* Cambridge: Harvard University Press, 1981.

――――. "Hu Yaobang's Intellectual Network and the Theory Conference of 1979." *The China Quarterly*, no. 126 (1991).

Goldman, et al. *China's Intellectuals and the State: In Search of a New Relationship.* Harvard Contemporary China Series, no.3. Cambridge: Harvard University Press, 1987.

Goldman, Merle. *Sowing the Seeds of Democracy in China: Political Reform in the Deng Xiaoping Era.* Cambridge: Harvard University Press, 1994.

Gouldner, Alvin. *The Two Marxisms: Contradictions and Anomalies in the Development of Theory.* New York: Seabury Press, 1980.

――――. *The Future of Intellectuals and the Rise of the New Class.* New York: Seabury Press, 1979.

Gramsci, Antonio. *Selections From the Prison Notebooks.* London: Lawrence and Wishart, 1971.

Griffith, William. *The Sino–Soviet Rift.* Cambridge: MIT Press, 1964.

Gu Xin. "Hegelianism and Chinese Intellectual Discourse: A Study of Li Zehou," *The Journal of Contemporary China*, no. 8 (Winter–Spring 1995), pp. 1–27.

Gua Huaro. "The Glorious Philosophical Activities of Chairman Mao in the Early Period of the War of Resistance." *Zhongguo zhexue*, no. 1 (1979).

Guan Feng. "On the Identity of Opposites." *Hongqi*, no. 15 (1960), pp. 33–41.

Guan Jian. "Comrade Mao Zedong's Position and Role in the History of the Chinese Revolution." *Hongqi*, no. 11 (1981), pp. 11–18.

Guo Luoji. "Commenting on the So-Called 'Crisis of Faith.'" *Wenhuibao*, 13 January 1980.

Hamrin, Carol Lee. *China and the Challenge of the Future.* Boulder: Westview Press, 1990.

Hamrin, et al., ed. *China's Establishment Intellectuals.* Armonk, N.Y.: M.E. Sharpe, 1986.

Harding, Harry. *China's Second Revolution: Reform After Mao.* Washington, D.C.: Brookings Institution, 1987.

He Jianzhang. "Actively Support and Appropriately Develop Individual Economy in Cities and Towns." *Hongqi*, no. 24 (1981), pp. 13–16.

He Rongfei. "Does Prosperity Necessarily Mean 'Revisionism'?" *Hongqi*, no. 3 (1980), pp. 45–48.

He Zuoxiu. "Some Questions on the Criterion of Practice in the Study of Natural Sciences." *Hongqi*, no. 2 (1962), pp 13–24.

———. "Why Does Jin Guantao Want to Negate the Objectivity of Objective Reality? Commenting on 'The Philosophy of Man.'" *Qiushi*, no. 23 (1 December 1989).

———. "More on the Question of the Criterion of Practice in the Study of Natural Sciences." *JPRS*, 25624, 29 July 1964, pp. 38–53.

Hill, J.D. "Epistemology and Politics." Ph.D. dissertation, University of Michigan, 1981.

Hindess, Barry. *Philosophy and Methodology in the Social Sciences.* Hassocks, 1977.

Hinton, William. "A Trip to Fengyang County." *Monthly Review*, no. 6 (1983).

Hsuan Mo. "Deng Xiaoping's Dilemma." *Issues and Studies*, no. 8 (1981), pp. 13–25.

Hu Fuming. "More on the Source of Knowledge." *Shehui kexue*, no. 1 (1982), pp. 30–35.

———. "Politics and Ideology Cannot Serve as the Basis for Identifying Class." *Beijing Ribao*, 10 August 1979, p. 3. In *FBIS*, no. 25 (17 October 1979).

Hu Jiwei. "Report on a Series of Struggles in the Top Echelons of the CCP." *Zhengming*, no. 34 (1980), pp. 55–63. In *FBIS–Daily Report*, 15 August 1980, pp. U1–U17.

———. "Should One Listen to the Party's Words or Not?" in *The Moment of Sudden Awakening*, edited by Yu Guangyuan and Hu Jiwei. Beijing: Zhongwai chuban gongsi, 1989.

Hu Jiwei and Chang Dalin. "Exploring China's Theories on Democracy." *Renmin ribao*, 30 December 1988, p. 5.

Hu Maoren. "Materialism Refuted?" *Guangming ribao*, 27 November 1989, p. 3.

Hu Peizhao. "A Brief Discussion of Exploitation." *Jingji wenti*, no. 1 (1988).

Hu Qili. "Speech on May Day." *RMRB*, 14 May 1986.

Hu Qiaomu. "Act According to Economic Laws, Speed Up the Four Modernizations." *Renmin ribao*, 6 October 1978, pp. 1–3.

———. "On the Question of Humanism and Alienation." *Renmin ribao*, 27 January 1984, pp. 1–5.

———. "Some Current Problems on the Ideological Front." *Hongqi*, no. 23 (1981), pp. 2–22.

———. "On the Practice of Communist Ideology. *Renmin ribao*, 24 September 1982.

Hu Yaobang. "Usher in an All-Round New Situation in Socialist Modernization." Report to the Twelfth Party Congress. *Hongqi*, no. 18 (1982), pp. 6–32.

———. "The Radiance of the Great Truth of Marxism Lights Our Way Forward." *Beijing Review*, vol. 26, no. 12 (1983), pp. I–XV.

Hua Guofeng. "Report on the Work of the Government." *Beijing Review*, 6 July 1979.

Hua Shi. "An Inexorable Historical Development—A Discussion on Several Questions Regarding the Socialist Transformation of Agriculture in Our Country." *Hongqi*, no. 24 (1981), pp. 25–30.

Hua Shiping. "All Roads Lead to Democracy." Responses by Su Shaozhi, Wang Ruoshui, and Yan Jiaqi. *Bulletin of Concerned Asian Scholars*, Vol. 24, no. 1, pp. 56–58.

———. *Scientism and Humanism: Two Cultures in Post–Mao China (1978–1989)*. Albany: State University of New York Press, 1995.

Huang Dansen. "Some Questions Concerning the Theory of Man." *Zhexue yanjiu*, no. 4 (1983), pp. 23–27.

Huang Fanzhang. "Take a Correct Approach Towards the Contemporary Bourgeois Economic Theories." *Guangming ribao*, 20 November 1983.

Huang Kecheng. "On the Question of Party Style." *Renmin ribao*, 28 February 1981.

———. "On the Appraisal of Chairman Mao and the Attitude Towards Mao Zedong Thought." *Renmin ribao*, 11 April 1981.

Huang Kejian. "The Cultural Dilemma of Contemporary China," *Zhexue yanjiu*, no.2 (1989), pp. 10–19.

Huang Wansheng. "A Dialogue on the Critiques of the New Authoritarianism." *Wenhuibao*, 22 February 1989.

Huang Wenzhuan. "Correctly Understand the Social Characteristics of Our Country During the Present Stage—Also Commenting on a Certain Unhealthy Style of Study." *Renmin ribao*, 12 May 1981.

Hudson, G.F., Richard Lowenthal, and Roderick MacFarquhar. *The Sino–Soviet Dispute*. New York: Praeger, 1961.

Hughes, E.R. "Epistemological Methods in Chinese Philosophy." In *The Chinese Mind*, edited by Charles Moore. Honolulu: East West Center Press, 1967.

Ingersoll, David E. and Richard K. Matthews. *The Philosophic Roots of Modern Ideology: Liberalism, Communism, Fascism*. Englewood Cliffs: Prentice Hall, 1986.

Janos, Andrew, ed. *Authoritarian Politics in Communist Europe*. Berkeley: University of California, Institute of International Studies, 1976.

Jia Wei. "Is Class Nature an Attribute of Truth?" In *Zhexue zhenglun 1977–1980 nianchu* (Philosophical Debates, 1977–beginning of 1980), pp. 55–71. Edited by Chinese Academy of Social Sciences, Philosophy Research Branch, *Zhexue zhenglun*, Editorial Group. Xian: Shanxi People's Publishing House, 1980.

Jian Chunfeng. "Comrade Mao Zedong's Contribution to the Marxist Theory of Knowledge." *Hongqi*, no. 24 (1981), pp. 20–24.

Jiang Nandong, Li Shaogeng, and Yang Pishan. "Have China's Exploiters Been Eliminated as a Class?" *Hongqi*, no. 2 (1980), pp. 35–39.

Jiang Niantao. "Questioning and Argument." *Hongqi*, no. 11 (1979), pp. 17–19.

Jiang Siyi. "Eliminating the Evil Legacy of Feudalism Is an Important Task." *Renmin ribao*, 1 August 1986.

Jiang Yiwei. "If All Workers Are on the Contract System It Will Not Be Conducive to the Socialist Character of the Enterprise." *Jingji tizhe gaige*, no. 2 (1985), pp. 11–13.

Jiang Zemin. "Report to the Fourteenth Party Congress." *Renmin ribao*, 12 October 1992.

Jin Chunming. "Why Were 'Errors of Line' and 'Two Line Struggle' Not Mentioned in the 'Resolution'?" *Hongqi*, no. 18 (1981), pp. 39–41.

Jin Guantao. "Socialism and Tradition: The Formation and Development of Modern Chinese Political Culture." *The Journal of Contemporary China*, no. 3 (Summer 1993), pp. 3–17.

——. *The Philosophy of Man*. Taibei: Shangwu yinshuguan, 1988, pp. 3–17

——. "The Effect of the Deep Structure of Confucian Culture on the Sinification of Marxism." *Xinqimeng*, no. 2, Hunan: Jiaoyu Chubanshe, 1988.

Jin Guantao and Liu Qinfeng. "Explore a Method Which Unites Natural Sciences and Social Sciences." Shanghai: Shanghai renmin chubanshe, 1986.

——. *The Cycle of Growth and Decline — On the Ultrastable Structure of Chinese Society*. Hong Kong: The Chinese University Press, 1992.

Jin Jian. "Repudiation of the 'Theory of Focal Points.'" *Lilun Xuexi*, no 4 (1978), pp. 19–26. In *JPRS*, 72476, 19 December 1978, pp. 14–27.

Jin Sheng. "Human Rights, Equality and Democracy — Commenting on the Contents of 'Move on the Fifth Modernization.'" *Tansuo*, 29 January 1979, pp. 4–7.

Jin Shougeng. "An Important Principle of Dialectical Materialism." *Zhexue yanjiu*, no. 1 (1980), pp. 14–27.

Jin Wen. "On Current Classes and Class Struggle in Our Country." *Jiefang ribao*, 23 July 1979, pp. 1, 4. In *JPRS*, 74334, 9 October 1979, pp. 1–10.

Joffe, Ellis. "Party and Military Professionalism in Command?" *Problems of Communism*, September–October 1983, pp. 48–63.

Joseph, William. *The Critique of Ultraleftism in China, 1958–1981*. Stanford: Stanford University Press, 1984.

Kadar, Janos. "Lenin—The Theoretician and Organiser of Socialist Construction." In *For a Socialist Hungary*. Budapest: Corvina Press, 1974.

———. "Answers to the Questions of the Correspondent of 'New Age,'" Newspaper of the Indian Communist Party." November 1970. In *For a Socialist Hungary*.

Ke Weiran. "The Liberation of Thought and the Four Basic Principles." *Hongqi*, no. 12 (1980), pp. 28–32.

Kelly, David. "The Emergence of Humanism: Wang Ruoshui and the Critique of Socialist Alienation," in *Chinese Intellectuals and the State: In Search of a New Relationship*. pp. 159–182.

———. "Chinese Controversies Over the Guiding Role of Philosophy Over Science," *Australian Journal of Chinese Affairs*, no. 14 (1985), pp. 21–34.

———. ed. and trans. "Wang Ruoshui: Writings on Humanism, Alienation, and Philosophy." *Chinese Studies in Philosophy*, Spring 1985, pp. 25–38.

———. "Chinese Marxism Since Tiananmen: Between Evaporation and Dismemberment." In *China in the Nineties,* edited by David Goodman and Gerald Segal, Oxford: Clarendon Press, 1991.

Kelly, David and Gu Xin. "New Conservatism: Ideology of a 'New Elite.'" In *China's Quiet Revolution,* edited by David Goodman and Beverley Hooper. Melbourne: Longmans Cheshire, 1994.

Kelly, David and He Baogang. "Emergent Civil Society and the Intellectuals in China," in *Developments of Civil Society in Communist Systems,* edited by Robert F. Miller. North Sydney: Allen & Unwin, 1992.

Knight, Nick. "Introduction: The Study of Mao Zedong's Philosophical Thought in Contemporary China." *Chinese Studies in Philosophy*, vol. 23, nos. 3–4 (Spring Summer 1991), pp. 3–56.

Kolakowski, Leszek. *Main Currents of Marxism*, 3 vols. New York: Oxford University Press, 1978.

Konrád, George and Ivan Szelenyi. *The Intellectuals on the Road to Class Power.* New York: Harcourt Brace Jovanovich, 1979.

Kovrig, Bennett. "Hungarian Socialism: The Deceptive Hybrid." *Eastern European Politics and Societies*, vol. 1, no. 1 (1987), pp. 113–134.

Kraus, Richard. *Class Conflict in Chinese Socialism.* New York: Columbia University Press, 1981.

———. "The Lament of Astrophysicist Fang Lizhi: China's Intellectuals in a Global Context," in *Marxism and the Chinese Experience*, pp. 294–315.

Krejci, Jaroslav. *Social Change and Stratification in Postwar Czechoslovakia.* New York: Columbia University Press, 1972.

Krup, Elizabeth. "The Maoist Influence on Current Educational Policy in China." MA thesis, University of Michigan, 1987.

Kuhn, Thomas. *The Structure of Scientific Revolutions.* 2d ed., enlarged. *International Encyclopedia of Unified Sciences*, vol. 2, no. 2. Chicago: University of Chicago Press, 1970.

Laclau, Ernesto and Chantal Mouffe. *Hegemony and Socialist Strategy.* London, 1985.

———. "Post-Marxism Without Apologies," *New Left Review*, vol. 166, 1987.

Lakor, Sandos. "Questions of Social Equality." In *Modern Hungary: Readings From the New Hungarian Quarterly*, edited by Denis Sinor. Bloomington: Indiana University Press, 1977.

Lan Qiuliang and Chen Xilian. "Discussing the Socialist Principle of Equality." *Renmin ribao*, 3 March 1986.

Lan Ying. "The New Development of the Ideological Line of Seek Truth From Facts." *Shehui kexue*, no. 4 (1981), pp. 1–5.

Lardy, Nicholas. "Is China Different? The Fate of its Economic Reform." In *The Crisis of Leninism and the Decline of the Left*, edited by Daniel Chirot. Seattle: University of Washington Press, 1991.

Lee, Ou-fan Lee. "The Crisis of Culture," in *China Briefing 1990*, edited by Anthony Kane. Boulder: Westview Press, 1990.

Lefebvre, Henri. *The Sociology of Marx.* New York: Pantheon Books, 1968.

Lei Zhenwu. "Uphold Materialism, Thoroughly Implement Practice as the Criterion of Truth." *Zhexue yanjiu*, no. 9 (1979), pp. 3–9.

Lenin, V.I. *Materialism and Empirio–Criticism. Collected Works of Lenin*, vol. XXXVIII. Moscow: Progress Publishers, 1972.

———. "The State and Revolution." In *Selected Works of Lenin*, vol. III. Moscow: Foreign Languages Publishing House, 1947, pp. 141–225.

———. "What Is to Be Done? Burning Questions of Our Movement." *Collected Works*, vol. V. Moscow: Progress Publishers, 1964.

———. "A Great Beginning." June 1919. *Selected Works of Lenin*, Moscow: Foreign Languages Publishing House, 1950.

———. "Greetings to Hungarian Workers." *Collected Works*, vol. XXIV.

———. "The Discussion on Self-Determination Summed Up." *Collected Works*, vol. XIX.

Leningrad Institute of Philosophy. *A Textbook of Marxist Philosophy.* Translated, revised, and edited by John Lewis. London: Camelot Press Ltd., 1937.

Lewis, John. *The City in Communist China.* Stanford: Stanford University Press, 1971.

Lewis, Paul, ed. *Eastern Europe: Political Crisis and Legitimation.* London: Croom Helm Press, 1984.

Li Da. "An Outline of Sociology." *Li Da wenji.* Vol. III. Beijing: People's Publishing House, 1984.

Li Dazhao. "My Marxism." *Li Dazhao wenji*, Beijing: People's Publishing House, 1962, pp. 173–211.

———. "Chinese Socialism and World Capitalism." *Li Dazhao wenji*, pp. 356–357.

Li Guangyuan. "Socialism and the Personal Interest of Workers." *Hongqi*, no. 3 (1979), pp. 66–69.

Li Honglin. "Science and Blind Faith." *Renmin ribao*, 2 October 1978. In *Kexue he mixin*, Tianjin: Tianjin People's Publishing House, 1980, pp. 90–108.

———. "Historical Initiative and Historical Limitation." *Guangming ribao*, 3 January 1980.

———. "Mao Zedong Thought Is Science." *Kexue he Mixin*, Tianjin: Tianjin People's Publishing House, 1980, pp. 48–56.

———. "What Kind of Democracy Do We Want?" *Guangming ribao*, 11 March 1979.

———. "Exposing and Criticising the Gang of Four Constitutes a Decisive Battle of a Historical Nature." *Lishi yanjiu*, no. 3 (1978), pp. 3–15.

———. "The 'Theory of Bourgeois Rights' of the Gang of Four Must Be Criticised." *Zhexue yanjiu*, no. 7 (1978), pp. 30–38.

Li Jinquan. "On the Historical Status of Confucianist Humanistic Thought." *Zhexue yanjiu*, no. 11 (1989), pp. 47–52.

Li Jingyuan. "The Results and Purpose of Practice." *Zhexue yanjiu*, no. 6 (1980), pp. 52–54.

Li Junru. "The 'Fountainhead of Knowledge' and the 'Origin of the World.'" *Shehui kexue*, no. 6 (1980), pp. 103–104.

Li Mingsan. "Why Common Prosperity Does Not Mean Concurrent Prosperity?" *Hongqi*, no. 15 (1984), pp. 46–47.

Li Shaochun. "China's Ancient Feudal Despotism." *Guangming ribao*, 14 August 1979.

Li Shichao. "Comment on Kang Sheng's Historical Idealist Viewpoint of Determining Class Status According to Political and Ideological Criteria." *Renmin ribao*, 4 August 1980.

Li Shu. "Thirty Years of Social Science in China." *Lishi yanjiu*, no. 11 (November 1979), pp. 3–16.

———. "Identify the Essence and Absorb It." *Lishi yanjiu*, 1989. In *JPRS*, 74564, p. 36.

Li Xiulin, Ding Yelai and Zhang Hangsheng. "The Practice Criterion and the Guidance of Theory." *Zhexue yanjiu*, no. 10 (1978), pp. 14–20.

Li Xiulin, and Zhang Hangsheng. "Class Struggle Without Exploiting Classes." *Renmin ribao*, 31 October 1979.

———. "Is Class Really a General Social Formation?" *Renmin ribao*, 24 January 1980.

Li Yanshi. "Power and Truth." *Hongqi*, no. 11 (1979), pp. 15–17.

Li Yu-ning. *The Introduction of Socialism to China*. New York: Columbia University Press, 1971.

Li Zehou. *A Critique of Critical Philosophy*. Beijing: Renmin chubanshe, 1979.

———. *Ancient Chinese Intellectual History*. Beijing: Renmin chubanshe, 1985.

Liao Gailong. "Historical Experience and Our Road of Development." *Zhonggong yanjiu*, no. 19 (1981), pp. 108–77. *Issues and Studies*, no. 10 (1981), pp. 65–94;11: 81–110; 12: 79–104.

———. "Concerning the Question of the Superiority of the Socialist System." *Zhexue yanjiu*, no. 6 (1979), pp. 7–14.

———. "Advance Along the Path of All-Round Socialist Construction—In Commemoration of the 100th Death Anniversary of Marx." *Jiaoxue yu yanjiu*, (*Zhonguo renmin daxue*), no. 2 (1983), pp. 6–15.

———. "The Road of All-Round Socialist Construction." *Yunnan shehui kexue*, no. 2 (1982), pp. 1–8.

———. "Answers and Explanations Regarding Some Questions Which Have Been Posed in Connection With the Study of the 'Resolution.'" *Yunnan shehui kexue*, no. 2 (1982).

———. "Mao Zedong Thought and Building Socialism with Chinese Characteristics). *Wenhuibao*, 12 December 1983, p. 3.

———. "Again Discussing Mao Zedong Thought and 'Socialism With Chinese Characteristics.'" *Mao Zedong sixiang yanjiu* (*Chengdu*), no. 2 (1985), pp. 1–7.

———. "Zhou Enlai Thought on Socialist Construction." *Mao Zedong sixiang yanjiu* (*Chengdu*), no. 3 (1985), pp. 1–6.

Liebarthal, Kenneth. "The Political Implications of Document No. 1, 1984." *The China Quarterly*, no. 101 (1985).

Lin Boye and Shen Che. "Commenting on the So-Called Opposition to the Class of Bureaucrats." *Hongqi*, no. 5 (1981), pp. 12–18.

Lin Min. "The Search for Modernity: Chinese Intellectual Discourse and Society,1978–88—the Case of Li Zehou.," *The China Quarterly*, no. 132 (December 1992), pp. 969–998.

Lin Tongqi, Henry Rosemont Jr., and Roger T. Ames. "Chinese Philosophy: A Philosophical Essay on the 'State-of-the-Art,'" *The Journal of Asian Studies*, vol. 54, no. 3 (1995), pp. 727–758.

Lin Yuhua. "The General Character of the Transition Period and Its Specific Pattern." *Shehui kexue*, no. 1 (1980), pp. 30–34.

———. "Some Problems Concerning the Principal Contradiction at the Present Stage." *Shehui kexue*, no. 3 (1979), pp. 21–26.

Lin Yusheng, et. al. *May Fourth: Pluralistic Reflections.*" Hong Kong: Joint Publishing Co., 1989.

Liu Ben. "The Origin of Knowledge and the Criterion of Truth." *Zhexue yanjiu*, no. 9 (1980), pp. 12–19.

Liu Da. "Rectify Our Understanding of Intellectuals." *Hongqi*, no. 1 (1980), pp. 36–38, 41.

Liu Binyan. "Listen Carefully to the Voice of the People." *Renmin ribao*, 26 November 1979.

Liu Fen and Zhang Zhuanfang. "The 'Struggle' of Contradiction Is the Dynamic of the Development of Things." *Zhexue yanjiu*, no. 8 (1979), pp. 41–47.

Liu Guogang. "Several Problems in Current Economic Reform and Readjustment," *Xinhua wenzhai*, no. 6 (1984), pp. 46–48.

Liu Huiyong. "We Must Rectify a Misunderstanding of the Marxist Theory of Ownership." *Jingji wenti*, no. 2 (1989).

Liu Shiding. "Political Structural Reform Must Be Coordinated With Economic Structural Reform." *Minzhu yu fazhai*, no. 8 (1986), pp. 20–21.

Liu Xinyu. "What is the Principal Contradiction in Our Society at the Present Stage?" *Shehui kexue*, no. 3 (1979), pp. 16–20.

Lu Guoying. "A Probe Into the Classification and Solution of Contradictions." *Zhexue yanjiu*, no. 2 (1980), pp. 18–26.

Lu Zhichao. "Assess Socialist Society With the Theory of Development of Dialectical Materialism." *Hongqi*, no. 14 (1983), pp. 13–17.

———. "Mao Zedong Thought Is the Shining Banner of the Chinese People." *Hongqi*, no. 16 (1981), pp. 29–34.

Lukacs, Georg. *History and Class Consciousness*. London: Merlin Press, 1971.

Luo Bing. "The Differences Between Chen Yun and Deng Xiaoping." *Zheng-ming*, no. 6 (1984).

Ma Jihua. "Is Socialist Society a Transition Period." *Shehui kexue*, no. 1 (1980), pp. 35–39.

Ma Hong. "Marxism and China's Socialist Economic Construction—Written to Commemorate the Centenary of Marx's Death." *Social Sciences in China*, no. 3 (1983), pp. 95–110.

Ma Ming. "Neither Purpose Nor Interest Is the Criterion to Test the Truth." *Zhexue yanjiu*, no. 8 (1980), pp. 13–16, 12.

Ma Qibin, and Chen Dengcai. "Why Is It That Mao Zedong Thought Does Not Include the Errors Made by Mao Zedong in His Later Years?" *Hongqi*, no. 20 (1981), pp. 36–38.

Ma Qibin, Chen Dengcai, and Chen Wei. "The Formation and Development of Mao Zedong Thought." *Hongqi*, no. 12 (1981), pp. 22–31.

Ma Shu-Yun. "The Chinese Discourse on Civil Society." *The China Quarterly*, no. 137 (March) 1994, pp. 180–193.

Ma Zhongtu. "Unfold Ideological Struggle on Two Fronts Correctly and in Good Time." *Hongqi*, no. 8 (1983), pp. 33–36.

Macfarquhar, Roderick, Timothy Cheek, and Eugene Wu. *The Secret Speeches of Chairman Mao."* Cambridge: Harvard University Press, 1989.

"Making Up the Lesson Must Be Applied to Reality." *Renmin ribao*, 3 September 1978.

Mandel, Ernest. *Marxist Economic Theory*. London: Merlin Press, 1962.

Manion, Melanie. "Discussions on Practice: Definition of the Parameters of Choice in the People's Republic of China, Post-Mao." M.A. dissertation, School of Oriental and African Studies, University of London, 1982.

Mao Chongjie. "Is Man the Starting Point for Marxism?" *Zhexue yanjiu*, no. 3 (1983), pp. 34–41.

Mao Zedong. "Analysis of Classes in Chinese Society." *Selected Works of Mao Tse-tung*, vol. 1. Peking: Foreign Languages Press, 1967, pp. 13–22.

———. "How to Differentiate the Classes in the Rural Areas?" *Selected Works*, vol. 1, pp. 137–140.

———. "On Practice." *Selected Works*, vol. 1, pp. 295–310.

———. "On Contradiction." *Selected Works*, vol. 1, pp. 85–133.

———. "On the Ten Great Relationships." *Mao Tse–tung Unrehearsed*, edited by Stuart Schram. Harmondsworth, Middlesex, England: Penguin Books, 1974, pp. 61–83.

———. "Where do Correct Ideas Come From." *Selected Readings From the Works of Mao Tse–tung*. Beijing: Foreign Languages Press, 1971, pp. 502–504.

———. "Speech at CCP National Conference on Propaganda." 12 March 1957. *Selected Readings*, pp. 480–498.

———. "Things Are Beginning to Change." *Selected Works*, vol. 5, 15 May 1957.

———. "The Situation in the Summer of 1957." *Selected Works*, vol. 5, July 1957.

———. "Talk at an Enlarged Central Work Conference" [30 January 1962]. *Mao Tse–tung Unrehearsed*, edited by Stuart Schram. Harmondsworth, Middlesex, England: Penguin Books, 1974, pp. 158–187.

———. "Speech at the First Zhengzhou Conference." *JPRS*, 61269-1, 20 February 1974.

———. "Comments on a Reply to Comrades A.V. Sanina and V.G. Venzher." *JPRS*, 61269, 20 February 1975, pp. 129–132.

———. "On the Correct Handling of Contradictions Among the People." Speaking Notes, 27 February 1957 in *The Secret Speeches of Chairman Mao*, edited by MacFarquhar et al., Harvard Contemporary China Series: 6. Cambridge: Harvard University Press, 1989.

———. "Directives on Strengthening the Dictatorship Over the Bourgeoisie." 9 February. *Peking Review*, no. 7 (1975), pp. 4; no. 9 (1975), p. 5.

Marx, Karl. *Thesis on Feuerbach*. Moscow: Progress Publishers, 1965.

———. *Critique of the Gotha Programme*. The Marxist-Leninist Library, vol 15, London: Lawrence and Wishart Ltd., 1943.

———. "The Civil War in France." *The Karl Marx Library: On Revolution*, vol. 1, edited and translated by Saul Padover. New York: McGraw-Hill, 1971, pp. 332–372.

———. "The Eighteenth Brumaire of Louis Napoleon." *The Karl Marx Library: On Revolution*, pp. 243–328.

Marx, Karl, and Frederick Engels. "Letter to E. Bloch." *Selected Correspondence of Karl Marx and Fredrich Engels*, Moscow: Progress Publishers. 1965.

———. *The German Ideology*, edited by C.J. Arthur. New York: International Publishers, 1976.

McClellan, David. *The Thought of Karl Marx*. New York: Harper and Row, 1971.

Meaney, Connie Squire. "Market Reform in a Leninist System: Some Trends in the Distribution of Power, Strategy, and Money in Urban China." *Studies in Comparative Communism*, vol. 22, nos. 2–3 (1989), pp. 203–220.

Mehnert, Klaus. *Peking and the New Left*. Berkeley: University of California Press, 1969.

Meisner, Maurice. *Li Ta–chao and the Origins of Chinese Marxism*. Cambridge: Harvard University Press, 1967.

Meng Xianzhong, Wang Yanbing, Liu Renke, Wang Youdang, and Hu Hao. "It Is Necessary to Reflect Correctly the Results of Practice." *Zhexue yanjiu*, no. 6 (1980).

Meyer, Alfred. *Leninism*. Cambridge: Harvard University Press, 1957.

―――. *Marxism: The Unity of Theory and Practice*. Ann Arbor: University of Michigan Press, 1969.

Miller, Lyman. "The Politics of Reform in China." *Current History*, September 1981, pp. 258–262, 273.

Misra, Kalpana. *Rethinking Marxism in Post–Mao China: The Erosion of Official Ideology, 1978–84*. Ph.D. dissertation in Political Science, University of Michigan, 1992.

Moody, Peter. *Chinese Politics After Mao*. New York: Praeger Publishers, 1983.

Moskovic, L.N. *The End of Ideology Theory: Illusions and Reality*. Moscow: Progress Publishers, 1974.

Munro, Donald. *The Concept of Man in Early China*. Ann Arbor: University of Michigan Press, 1969.

―――. *The Concept of Man in Contemporary China*. Ann Arbor: University of Michigan Press, 1977.

―――. "The Malleability of Man in Chinese Marxism." *The China Quarterly*, no. 48 (1971), pp. 609–640.

―――. "The Chinese View of Alienation." *The China Quarterly*, no. 59 (1979), pp. 580–582.

―――. "The Yang Hsien-chen Affair." *The China Quarterly*, no. 22 (1965), pp. 75–82.

Nee, Victor and David Mozingo, ed, *State and Society in Contemporary China*. Ithaca: Cornell University Press, 1983.

O'Briere, S.J. *Fifty Years of Chinese Philosophy*. Westport, Conn.: Greenwood Press, 1979.

Ollman, Bertel. *Alienation: Marx's Concept of Man in Capitalist Society*. Cambridge, England: Cambridge University Press, 1976.

"On Current Classes and Class Struggle in Our Country." *Jiefang ribao*, 23 July 1979. In *FBIS*, no. 22 (9 October 1979), pp. 1–10.

Ossowski, Stanislaw. *Class Structure in the Social Consciousness*. London: Routledge and Kegan Paul, 1963.

Parkin, Frank. *Marxism and Class Theory: A Bourgeois Critique*. New York: Columbia University Press, 1979.

People's Republic of China, Communist Party of China. *Eighth National Congress of the Communist Party of China*. Peking: Foreign Languages Press, 1956.

Petracca, Mark and Meng Xiong. "The Concept of Chinese Neo-Authoritarianism." *Asian Survey*, vol. XXX, no. 11 (November 1990), pp. 1099–1117.

Poulantzas, Nicolas. *Classes in Contemporary Capitalism*. London: New Left Books, 1975.

Price, Jane. *Cadres, Commanders and Commissars: The Training of the Chinese of the Chinese Communist Leadership, 1920–45*. Boulder: Westview Press, 1976.

"Proposal for the Reform of the Ownership System of Our Country." *Renmin ribao*, 26 September 1986.

Pye, Lucian. "The Legitimacy Crisis." *Crisis and Sequences in Political Development*, ed. by Leonard Binder, et. al. Princeton: Princeton University Press, 1971.

———. "The State and the Individual: An Overview Interpretation." *The China Quarterly*, no. 127 (September 1991), pp. 443–466.

Qi Xin. "The New Power Struggle of the Chinese Communists." *Qishi niandai*, no. 106 (1978).

———. "The Class Situation and the Principal Contradiction in Mainland China—An Important Theoretical Issue at the Second Session of the Fifth NPC." *Qishi niandai*, August 1979. In *FBIS*, 13 August 1979, pp. U1–U5.

———. "About Deng Xiaoping's Talks on the Problem of Privileges—and About the Social Background of the Drama 'If I Were the Real One.'" *Qishi niandai*, no. 1 (1980), pp. 74–75. In *JPRS*, 75142, 15 February 1980, pp. 83–87.

Qi Zhenhai. "The Relativity and Absoluteness of the Criterion of Practice." *Zhexue yanjiu*, no. 7 (1978), pp. 8–14.

Qi Zhenhai and Liu Jiyue. "Marxist Philosophy Versus Voluntarism." *Journal of Beijing Normal University*, Social Science edition, no. 3 (1980), pp. 47–54.

Qi Zhenhai, and Xu Hongwu. "A Brief Discussion on the Two Forms of Revisionism." *Shehui kexue zhanxian*, no. 3 (1980), pp. 21–25.

———. "Recognise the Main Signs of Revisionism." *Hongqi*, no. 2 (1980), pp. 40–43.

Qin Xiaoying. "Escaping From a Historical Cycle." *Chinese Sociology and Anthropology*, vol. 23, no. 4 (Summer 1991), pp. 7–30.

"Resolution on Certain Questions in the History of Our Party Since the Founding of the PRC." Adopted by the Sixth Plenary Session of the Eleventh Central Committee of the CCP on 27 June 1981. *Beijing Review*, no. 27 (1981), pp. 10–39.

"Resolution of the Central Committee of the CPC on the Guiding Principles for Building a Socialist Society With an Advanced Culture and Ideology." September 1986. In *FBIS*, 29 September 1986, pp. K2–K12.

Rong Jian. "Does China Need an Authoritarian Political System in the Course of Modernization?" *Chinese Sociology and Anthropology*, Winter 1990–91.

Rosen, Stanley. "Recentralization, Decentralization, and Rationalization: Deng Xiaoping's Bifurcated Education Policy." *Modern China*, no. 3 (1985), pp. 301–346.

Rosen, Stanley and Gary Zou, eds. "The Chinese Debate on Neo-Authoritarianism," *Chinese Sociology and Anthropology*, Winter 1990–91, Spring 1991, and Summer 1991.

Rozman, Gilbert. *The Chinese Debate on Soviet Socialism, 1978–85*. Princeton: Princeton University Press, 1987.

Ru Xin. "Is Humanism Revisionism?" *Renmin ribao*, 14 August 1980, p. 5.

———. "New Tasks Facing Marxist Philosophy." *Renmin ribao*, 20 July 1983, p. 5.

———. "Young Hegel's Thought on Labour and Alienation." *Zhexue yanjiu*, no. 8 (1978), pp. 44–52.

Ruben, David-Hillel. *Marx and Materialism: A Study in the Marxist Theory of Knowledge*. Sussex: Harvester Press, 1979.

Sautman, Barry. "Sirens of the Strongman: Neo-Authoritarianism in Recent Chinese Political Theory." *The China Quarterly*, no. 129 (March 1992), pp. 77–102.

Scanlan, James. *Marxism in the USSR: A Critical Survey of Soviet Thought*. Ithaca: Cornell University Press, 1985.

Schoenhal, Michael. "The 1978 Truth Controversy." *The China Quarterly*, no. 126 (1991), pp. 243–268.

Schram, Stuart. *Ideology and Politics Since the Third Plenum, 1978–84*. Research notes and studies, no. 6. London: Contemporary China Institute, School of Oriental and African Studies, 1984.

———. *Mao Tse–tung Unrehearsed, Talks and Letters: 1956–71*. Harmondsworth, Middlesex, England: Penguin Books, 1974.

Schwarcz, Vera. *The Chinese Enlightenment*. Berkeley: University of California Press, 1986.

Schwartz, Benjamin. *Communism and China: Ideology in Flux*. Cambridge: Harvard University Press, 1968.

———. *Chinese Communism and the Rise of Mao*. Cambridge: Harvard University Press, 1951.

Seymour, James. *The Fifth Modernization: China's Human Rights Movements, 1978–79*. Stanfordville, N.Y.: Human Rights Publishing Group, 1980.

Sha Yexin and Wu Yiye. "Chase Away the Ghost of Feudalism." *Wenhuibao*, 10 July 1980, p. 3. In *JPRS*, 76394, 9 September 1980. pp. 5–11.

Shao Huaze. "Correctly Analyze and Understand the 'Great Cultural Revolution.'" *Hongqi*, no. 17 (1981), pp. 43–48.

Shi Zhonglian. "New-Confucianism and the Living Spirit of China's Civilization." *Zhexue yanjiu*, no. 9 (1989), pp. 31–36.

Shi Zhongquan. "How Should China's Socialist Society be Assessed?" *Hongqi*, no. 11 (1981), pp. 2–10.

———. "An Example of Summing Up Historical Experience—Studying the 'Resolution.'" *Hongqi*, no. 14 (1981).

Shi Zhu. "The 'Leftist' Line of Lin Biao and the Gang of Four and its Social and Historical Root Causes." *Hongqi*, no. 4 (1979), pp. 21–26.

Solinger, Dorothy, ed. "Commerce: The Petty Private Sector and the Three Lines in the Early 1980s." *Three Visions of Socialism*, edited by Dorothy Solinger. Boulder: Westview Press, 1984.

————. "Urban Entrepreneurs and the State: The Merger of State and Society," In Arthur Rosenbaum, ed., *State and Society in China*. Boulder: Westview Press, 1992.

Special Commentator. "Practice Is the Sole Criterion for Testing Truth." *Guangming ribao*, 11 May 1978, p. 2.

Staff Commentator. "Deepen and Expand the Scientific Study of Marxism-Leninism–Mao Zedong Thought." *Zhexue yanjiu*, no. 11 (1978), pp. 2–7.

————. "Conscientiously Make Up This Lesson on the Discussions on the Criterion of Truth." *Hongqi*, no. 9 (1979), pp. 2–4.

————. "Rectify the Attitude Towards Marxism." *Renmin ribao*, 3 October 1979, pp. 1–4.

————. "Seek Truth From Facts, Where There Are Errors, They Must Be Corrected." *Renmin ribao*, 15 November 1978, pp. 1, 4.

Staff Special Commentator. "Win Complete Victory in the Struggle to Expose and Criticise the Gang of Four." *Renmin ribao*, 4 October 1978, pp. 1, 2.

————. "Eliminate Superstition, Master Science." *Zhongguo qingnian*, no. 1 (1978), pp. 5–8.

————. "On the Characteristics of Chinese Society at the Present Stage." *Guangming ribao*, 14 May 1981, p. 1.

————. "To Uphold the People's Democratic Dictatorship Is an Unshakeable Political Principle." *Guangming ribao*, 23 April 1981, p. 1.

————. "The People's Democratic Dictatorship is in Essence the Dictatorship of the Proletariat." *Guangming ribao*, 21 April 1981, p. 1.

Starr, John. *Continuing the Revolution*. Princeton: Princeton University Press, 1979.

Su Dongbin. "China Is Heading Towards 'New Socialism.'" *Guangming ribao*, 27 March 1989, p. 3.

Su Shaozhi. "On the Principle Contradiction Facing Our Society Today." *Xueshu yuekan*, no. 7 (1979), pp. 14–15. In *JPRS*, 74813, 21 December 1979, pp. 12–15.

————. "The Aim of Socialist Production Is to Satisfy People's Needs. *Wenhuibao*, 26 November 1979. In *Xinhua yuebao*, no. 1 (1980), pp. 72–74.

————. "The Most Important Development of Marxism." *Renmin ribao*, 21 July 1981. In *Xinhua wenzhai*, no. 9 (1981), p. 7.

————. " Earnestly Study the New Situation in the New Period and Advance Marxism." *Xuexi yu tansuo*, no. 1 (1983), pp. 17–22.

————. "Some Questions in China's Socialist Economic Construction." (1981). In *Selected Studies on Marxism*, Beijing: Chinese Academy of Social Sciences, Institute of Marxism-Leninism, 1988.

———. "Tentative Views on the Reform of the Economic Mechanism in Hungary." (1983) *Selected Studies on Marxism*, 1988.

———. "In the Midst of Overall Reform Develop Marxism and Construct Socialism with Chinese Characteristics." *Renmin ribao*, 11 March 1983, p. 5.

———. "Some Theoretical Questions on Hungary's Economic Structural Reform." *Xinhua yuebao wenzhaiban*, no. 7 (1980), pp. 66–70.

———. "Some Important Questions for Research on Our Development Strategy." *Shehui kexue zhanxian*, no. 1 (1982). In *Xinhua wenzhai*, no. 6 (1982), pp. 47–49.

———. "Develop Marxism Under Contemporary Conditions—In Commemoration of the Centenary of the Death of Karl Marx." (1983). *Selected Studies on Marxism*, 1988.

———. "Tentative Views on the Class Situation and Class Struggle in China at the Present Stage." (1981). *Selected Studies on Marxism*, 1988.

———. "Uphold and Develop Mao Zedong Thought." *Makesizhuyi yanjiu* (congkan), no. 1 (1984), pp. 18–25.

———. "On Distinguishing Criteria of Socialist Structures." *Guangming ribao*, 21 October 1985, p. 3.

———. "The Resolution Is a Guiding Document of Marxism." *Zhejiang xuekan* (*Hangzhou*), no. 1 (1985), pp. 4–10. In *Renda Fuyin*, no. 3 1985, pp. 5–11.

———. "Prospect for Socialism as Viewed From China's Experience and Lessons." (1985). *Selected Studies on Marxism*, 1988.

———. "Some Questions Concerning the Writing of the History of Marxism." (1985). *Selected Studies on Marxism*, 1988.

———. "Political Structural Reform and the Opposition to Feudal Influences." *Renmin ribao*, 14 August 1986.

———. "Feudal Remnants Block China's Path." *China Daily*, 22 July 1986.

———. "Remarks at the *Honqi* Symposium on 'Building Socialism With Chinese Characteristics.'" *Hongqi*, no. 14 (1986).

———. "Economic Development and Democratization." *Selected Studies on Marxism*, 1988.

———. "Some Problems of the Political Reform in China." *China Information*, vol. 3, no. 2 (Autumn 1988).

———. "The Historical Destiny of Marxism in China From 1949–89." *Pai Hsing*, no. 201 (1 October 1989), pp. 31–33. Translated in *JPRS-CAR-90-010*, 7 February 1990, pp. 22–24 and *JPRS-CAR-90-011*, 12 February 1990, pp. 11–14.

———. "Rethinking Socialism in the Light of Chinese Reforms." *China Information*, vol. 5, no. 4 (Spring 1991).

Su Shaozhi et al. "A Symposium on Marxism in China Today: An Interview with Su Shaozhi, With Comments by American Scholars and a Response by Su Shaozhi." *Bulletin of Concerned Asian Scholars*, no. 1 (1988), pp. 11–35.

Su Shaozhi, and Ding Xueliang. "Marx's Predictions on the Era of Information." *Renmin ribao*, 24 August 1984, p. 5.

Su Shaozhi, and Feng Lanrui. "The Question of the Stages of Social Development After the Seizure of Power by the Proletariat." *Jingji yanjiu*, no. 5 (1979), pp. 14–19.

Su Shaozhi, and Guo Shuqing. "The Relationship Between Marxist Theory and the Yugoslav Self-Management System." *Dangdai guowai shehuizhuyi*, no. 2 (1984), pp. 9–16.

Su Shaozhi and Wang Yizhou. "Two Historic Tasks of Reform." *Renmin ribao*, 5 March 1988, p. 5.

———. "Several Problems Concerning Political Structural Reform." *Baike zhishi*, no.1 (1987), pp. 2–5.

Suchting, Wal. "Marx's Thesis on Feuerbach. A New Translation and Notes Towards a Commentary." *Issues in Marxist Philosophy Volume 2: Materialism*, edited by John Mepham and David-Hillel Ruben, pp. 5–34. Brighton: Harvester Press, 1977.

Sun Changjiang. "From the Practice Criterion to the Production Criterion." *RMRB*, 9 May 1988.

Sun Ruiyuan. "Why Is It That Not All Ideological Differences in the Party Reflect Class Struggle in Society?" *Hongqi*, no. 19 (1981), pp. 38–40.

Sun Yuecai. "Three Points Regarding the Theory of Man." *Shehui kexue*, no. 9 (1983), pp. 47–50.

Sweezy Paul, and Charles Bettelheim. *On the Transition to Socialism*. New York: Monthly Review Press, 1971.

Swingewood, Alan. *Marx and Modern Social Theory*. London: Macmillan Press, 1975.

Tang Tsou. *The Cultural Revolution and Post–Mao Reforms: A Historical Perspective*. Chicago: University of Chicago Press, 1986.

Tao Delin. "A Few Problems Concerning the Criterion of Truth." *Zhexue yanjiu*, no. 10 (1978), pp. 12–13.

Teng Wensheng. "Historical Experience Shows the Correct Road to Our Country's Modernization." *Hongqi*, no. 17 (1981), pp. 37–42.

Tian Jujian. "Feudal Remnants Must Be Analyzed in Depth." *Renmin ribao*, 13 September 1986.

Ticktin, Hillel. "The Political Economy of Class in the Transitional Epoch." *Critique*, nos. 20–21 (1987), pp. 7–25.

Ting Gong and Feng Chen. "Neo-Authoritarian Theory in Mainland China." *Issues and Studies*, January 1991, pp. 84–98.

Tong, James, ed. "Underground Journals in China, Part I and II. " *Chinese Law and Government*, vol. 13, nos. 3–4 (1980), and vol. 14, no. 3 (1981).

Trotsky, Leon. "Social Relations in the Soviet Union." *The Stalinist Legacy*, edited by Tariq Ali. Harmondsworth, Middlesex, England: Penguin Books, 1984.

———. *The Third International After Lenin*. New York: Pathfinder Press, 1970.

Tu Lei and Wu Chunguang. "Practice Is the Only Objective Criterion by Which to Verify Truth." *JPRS*, 25624, 29 July 1964, pp. 30–37.

Tu Wei-ming. *Way, Learning and Politics: Essays on the Confucian Intellectual*. Albany: State University of New York Press, 1993.

———. "Intellectual Effervescence in China." *Exit from Communism, Daedalus*. Spring 1992, pp. 251–292.

———. "The Modern Chinese Intellectual Quest." *Way, Learning and Politics: Essays on the Confucian Intellectual*.

———. ed. *The Triadic Chord: Confucian Ethics, Industrial East Asia and Max Weber*. Singapore: Institute of East Asian Philosophy, 1991.

Wakeman, Frederick Jr. *History and Will: Philosophical Perspectives of Mao Tse–tung's Thought*. Berkeley: University of California Press, 1973.

Wang Dingyuan. "The 'Z' Shaped Development of the Cooperative System in Socialist Agriculture." *Shehui kexue*, no. 11 (1983), pp. 20–25.

Wang Guofa. "Democracy Should Not Go Beyond Social Development." *Liaowang*, 7 August 1989, p. 17. In *FBIS*, 21 August 1989, pp. 32–33.

Wang Hongchang and Liu Mengyi. "Does a Bureaucratic Class Exist Within the Party?" *Zhongguo qingnianbao*, 7 February 1981. In *FBIS Daily Report*, 23 February 1981, pp. L27–L30.

Wang Huning. "Political Aesthetics and Political Development." *Shehui kexue zhanxian*, no. 1, pp. 134–141.

Wang Jianwei. "The Principled Difference Between the Marxist Criterion of Practice and That of Pragmatism." *Zhexue yanjiu*, no. 6 (1980), pp. 51, 56–58.

Wang Jiuying. "A Brief Analysis of the Causes of Inequities in Social Distribution in Our Country." In *Guangming ribao*, 15 October 1988.

Wang Li, Jia Yixue, and Li Xin. "The Dictatorship of the Proletariat and the Great Proletarian Cultural Revolution." *Peking Review*, 23 December 1966.

Wang Mengui. "Exploring the Road of Our Country's Socialist Construction." *Hongqi*, no. 15 (1981), pp. 33–40.

Wang Renzhong. "Typical Example of Seeking Truth From Facts." *Zhongguo qingnian*, no. 4 (1978). Also in *Guangming ribao*, 9 December 1978.

Wang Ruoshui. "Do Thought and Existence Not Have Identity?" *Zhexue yanjiu*, no. 1 (1960), pp. 7–16.

———. "The Greatest Lesson of the Cultural Revolution Is That the Personality Cult Should Be Opposed," Speech at the Theory Conference, 13 February 1979. *Mingbao*, Hong Kong, no. 2 (1980), pp. 2–15. In *JPRS*, 12 March 1980, pp 78–99.

———. "The Aim of Practice Is the Criterion to Evaluate the Success or Failure of Practice," *GMRB*, 12 May 1980, p. 3.

———. "The Theory of Knowledge Must Not Forget People," *GMRB*, 12 February 1981, p. 4.

———. "The Fate of Dialectics." *Shehui kexue zhanxian*, no. 3 (1981), pp. 1–19.

———. "Discussing the Problem of Alienation. *Xinwen zhanxian*, no. 8 (1980). In *Wang Ruoshui: Writings on Humanism, Alienation and Philosophy*, translated and edited by David Kelly. *Chinese Studies in Philosophy*, Spring 1985, pp. 25–38.

———. "In Defense of Humanism." *Wenhuibao*, 17 January 1983, p. 3.

———. "Marxism and Intellectual Emancipation." *Xin Shiqi*, no. 4 (1980), pp. 2–3. *Renmin ribao*, 8 August 1980, p. 5.

———. "The Double Hundred Policy and Civil Rights." *SWB/FE*, 8360, 10, September 1986, pp. BII8–9.

———. "The Cult of the Individual and Intellectual Alienation." *Jingbao*, April 1988, pp. 24–27, and May 1988, pp. 40–44.

———. "Issues on Realism and Theory of Reflection." *Wenhuibao*, 12 July 1988, p. 3.

———. "The Maid of Chinese Politics: Mao Zedong and His Philosophy of Struggle." *The Journal of Contemporary China*, no. 10 (Fall 1995), pp. 66–80.

Wang Xizhe. "Mao Zedong and the Cultural Revolution." *Chinese Law and Government*, 1985, pp. 1–98.

Wang Xiaoqiang. "The Peasantry and the Struggle Against Feudalism." *Lishi yanjiu*, no. 10 (1979), pp. 3–12.

———. "A Repudiation of Agrarian Socialism." *Nongye jingji wenti*, no. 2 (1980). In *Xinhua yuebao wenzhaiban*, no. 5 (1980), pp. 7–13.

Wang Yizhou. "Why We Cannot Agree With the New Authoritarianism." *Chinese Sociology and Anthropology*, vol. 23, no. 4 (Summer 1991), pp. 56–66.

Wang Zhe. "Pseudo-Leftists and Genuine Rightists—Viewing the Counter Revolutionary Revisionism of the Gang of Four From the Question of Class Struggle." *Renmin ribao*, 12 December 1977.

Wang Zhen. "Guard Against and Remove Spiritual Pollution on the Ideological Front, Raise High the Banner of Marxism and Socialism." *Renmin ribao*, 25 October, 1983, p. 1.

Wang Zhengping. "What Is the Basis for Determining Whether the Exploiting Classes Have Been Eliminated." *Beijing Review*, no. 22 (1980).

———. "Is Class Only an Economic Formation?" *Renmin ribao*, 4 January 1980.

———. "A Brief Analysis of Socialism Is the 'Reconstruction of Individual Ownership.'" *Guangming ribao*, 13 September 1989.

Wang Zhiliang. "Economic Reform Must Adhere to a Socialist Direction." *Guangming ribao*, 9 September 1989.

Watson, James. *Class and Social Stratification in Post–Revolution China*. Cambridge: Cambridge University Press, 1984.

Wei Zhongduan and Cui Zhengqi. "Why Do We Say That Class Struggle at the Present Stage in Our Country Is a Special Form of Class Struggle?" *Wenhuibao*, 17 July 1979.

Wen Yanmao. "On the Question of Our Country's Transition From New Democracy to Socialism." *Hongqi*, no. 18 (1981), pp. 32–38.

White Gordon. "Restructuring the Working Class: Labor Reform in Post-Mao China," *Marxism and the Chinese Experience*, pp. 152–168.

Williams, James. "Fang Lizhi's Expanding Universe." *The China Quarterly*, no. 123, (1990), pp. 459–484.

———. ed. and trans. "The Expanding Universe of Fang Lizhi: Astrophysics and Ideology in People's China." *Chinese Studies in Philosophy*, vol. 19, no. 4 (1988).

Winburg, George, and John Shumaker. *Statistics: An Intuitive Approach*. Monterey, Calif.: Brooks and Cole Publishing Company, 1974.

Woei Lian Chong. "The Tragic Duality of Man: Liu Xiaobo on Western Philosophy from Kant to Sartre," Kurt Werner Radtke and Tony Saich, eds. *China's Modernization: Westernization and Acculteration*. Stuttgart: Franz Steiner Verlag, 1993.

———. "Mankind and Nature in Chinese Thought: Li Zehou on the Traditional Roots of Maoist Voluntarism." *China Information*, vol. XI, nos. 2–3 (Autumn–Winter 1996), pp. 138–175.

Womack, Brantly. "Politics and Epistemology in China Since Mao." *The China Quarterly*, no. 80 (1979), pp. 768–792.

———. *Contemporary Chinese Politics in Historical Perspective*. Cambridge: Cambridge University Press, 1991.

Wortzel, Larry. *Class in China: Stratification in a Classless Society*. Westport, Conn.: Greenwood Press, 1987.

Wright, Erik Olin. *Class, Crisis, and the State*. London: New Left Books, 1978.

Writing Group of the Shantung Provincial Committee of the Chinese Communist Party. "Adhere to the Method of Class Analysis, Correctly Understand the Struggle Between the Two Lines." *Hongqi*, no. 13 (1971).

Writing Group of the Military Affairs Institute. "Some Questions on Class and Class Struggle." *Guangming ribao*, 22 August 1979. In *Xinhua yuebao wenzhaiban*, no. 10 (1979), pp. 1–6.

Wu Daying and Liu Han. "The Theory and Practice of Class Struggle—to Clear the Confusion Created by the Gang of Four on the Question of Class Struggle." *Xueshu yuekan*, no. 3 (1979), pp. 26–29. In *JPRS*, 74334, 9 October 1979, pp. 11–18.

Wu Jiang. "Correct Handling of Contradictions Among the People is a General Subject." *Hongqi*, no. 2 (1979), pp. 2–7.

———. "Again Studying the Basic Economic Law of Socialism." *Hongqi*, no. 12 (1980), pp. 2–18.

———. "On the Historical Stage of Socialist Construction." *RMRB*, 5 May 1988.

Wu Jianguo. "Fully Realize the Flaws of Bourgeois Liberalization: Correctly Understand the Intrinsic Unity of the Two Basic Points." *Guangming ribao*, 6 July 1989.

———. "Reflections on the Question of Freedom." *Hongqi*, 1 September 1986, pp. 32–38.

Wu Jiaxiang. "Several Options for Property Rights Reforms." *Zhongguo fazhan yu gaige*, no. 4 (1988), pp. 45–47.

———. "An Outline for Studying the New Authoritarianism." *The New Authoritarianism*, edited by Liu Jin and Li Lin. Beijing: Beijing Institute of Economics Press, 1989, pp. 47–53.

———. "The New Authoritarianism: An Express Train Towards Democracy by Building Markets." *The New Authoritarianism*. pp. 39–46.

Wu Jiaxiang and Zhang Binjiu. "Radical Democracy or Stable Democracy?" *Guangming ribao*, 31 March 1989, p. 3.

Wu Jinglian. "Again Discussing the Maintenance of a Beneficial Environment for Economic Reform." *Jingji yanjiu*, no. 5 (1985).

———. "Some Thoughts on the Choice of Reform Strategies." *Jingji yanjiu*, no. 2 (1987), pp. 3–14.

Wylie, Raymond. *The Emergence of Maoism: Chen Po–ta and the Search for Chinese Theory, 1935–45*. Stanford: Stanford University Press, 1980.

Xia Guanghua. "The Political Line Must Be Tested Through the Practice of Economic Construction." *Shehui kexue*, no. 3 (1979), pp. 3–4.

Xia Zhentao. "The Essential Factors and Characteristics of Practice and the Criterion of Truth." *Zhexue yanjiu*, no. 5 (1980), pp. 7–17.

Xiao Gongqin. "On Transformative Authoritarianism." *The New Authoritarianism*.

Xiao Gongqin. "A Painful Dilemma: A Dialogue on the Theory of 'New Authoritarianism.'" *Wenhuibao*, 17 January 1989, p. 5.

Xiao Lu. "Is Contradiction Between the Advanced Social System and the Backward Productive Forces a Scientific Issue?" *Zhexue yanjiu*, no. 7 (1979), pp. 19–26. In *JPRS*, 74224, 21 September 1979, pp. 16–25.

Xiao Qian. "On the Marxist View of Practice." *Hongqi*, no. 14 (1980), pp. 38–45.

Xiao Yougen. "Strive to Eliminate the Evil Influence of Inflating Class Struggle." *Nanfang ribao*, 6 November 1979, p. 2. In *JPRS*, 74813, 21 December 1979, pp. 27–31.

Xing Fensi. "Several Questions About Alienation." *Jingji ribao*, 4 November 1983. In *FBIS*, 29 November 1983, pp. K13–23.

———. "The Alienation Issue and Spiritual Pollution." *Renmin ribao*, 5 November 1983, p. 5.

Xiong Fu. "The Yugoslav People Are Advancing Along the Socialist Road." *Hongqi*, no. 18 (1981), pp. 19–24.

———. "Study the Report to the Twelfth CCP Congress From the High Plane of Communist Ideology." *Hongqi*, no. 18 (1982), pp. 31–43.

———. "The May Fourth Movement and the Historical Road of Chinese Intellectuals." *Hongqi*, no. 9 (1980), pp. 14–21.

Xu Chengqing and Huang Shuxun. "Why Can Economically Backward Countries Enter Socialism First?" *Hongqi*, no. 10 (1983), pp. 12–17.

Xu Chongde. "'Practice Is the Source of Knowledge' Is a Twisting of the 'Primacy of Practice.'" *Shehui kexue*, no. 5 (1982), pp. 34–36.

Xu Dixin. "Chairman Mao's Devlopment of Marxism on the Question of Changing the Relations of Production and Developing the Productive Forces." *Jingji Yanjiu*, no. 1 (1978), pp. 7–20. *JPRS*, 71060, 4 May 1978, pp. 56–64.

Xu Junji and Zhou Zhiliang. "The Source and Manifestation of Revisionism." *Hongqi*, no. 1 (1980), pp. 42–45.

Xu Kun. "Class Conditions and Class Struggle in Our Country at the Present Stage." *Shehui kexue*, no. 3 (1979), pp. 60–64, 70.

Xue Mu. "How Should We Correctly View Small-Scale Production After the Basic Completion of Socialist Transformation?" *Hongqi*, no. 21 (1981), pp. 41–43.

Xue Muqiao. *Current Problems of the Chinese Economy*. Beijing: People's Publishers, 1980.

———. "Some Opinions on the Reform of the Economic System." *Renmin ribao*, 10 June 1980.

———. *China's Socialist Economy*. Beijing: Foreign Languages Press, 1981.

———. "Postscript to 'a Study of Questions Concerning China's Economy.'" *Hongqi*, no. 21 (1981), pp. 23–30.

———. "Reform of the Economic Structure and the Economic System." *Hongqi*, no. 14 (1980), pp. 6–15.

———. "The New Trend in Economic Development in China," speech at a Symposium in Hong Kong. Excerpts in *Shijie jingji daobao*, 30 October 1980.

———. "Continuously Develop the Science of Marxism." *Renmin ribao*, 20 March 1987.

Yan Jiaqi. "Democracy and Social Equity: A Comparative Analysis of the Role of the Government." *GMRB*, 7 July 1988.

———. "Socialist Countries Must Also Properly Resolve the Problem of the 'Political System.'" *Guangming ribao*, 8 December 1980.

———. "From 'Non-Procedural' to Procedural Politics." *Shehui kexue*, 15 August 1988, pp. 3–7.

———. "Conversation With Wen Yuankai." *Yan Jiaqi and China's Struggle for Democracy.*

Yan Qiushi. "Ideological and Political Work Is a Branch of Science." *Renmin ribao*, 14 August 1980, p. 5.

Yang Baikui. "Democracy and Authority in the Course of Political Development." *Chinese Sociology and Anthropology*, vol. 23, no. 3 (Spring 1991), pp. 67–80.

Yang Changfu. "On the Meaning of the Economic Base." *Zhexue yanjiu*, no. 11 (1979), pp. 31–36, 40.

Yang Fan. "First Anniversary of the Market Economy." *Fazhan yu guanli*, no. 1 (1993).

Yang Fengchun. "Why Were the Class Roots of the 'Great Cultural Revolution' Not Analyzed in the 'Resolution'?" *Hongqi*, no. 18 (1981), pp. 41–43.

Yang Jianbai. "On Social Individual Ownership." *Shehui kexue*, no. 3 (1988).

Yang Qixian. "The Nature and Functions of the Stock System Under Socialist Conditions." *Renmin ribao*, 3 July 1987.

Yang Xianzhen. "Adhere to the Principle of the Basic Question of Philosophy; Study the Documents of the Central Work Conference." *Guangming ribao*, 2 March 1981. In *FBIS*, 23 March 1981.

———. "The Fate of Materialism." *Shehui kexue zhanxian*, no. 1 (1982), pp. 19–25.

Yanowitch, Murray and Wesley Fischer, eds. *Social Stratification and Mobility in the USSR*. White Plains: International Arts and Sciences Press, 1973.

Yao Bomao, "The Source of Knowledge is Practice, Not Matter." *Shehui kexue*, no. 5 (1982), pp. 30–33.

———. "Reevaluating the Theory of an Integrated Economic Base." *Guangming ribao*, 3 July 1980.

Yao Wenyuan. "On the Social Basis of the Lin Biao Clique." *Hongqi*, no. 4 (1975), pp. 20–29.

Yan Sun. *The Reassessment of Chinese Socialism, 1976–1992*, Princeton: Princeton University Press, 1995.

Ye Jianying. "Comrade Ye Jianying's Speech at the Meeting in Celebration of the Thirtieth Anniversary of the PRC." *Beijing Review*, no. 22 (1979).

Yi Chen. "Louis Althusser and Structuralism." *Hongqi*, no. 9 (1983), pp. 25–32.

Yong Jian and Fan Hengsan. "On the Opening of Ownership." *Xinhua wenzhai*, no. 4 (1989), pp. 36–39.

Yu Guangyuan. "Discussing the 'Theory of the Goal of a Socialist Economy.'" *Renmin ribao*, 22 October 1979.

———. "Ownership, Socialism, Socialist Ownership." *Shehui kexue yuekan*, no. 3 (1981), pp. 38–51.

———. "On the Liberation of Thought." *Ziran bianzhengfa tongxun*, no. 1 (1981), pp. 1–2.

———. "Reform Is Also a Philosophical Revolution." *Xuexi yu yanjiu*, no. 10 (1984), pp. 9–11.

———. "Develop the Study of Marxism One Step Further." *Makesizhuyi yanjiu* (congkan), no. 1 (1983), pp. 1–6.

———. "Perceive the Reform of the Period of Socialist Construction From the Point of View of World and Chinese History." *Zhonguo shehui kexue*, no. 1 (1985), pp. 53–68.

———. "Develop Economics for Even Better Construction of Socialist Modernization." *Jingji yanjiu*, no. 10 (1981).

———. "The Basic Attitude Towards Socialist Ownership." *Xinhua yuebao*, no. 9 (1980), pp. 7–14.

———. "On the Scientific Study of Questions Relating to China's Socioeconomic Development Strategy." *Renmin ribao*, 16 August 1982. In *Xinhua wenzhai*, no. 10 (1982), pp. 40–42.

———. "The Objective Laws of Socialist Revolution and Socialist Construction and the Progressive Role of Marxism." *Tianjin shehui kexue*, no. 2 (1983), pp. 2–6.

———. "What Must Be Done to Develop Marxism—This Question Must Be Discussed at the Commemoration of Marx's Death Centennial." *Xuexi yu tansuo*, no. 1 (1983), pp. 4–5.

———. "Develop Marxism as a Science for Socialist Construction." *Zhongguo shehui kexue*, no. 4 (1983), pp. 3–12.

———. "The Reaction of Consciousness on Matter." *Zhexue yanjiu*, no. 11 (1979), pp. 7–13.

———. "Actively Promote Marxism as the Science of Socialist Construction." *RMRB*, 5 August 1985, p. 5.

———. "For the Victory of Reform and Opening and the Cause of Socialist Construction for Modernization." *Renmin ribao*, 28 April 1989.

————. "Commemorating the Tenth Anniversary of the Discussion on the Question Regarding the Criterion of Truth." *Renmin ribao*, 6 May 1988, p. 5.

Yu Guangyuan and Hu Jiwei. *The Moment of Sudden Awakening*. Beijing: Zhong-wai chuban gongsi, 1989.

Yu Haocheng. "Protection of Human Rights Is a Just Cause in the Advance of Mankind." *Shijie zhishi*, 1 December 1988, pp. 2–5. In *JPRS*, 89018, 1 March 1989.

————. "Does China Need the New Authoritarianism?" *Chinese Sociology and Anthropology*, vol. 23, no. 4 (Summer 1991), pp. 44–55.

Yu Mingren. "It Is Imperative to Criticise the Theory of the 'Three-Stage Development of the Bourgeoisie.'" *Renmin ribao*, 8 April 1978, p. 2. *JPRS*, 71088, 10 May 1978, pp. 11–14.

Yu Yiding. "On Emancipating the Mind and Opposing Bourgeois Liberalization." *Hongqi*, no. 23 (1981), pp. 23–28.

Yuan Kuiren and Li Jin. "Practice Is the Only Source of Knowledge—Deliberating With Comrade Ze Ming." *Shehui kexue*, no. 6 (1980), pp. 105–8.

Yuan Mu. "Uphold Mao Zedong Thought, Develop Mao Zedong Thought—Studying the 'Resolution on Certain Questions in the History of Our Party Since the Founding of the PRC.'" *Hongqi*, no. 15 (1981), pp. 41–48.

Yue Ping. "Carry Forward Marxist Theory—In Preparation for the Centenary of the Death of Karl Marx." *Guangming ribao*, 30 May 1982.

Yun Xiliang. "The Interests of the State, Enterprises and Individuals." *Hongqi*, no. 16 (1983), pp. 7–12.

Ze Ming. "Refutation of 'Practice Is the Only Source of Knowledge.'" *Shehui kexue*, no. 2 (1980), pp. 61–66.

————. "Another Refutation of 'Practice Is the Only Source of Knowledge.'" *Shehui kexue*, no. 1 (1982), pp. 30–35.

Zhang Bingjiu. "The Progress and Coordination Between Economic and Political System Reform." In *The New Authoritarianism*, pp. 1–26.

Zhang Chunhan. "Overcome Narrow Thinking, Deepen the Discussions on the Criterion of Truth". *Hongqi*, no. 11 (1979), pp. 11–14.

Zhang Chunqiao. "On Exercising All-Round Dictatorship Over the Bourgeoisie." *Hongqi*, no. 4 (1975), pp. 3–12.

Zhang Decheng. "Adhere to the Four Cardinal Principles and the Struggle on Two Fronts." *Hongqi*, no. 20 (1983), pp. 31–34.

Zhang Enci. "Truth Cannot Be the Criterion by Which Truth Is Tested." *Zhexue yanjiu*, no. 9 (1978), pp. 27–30.

Zhang Gong. "In Which Fields Should We Continue to Carry Out Revolutionary Struggle Under Socialist Conditions." *Hongqi*, no. 19 (1981), pp. 40–42.

Zhang Huajin and Ma Jihua. "Scientific Proposition of the Dialectical Material-ist Theory of Knowledge—Deliberating With Comrade Ze Ming." *Shehui kexue*, no. 5 (1980), pp. 98–101.

Zhang Lizhou. "Deepen the Discussion on the Criterion of Truth." *Sixiang zhanxian*, no. 4 (1979), pp. 1–5.

Zhang Luxiong. "Will Letting Some People Get Rich First Cause Social Polariza-tion?" *Hongqi*, no. 17 (1984), pp. 38–39.

Zhang Shihong. "Eliminate the Metaphysical Poison in the Theory of Truth—Understanding the Relative and Absolute Nature of Truth." *Shehui kexue*, no. 5 (1980), pp. 95–97.

Zhang Weiguo. "Li Honglin on Reunderstanding Socialism." *Shijie jingji daobao*, 11 April 1988, p. 7.

———. "Whither the State Ownership System?" *Shijie jingji daobao*, 3 April 1989, p. 10.

Zhang Xianyang. "Marxism: Reflection and Transcendence." *Wen huibao*, Hong Kong, 29 January 1989, p. 2.

Zhang Xianyang and Wang Guixiu. "Proletarian Democracy and Bourgeois Democracy." *Renmin ribao*, 6 September 1979.

Zhang Yun. "Refuting the Theory of Family Lineage." *Renmin ribao*, 17 May 1978, p. 3. In *JPRS*, 71366, 27 June 1978, pp. 57–58.

Zhang Yunyi. "Dialogue on the Existence of Class Struggle After the Abolition of Exploiting Classes." *Guangming ribao*, 31 October 1983.

Zhang Zhiqing. "The Market Economy and the Way Out for China's Reform." *Jingji kexue*, no. 2 (1989).

Zhao Ziyang. "Advance Along the Road of Socialism With Chinese Characteris-tics." Report Delivered at the Thirteenth National Congress of the Commu-nist Party of China on 5 October 1987. *Beijing Review*, 9–15 November 1987, pp. 23–49.

Zheng Wen. "China Can Never Copy Wholesale the Western Democratic Sys-tem." *Jingji ribao*, 18 July 1989, p. 3.

Zhexue yanjiu, Editorial Department, ed. *Selections From the Discussions on "Practice Is the Sole Criterion for Testing Truth."* 2 vols, Beijing: Chinese Acad-emy of Social Sciences, 1979.

———. *Selections from the Discussion on Whether or Not Truth Has a Class Nature.* Jinan: Shandong People's Publishing House, 1980.

Zhi Jiao. "By Inciting Anarchism, the Gang of Four Aimed at Subverting the Dictatorship of the Proletariat." *Hongqi*, no. 5 (1978), pp. 38–44.

Zhou Yang. "The Three Great Movements for the Liberation of Thought," speech at the Academic Conference Convened by the Chinese Academy of

Social Sciences to Commemorate the Sixtieth Anniversary of the May Fourth Movement". *Renmin ribao*, 7 May 1979, pp. 2–4.

———. "A Probe Into Some Theoretical Problems of Marxism." *Renmin ribao*, 16 March 1983, pp. 4–5.

———. "Emancipate Thought, Truthfully Reflect Our Epoch." *Wenhuibao*, no. 4 (1981). In *Xinhua wenzhai*, no. 4 (1981), pp. 132–137.

Zhu Shuxian. "Also Discussing the Question of Stages of Social Development After the Seizure of Power by the Proletariat." *Jingji yanjiu*, no. 8 (1979), pp. 14–18.

Zhu Yuanshi. "The Cause of the Outbreak of the 'Great Cultural Revolution' and Its Lessons." *Hongqi*, no. 16 (1981), pp. 43–48.

Zuo Mu. "Problems of the Reform of China's Ownership Structure." *Jingji yanjiu*, no. 1 (1986), pp. 6–10.

Index